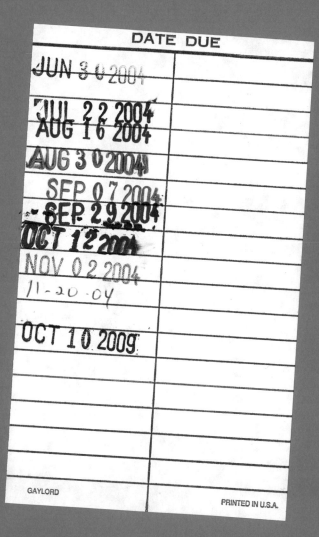

LINCOLN'S LAST MONTHS

LINCOLN'S
LAST MONTHS

★ ★ ★ ★ ★

WILLIAM C. HARRIS

THE BELKNAP PRESS OF
HARVARD UNIVERSITY PRESS
CAMBRIDGE, MASSACHUSETTS
LONDON, ENGLAND
2004

Library of Congress Cataloging-in-Publication Data

Harris, William C. (William Charles), 1933–
Lincoln's last months / William C. Harris.
p.   cm.
Includes bibliographical references and index.
ISBN 0-674-01199-6 (alk. paper)
1. Lincoln, Abraham, 1809–1865. 2. Presidents—United States—Biography.
3. United States—Politics and government—1861–1865. I. Title.

E457.45.H37 2003
973.7′092—dc22
[B]
2003057907

For
Lachlan Cotner,
Jill Harris,
and
Lorene Glenn

CONTENTS

LINCOLN'S LAST MONTHS

INTRODUCTION

Abraham Lincoln is the central figure in America's great epic—the Civil War. Lincoln's rise from a hard frontier and a largely self-educated background to become the finest exemplar of America's democratic and republican values has had an appeal for all generations, not only in the United States but also abroad. During the most critical period in American history, when the young republic and its democratic principles faced their greatest threat, this son of the West provided the leadership to preserve the Union. He eloquently expressed the universal ideals involved in the war and firmly took the steps necessary to end slavery. Lincoln himself came to believe he was the humble instrument of God in his struggle to achieve these purposes. Despite the bitter animosities generated by the war, Lincoln, with rare exception, lived the principles of magnanimity and tolerance toward his enemies in the South and his detractors in the North.

Lincoln's integrity and his steadfastness in standing behind his promises became increasingly apparent during the later stages of the Civil War and contributed to his legendary stature in history. The aftermath of his assassination produced an even greater recognition of his virtuous character, humaneness, and statesmanship, raising him to a nearly godlike status in the minds of Americans and others. Years later, at the dawn of a century that witnessed horrible violations of the Lincolnian example, the eminent Russian novelist Leo Tolstoy proclaimed Lincoln "a Christ in miniature, a saint of humanity whose name will live thousands of years in the legends of future generations."[1] In our time, Lincoln's life and character, in addition to his democratic ideals, have become an inspiration for Americans and an important link to the nation's presumably more innocent past.

Lincoln had great faith in constitutional processes, self-government, and the inherent equality of all people as set forth in the Declaration of Independence. Though he had no illusions about the perfectibility of humankind, he expected that after the war Americans, unencumbered by rebellion and slavery, would prosper and the ideals of liberty and equality would flourish. Since his early days in Illinois, Lincoln had envisioned democratic America as a model for the world, one based on moral example rather than military, economic, or political power. In his view, the Civil War was fought to vindicate before the world and sustain in America the principles of self-government and constitutional liberty. The issue in the war, he announced in his message to Congress of July 4, 1861, "embraces more than the fate of these United States. It presents to the whole family of man, the question, whether a constitutional republic, or a democracy—a government of the people, by the same people—can, or cannot, maintain its territorial integrity, against its own domestic foes."[2] At Gettysburg on November 19, 1863, Lincoln reaffirmed his commitment—and, by extension, America's—to this noble cause in the Civil War.

But by 1864 his ideals and purposes were in grave danger of being compromised or worse. The war dragged on that summer as Confederates under General Robert E. Lee and other commanders fought successfully, despite heavy casualties, to check the Federal offensives designed to end the rebellion. In the autumn Lincoln faced a presidential election that might change the war's ending and leave many blacks in slavery. Despite his anxiety and his realization that the military situation was the key to the election, Lincoln entrusted the battlefield decisions to U. S. Grant and his generals and turned to the presidential contest. Considerable opposition to his re-election had arisen, even within his Republican (Union) party, as the military stalemate continued, but dramatic Federal victories at Atlanta and elsewhere ultimately reversed the downward political trend. The Democratic party platform, proclaiming the war a failure and calling for an immediate cease-fire, virtually acknowledged Confederate independence and thereby contributed to a surge in support for Lincoln late in the presidential campaign. Lincoln and his party did indeed win the election, but his Democratic opponent, George B. McClellan, who repudiated the war-failure plank in his party's platform, managed to get 44 percent of the popular vote.

After the election Lincoln secured, by a slim margin, congressional approval of the Thirteenth Amendment abolishing slavery and validating his Emancipation Proclamation. With less success, he sought an early peace and the restoration of the Union. Despite the fact that the war was coming to a successful end on his terms—reunion and an end to slavery—Lincoln entered his second term with great trepidation. He was a tired and haggard man who wanted relief from his presidential responsibilities but who persevered to achieve his goals. He faced monumental challenges in the months ahead, challenges involving the composition of his new administration, the surrender of Confederate armies, conditions in the postwar South, the status of blacks in freedom, foreign affairs, and Indian troubles in the West. He confronted the critical issues relating to the end of the war with deep personal conviction and shrewd political agility.

Abraham Lincoln was not a president who sought power and control. Rather, he expanded presidential authority because doing so was necessary to meet the threat to the Union and ultimately to destroy slavery, the root cause of the war. In his December 1864 annual message to Congress Lincoln confirmed that "the Executive power itself will be greatly diminished by the cessation of actual war." Likewise, he expected the wartime powers of the federal government to be substantially reduced after the suppression of the rebellion, whereupon the states would again be the center of governmental activity. Secretary of the Navy Gideon Welles wrote that in the early months of 1865 Lincoln "anticipated with undisguised satisfaction the time . . . when the General Government would be able to dispense with the exercise of arbitrary and questionable authority." Lincoln never sought to subvert the Constitution to ends other than a permanent Union, nor did he extend presidential power for purposes of self-aggrandizement.[3]

After issuing the Emancipation Proclamation on January 1, 1863, Lincoln remained firm in his commitment to ending slavery. At the same time he did not contemplate an active role for the federal government in establishing civil rights for blacks in the South. He seemed willing to leave this authority to the restored state governments. But he preferred—not demanded—that these regimes, at least in Louisiana, adopt qualified black suffrage and provide for the education of young African Americans, neither of which the restored state governments were willing to do. In his debates with Stephen A. Douglas in 1858, Lincoln had said that he did "not understand there is any place where an alteration of the social and political relations of the Negro and the white man can be made except in the State Legislature." Nonetheless, by 1864–1865 he had developed considerable empathy for blacks and wanted their freedom to become a reality, not a halfway station between slavery and liberty. The black spokesman Frederick Douglass, who often criticized the president's policies, saw this growth and later wrote of him: "In all of my interviews with Mr. Lincoln I was impressed with his entire freedom from popular prejudice against the colored race."[4]

On the issue of blacks in freedom and other crucial matters, the president by 1864 rarely consulted with his full cabinet, though he frequently talked in an ad hoc fashion with individual members. Lacking administrative experience and not wanting to intervene in the regular operations of the government, he permitted members of his cabinet to run their departments without interference, except when their actions affected the war effort or important political issues. He virtually ignored, for example, the growing conflict between Indians and settlers in the West and the need to reform policies toward Indians after years of abuse. He also paid little practical attention to financial issues or to foreign relations. A notable exception was his handling of a serious controversy with Great Britain in late 1864 and early 1865 over Confederate military operations from Canada against the North. To a lesser extent, he also became involved in challenging the French presence in Mexico. For him, however, the struggle to unite the country was the main priority.

Lincoln largely pursued a hands-off policy regarding congressional legislation as well. As president-elect in February 1861, he had explained his view of the president's relationship to Congress: "By the constitution, the executive may recommend measures which he may think proper, and he may veto those he may think improper; and it is supposed that he may add to these, certain indirect influences to affect the action of congress." "My political education"—by which he meant his grounding in Whig party doctrine—"strongly inclines me against a very free use of any of these means, by the Executive, to control the legislation of the country. As a rule, I think it better that congress should originate, as well as perfect its measures, without external bias."[5]

After the war began, Lincoln concluded that he did not want Congress, consisting of obstructionists on both the left and the right, to interfere and complicate the work of winning the war and restoring the Union. The Constitution, he assumed, gave the president as commander in chief the primary responsibility for suppressing the rebellion and restoring the Southern states to "their proper practical relation with the Union." Nonetheless, he recognized that Congress possessed certain constitutional powers that he could not—and did not wish to—ignore. The authority to raise money and troops and to sustain his suspension of the writ of habeas corpus were the most important of these powers. Lincoln's annual messages to Congress usually outlined recommendations for legislative action, but he rarely lobbied Congress for their approval.

An important exception to this passive policy toward congressional legislation was his vigorous effort on behalf of the Thirteenth Amendment. In his annual message on December 6, 1864, he pressed Congress to pass a resolution initiating the antislavery amendment, and in January he followed up with a successful lobbying campaign to secure the support of key Democrats and border-state conservatives in the House of Representatives. When Congress approved the resolution, the president proclaimed it "a King's cure for all the evils" of slavery; downplaying his own role, he congratulated Congress, the country, and "the whole world upon this great moral victory."[6]

Lincoln did take a stand against Congress on challenges to his authority. A notable instance occurred in July 1864 when he pocket vetoed the Wade-Davis Reconstruction Bill, a veto that threatened to split his party on the eve of the critical presidential campaign. Except for the seating of senators and representatives from the restored Southern governments, Lincoln rejected congressional interference in his reconstruction efforts. He refused to support a bill introduced by Representative James M. Ashley of Ohio in December 1864 that would have given Congress an important role in reconstruction policy.

Despite his differences with Congress, Lincoln's stature with its members, especially those in his own party, grew after the 1864 election. In addition to a belated appreciation of his leadership in the Union cause, Republicans in Congress—a clear majority of the membership—recognized that the election had greatly strengthened Lincoln's political position and that they would continue to have to deal with him in matters of patronage, the lifeblood of nineteenth-century politics. The Radical congressman George W. Julian complained in his journal that his Republican colleagues "don't want any quarrel with Lincoln" and that since the election "Old Abe, through his patronage, is the virtual dictator of the country."[7] Though Julian exaggerated Lincoln's power, "Old Abe" no doubt had become master of affairs in Washington.

The last months of Abraham Lincoln's life began with the campaign and election of 1864 and ended with the shot fired at Ford's Theatre by John Wilkes Booth. Lincoln's policies and actions during the final months of the Civil War illuminate the man, his presidency, and the war he helped bring to an end. Accounts of his relationship with Mary Todd Lincoln, blacks, white Southerners, western Indians, the Federal military, and Congress are integral parts of this story, as are the changing American and European views of the president. Lincoln's apotheosis as an American icon began before his death. His reputation grew as his efforts to restore the Union and secure an early peace led him to extend lenient terms to white Southerners. Exploring these final months and the grinding burdens of the presidency for the man in the White House will enhance our understanding of the scope and greatness of Lincoln's character and achievements.

CHAPTER 1

RE-ELECTION

Election day, November 8, 1864, dawned "dull, gloomy, and rainy" in Washington; it would end in a downpour. The White House stood virtually deserted and few visitors disturbed Abraham Lincoln on this important day in his life and in the history of the republic. The president was running for his second term in office, and the events of recent months had made him very apprehensive about the election. The newspaperman Noah Brooks, arriving around noon, found Lincoln "entirely alone" and spent much of the afternoon with him. To Brooks, Lincoln admitted his anxiety. "I am just enough of a politician," he said, "to know that there was not much doubt about the result of the Baltimore Convention" nominating him for the presidency, "but about this thing, I am far from being certain."[1]

★ ★ ★

Others, too, believed that Lincoln's bid for re-election might fail. Doubts had surfaced soon after the Republicans' national convention at Baltimore in June 1864. Renaming themselves the National Union party in order to attract Democratic and conservative supporters of the war, the Republicans, in addition to renominating Lincoln for president, adopted a platform approving the administration's war policies and endorsing a constitutional amendment to abolish slavery. The convention nominated Andrew Johnson, the Union military governor of Tennessee and a former United States senator, to replace the incumbent vice president, Hannibal Hamlin, as Lincoln's running mate, a choice that the president approved but did not dictate.[2]

While the political leaders prepared for the presidential campaign, General-in-Chief U. S. Grant launched a spring military offensive designed to crush the rebel armies in Virginia, Georgia, and Louisiana. By the summer, however, the Northern public, having expected the rebellion to collapse, found its troops still mired in a bloody conflict with no early end in sight. War weariness replaced the early optimism. As is often the case when demoralization takes hold, Northern and border-state supporters of the war blamed their leaders and especially Lincoln for the failure to defeat the Confederate armies. Opposition to the president flared even within his own party. Some Republicans, led by Radicals like Senators Benjamin F. Wade of Ohio and Charles Sumner of Massachusetts, believed that Lincoln was incapable of firm and decisive leadership. Many Republican leaders grimly concluded that Lincoln and the party were doomed to defeat at the polls unless the Union's military fortunes changed dramatically, or unless the Democrats made a huge mistake when they met in Chicago in August to select a candidate for president and adopt a platform. As it turned out, both these eventualities occurred.

Since 1862 the Democratic party had vigorously opposed Lincoln's war policy. Democrats argued that Lincoln's insistence on emancipation had made negotiations to end the war on the basis of reunion impossible. The national Democratic party met at a time when the Union's military fortunes had reached a low point and opposition to Lincoln had swelled. Peace Democrats, or "Copperheads" as the Republicans called them, seized control of the Chicago convention and secured the approval of a platform declaring the war a failure and demanding an immediate cessation of hostilities "with the view to an ultimate convention of the states, or other peaceable means" for the purpose of restoring the Union. The platform confirmed the Democratic party's commitment to "the rights of the states unimpaired"—meaning slavery—and condemned the Lincoln administration's suppression of civil liberties in the Union states.[3]

Confederate President Jefferson Davis could not have asked for a better platform than the one the Northern Democrats served up in Chicago. It was clear to many observers, both North and South, what the effect of a cessation of hostilities would be. Once the fighting had ceased, the rebellious states would reject negotiations for a voluntary return to the Union, and the Confederacy would win its independence from a war-weary North that lacked the will to continue the fight. The Democrats created confusion in their own ranks by nominating for president General George B. McClellan, who, after much soul-searching, announced that he could not support the party's war-failure and peace planks. However, the general approved other parts of the platform, including the rights of the states to control their institutions and protect the civil liberties of their citizens. Despite McClellan's opposition to a peace short of reunion, the Democrats had made a colossal error in calling for a cessation of hostilities. The Republicans exploited their miscalculation during the final weeks before the election.

The Union's military situation began to improve two days after the Democratic convention adjourned, when Atlanta, a strategic center in the lower South, fell to General William Tecumseh Sherman's army. Other Union successes soon followed, virtually ensuring the defeat of the Democratic party at the polls.

Still, Lincoln and his supporters feared that the political contest, in the midst of a brutal war and after a divisive campaign, would degenerate into violent confrontations. Reports reached Washington that rebels and their Copperhead collaborators intended to set fires in New York and other Northern cities in a desperate effort to disrupt the election. Lincoln sadly remarked to his secretary John Hay, "It is a little singular that I, who am not a vindictive man, should have always been before the people for election in canvasses marked for their bitterness."[4]

★ ★ ★

The fears of election-day violence proved unfounded. From New York, where the worst disturbances had been expected, General Benjamin F. Butler, sent by the War Department to maintain order, telegraphed to Washington that the election was the quietest the city had ever seen. Similar encouraging reports from other areas soon reached the capital.[5]

At seven o'clock on election night Lincoln trudged in the rain and darkness from the White House and crossed the wooded grounds to the nearby War Department to await the telegraphic returns. As he arrived, the president received a dispatch reporting that the city of Philadelphia had given the Union ticket a majority of ten thousand votes. Returns from Boston and Baltimore immediately followed, all favorable to Lincoln and his party, but there was no indication from the states themselves. When Major Thomas T. Eckert, chief of the telegraph office, entered the room, shaking rain from his cloak and saying he had fallen in the mud, the president was reminded of an incident during his 1858 campaign against Stephen A. Douglas for the U.S. Senate. The day "was something like this, dark, rainy & gloomy," Lincoln said. "I had been reading the returns, and had ascertained that we had lost the Legislature and started to go home. The path had been worn hog-back & was slippery. My foot slipped from under me, knocking the other one out of the way, but I recovered myself & lit square, and I said to myself, 'It's a slip and not a fall.'"[6] Though the story was about an election that he had lost, the president's attempt at humor at his own expense relieved much of the tension in the room as the long wait began. The anecdote also perhaps suggested that a slip in the administration of public affairs, his own, was hardly a fall.

Before midnight, Lincoln, along with John Hay, went to Secretary of War Edwin M. Stanton's office, where Secretary of the Navy Gideon Welles and his chief assistant, Gustavus Vasa Fox, joined them. The president carefully told the newcomers "the particulars of each telegram which had been received." When Fox gloated at news of the defeat of Radical Congressman Henry Winter Davis of Maryland, a nemesis of the Navy Department and the president, Lincoln took exception: "You have more of that feeling of personal resentment than I. Perhaps I may have too little of it, but I never thought it paid . . . If any man ceases to attack me, I never remember the past against him." Recently, he said, Davis had grown "more sensible to his own true interests and has ceased wasting his time by attacking me." Then, in words suggesting that he had not completely forgotten or even forgiven the Maryland Radical, Lincoln related the history of Davis's "very strange" conduct toward him and also expressed his disappointment with Senator James W. Grimes of Iowa and Representative John Hickman of Pennsylvania, whom he had expected to be strong friends of his administration in Congress but who had opposed him.[7] The president remembered well those who acted against him but was also quick to forgive and welcome those who made conciliatory gestures.

As the election returns trickled in, Stanton read them to the group and Lincoln commented on their importance. The president sent over the first reports to Mrs. Lincoln, explaining to the group that "she is more anxious than I."[8] During a lull in the dispatches, Lincoln pulled out a copy of the writings of the humorist Petroleum V. Nasby (David Ross Locke). He would read a page or a story, pause to review the latest election dispatch, and then continue his reading, much to the annoyance of Stanton, who could not understand the pleasure that such amusement brought to the president's "care-worn" mind. An observer at the War Department on election night later wrote that "these jests" partly relieved "the natural gloom of a melancholy and desponding temperament [that] was Mr. Lincoln's prevailing characteristic." Stanton, however, was angry that, when the safety of the Union was at stake in the election, the man who was most responsible for that safety "could turn aside to read such balderdash and to laugh at such frivolous jests."[9] The humorless secretary of war did not recognize that Lincoln's "frivolous jests" were the president's way of alleviating anxiety and putting himself, as well as others, more at ease during a tense moment.

Soon after midnight it became clear that Lincoln and his party had swept the election. About two-thirty a group of well-wishers and a band arrived at the War Department, and the president, according to the admiring John Hay, answered from the window "with rather unusual dignity and effect." Lincoln told the jubilant crowd: "While deeply grateful for this mark of confidence in me, if I know my heart, my gratitude is free from taint of personal triumph. It is no pleasure to me to triumph over any one; but I give thanks to the Almighty for this evidence of the people's resolution to stand by free government and the rights of humanity." He declared "that all who have labored today in behalf of the Union organization, have wrought for the best interests of their country and the world, not only for the present, but for all future ages."[10]

Two days later, when well-wishers appeared at the White House, Lincoln delivered a brief prepared speech in which he announced: "It has long been a grave question whether any government, not *too* strong for the liberties of the people, can be strong *enough* to maintain its own existence, in great emergencies." The rebellion, he said, "brought our republic to a severe test; and a presidential election occurring in regular course during the rebellion added not a little to the strain . . . But the election was a necessity. We can not have free government without elections; and if the rebellion could force us to forego, or postpone a national election, it might fairly claim to have already conquered and ruined us." For Lincoln, the election had "demonstrated that a people's government can sustain a national election, in the midst of a great civil war. Until now it has not been known to the world that this was a possibility. It shows also how *sound* and how *strong* we still are."[11]

When he made these remarks, Lincoln probably knew that, while 44 percent of the electorate had voted against him, he had won all of the Union states except Kentucky, Delaware, and New Jersey. The final electoral vote stood at 212 for Lincoln to 21 for McClellan; Lincoln won 2,213,665 to McClellan's 1,802,237 popular votes. "But the rebellion continues," the president reminded his White House audience, "and now that the election is over, may not all, having a common interest, reunite in a common effort, to save our common country? For my own part I have striven, and shall strive to avoid placing any obstacle in the way." He asked his supporters to join with him in extending a conciliatory hand to Democrats and others who had differed with them in the election. And, as he had done on election night, he expressed his gratitude "to Almighty God for having directed my countrymen to a right conclusion" in the contest.[12]

* * *

Lincoln's exultation was mixed with relief that the Union cause had prevailed. During the summer of 1864, with the war stalemated in the South and the Copperhead-led peace movement growing in the North, the political clouds had looked dark indeed. Every military setback caused tension to mount in Washington and demoralization to spread in the North and the border Union states. On one occasion in mid-July a rebel force, consisting of more than ten thousand men under the command of General Jubal A. Early and operating from the Shenandoah Valley, reached the outskirts of Washington, only to be repulsed by Federal defenses hurriedly reinforced by veteran troops from Grant's army in Virginia. The Confederates retreated virtually unimpeded back to the Shenandoah Valley, but soon returned to western Maryland and raided as far north as Chambersburg, Pennsylvania, where Early's cavalry burned the town.

Privately seething and humiliated by Early's raid on Washington, Lincoln knew that public sentiment in the North would blame his administration for the near disaster and the lack of progress in suppressing the rebellion. He realized that if the military setbacks continued his party would face certain defeat in the fall elections. Publicly, however, Lincoln maintained his poise. He told a group of Baltimore citizens, "[We] must be vigilant but keep cool."[13] He set an example of courage and steadfastness at the height of Early's raid by visiting Fort Stevens, one of the defenses around Washington, and, though not by design, exposing himself to enemy fire.

Military setbacks for the Union continued into late July and August before the November elections. On July 30 a bold Federal effort to breach General Lee's defenses near Petersburg, Virginia, by blowing a hole in the center of the line was "a stupendous failure." The Battle of the Crater, as it was called, cost the Federals four thousand casualties and increased opposition to the Lincoln administration in the North. In Georgia, General Sherman's army, having lost about three thousand men in the bloody battle of Kennesaw Mountain, was stymied in its efforts to take Atlanta. Farther to the west, a daring raid by General Nathan Bedford Forrest on August 17 briefly recaptured Memphis and disrupted important Federal supply lines and facilities. Numerous minor engagements throughout the South continued to frustrate and sometimes rout Federal forces. Furthermore, disturbing reports reached Washington that during the summer Confederate sea raiders had intensified their activities against the Union commercial fleet. The C.S.S. *Tallahassee* alone captured thirty-one Northern ships in August. There seemed to be no relief in sight for the Union cause.

By mid-August 1864, with the elections looming and criticism of his administration's conduct of the war mounting, Lincoln's despair had turned to anguish. On August 19 he unburdened himself to two visitors from Wisconsin, both Democrats who supported the war: "My thoughts my solicitude for this great country follow me where ever I go. I don't think it is personal vanity, or ambition—but I cannot but feel that the weal or woe of this great nation will be decided in the approaching canvas." The Democratic party, Lincoln declared, had no program to save the Union, though he admitted that General McClellan, the presumed Democratic candidate, "is in favor of crushing out the rebellion." Still, "the slightest acquaintance with arithmetic will prove to any man that the rebel armies cannot be destroyed with democratic strategy"—by which he meant a peace that would concede emancipation and return the one to two hundred thousand black soldiers to slavery. Such a Democratic "strategy" not only would make Union victory impossible but also would result in armed black resistance and a racial war in the South. The Civil War could not be won by a policy of conciliation that would agree to the return of black soldiers to their masters, Lincoln insisted; if he supported such a policy, "I should be damned in time & in eternity." "The world shall know that I will keep my faith to friends & enemies, come what will." He affirmed that "no human power can subdue this rebellion without using the Emancipation lever as I have done. Freedom has given us the control of 200,000 able bodied men, born & raised on southern soil. It will give us more yet." He also said that "instead of alienating the south from us, there are evidences of a fraternal feeling growing up between our own & rebel soldiers."[14]

The two Democrats left the White House reassured in their support for the administration's war policy. Lincoln, who usually was persuasive in private conversations on vital issues, had no national media at his disposal to appeal directly to the people. Occasionally he wrote a letter for publication or to be read at a political rally. Only once during the 1864 presidential campaign did he write such a letter, and it was a brief statement for a mass meeting in Baltimore indicating his support for the ratification of a state constitutional amendment ending slavery in Maryland. The letter did not appeal for votes in the presidential election.[15] Lincoln depended upon the active support of editors and politicians, like his Wisconsin visitors, and their willingness to publicize his position on issues. He needed all the help he could get as war-weariness spread in the Union states.

Four days after his meeting with the Wisconsin Democrats, Lincoln, facing the likelihood that he would lose the election and, with it, the Union cause, drafted a remarkable proposal for saving the Union before the Democratic party's "strategy" was in place. His proposal was in the form of a sealed memorandum that he asked his cabinet to endorse without seeing it. Reflecting their respect for Lincoln, the cabinet members approved the memorandum without knowing its contents. The so-called blind memorandum read: "This morning, as for some days past, it seems exceedingly probable that this Administration will not be re-elected. Then it will be my duty to so co-operate with the President elect, as to save the Union between the election and the inauguration, as he will have secured his election on such ground that he can not possibly save it afterwards."[16] Only after the election did Lincoln reveal to his cabinet the memorandum's contents.

This document indicated the president's gloom regarding his party's electoral prospects and his willingness to put aside his opposition to McClellan and to work with him to end the war on the basis of reunion. Lincoln clearly did not believe that McClellan would be able to withstand the peace wing of his party after being inaugurated as president. Although this judgment may have been correct, it is unlikely that the Copperheads, after the Federal military victories of the fall and winter, could have obtained McClellan's agreement to a cease-fire and negotiations with the rebels. It is even more unlikely that McClellan would have cooperated with Lincoln after the election and before the inauguration in an all-out military effort to save the Union. That certainly was the sentiment of Secretary of State William H. Seward, who upon hearing the memorandum read to the cabinet scornfully remarked, "And the General would answer you 'Yes, Yes' and [do] nothing at all." But Lincoln responded, "At least, I should have done my duty and stood clear before my own conscience."[17]

★ ★ ★

The "blind memorandum" made no mention of emancipation as a condition for the restoration of the Union. In his despair, Lincoln momentarily considered abandoning emancipation. He reasoned that a victorious McClellan would not work with him to save the Union if he insisted on the abolition of slavery. It might be necessary to take the half loaf—Union—that McClellan would offer. Furthermore, Lincoln knew that restored Union governments in Louisiana, Arkansas, and Virginia had abolished slavery in their state constitutions as required by his plan of reconstruction announced in December 1863. Though the authority of these loyal governments did not extend throughout their states, McClellan was not likely to reverse their anti-slavery decisions. (Andrew Johnson's government in Tennessee was also considering state emancipation and would adopt it before the end of the war.)

The day after writing the memorandum, Lincoln, still convinced that he would lose the election, seemed willing to open negotiations with the Davis administration on the basis of reunion alone. Pressed by members of the national Republican committee to negotiate a peace without requiring emancipation, he drafted a letter authorizing Henry J. Raymond, editor of the *New York Times* and the new chairman of the committee, to go south and propose to Jefferson Davis that "upon the restoration of the Union and the National authority, the war shall cease at once, all remaining questions to be left for adjustment by peaceful means." But by the next day the president, after a night of anguished reflection, had changed his mind. He informed Raymond that to send a peace commission to Richmond at this juncture of the war and to break his promise to blacks who had been freed by the Emancipation Proclamation would be worse than losing the election: it would be an ignominious surrender of the purposes of the war.[18] The president thereby held fast on his antislavery position.

Few of Lincoln's presidential decisions carried as much moral weight as his decision to honor his commitment to end slavery, though at the time he feared it would further erode his chances for re-election. As he had demonstrated on other occasions, a promise was a promise and must be kept. Lincoln's earlier policy, expressed in his first inaugural address, of not interfering with slavery in the Southern states because of constitutional limitations, had lost validity when emancipation became a military necessity to restore those states to the Union. Still, Lincoln would not have issued his Emancipation Proclamation freeing slaves in rebel areas, nor would he have encouraged the adoption of a constitutional amendment ending the institution in the nation, had he not felt a strong moral revulsion against slavery itself. He had told his Wisconsin visitors on August 19 that the loss of black soldiers would make Union military defeat inevitable. He would not repudiate the promise of freedom to them and others of their race now by negotiating with the Confederates on the basis of reunion alone. Unlike the Democrats and apprehensive conservative Republicans, he also knew that Jefferson Davis would not seriously talk peace except to secure Confederate independence, a condition that Lincoln rejected outright.

* * *

There were those within the president's own party who believed he lacked nerve and decisiveness in the management of affairs. Radical Republicans like Senators Charles Sumner, Benjamin F. Wade, and Zachariah Chandler, though strong supporters of emancipation and the war, thought that Lincoln was slow to grasp the need for a vigorous policy to suppress the insurrection, end slavery, restore and maintain truly loyal governments in the South, and deal with rebel leaders. Some feared that the president, swayed by the public's longing for peace and influenced by conservative associates like Secretary of State Seward and Postmaster General Montgomery Blair, would ultimately compromise with the rebels in order to end the war and win re-election. Salmon P. Chase, the former treasury secretary whom Lincoln had removed from office in June over a patronage squabble, expressed this Radical concern in a letter to his daughter in September. His "apprehensions" regarding Lincoln, he wrote, "arise from the manifestations I see of a purpose to compromise, if possible, by sacrificing all that has been done for freedom in the rebel states—to purchase peace for themselves—the whites—by re-enslavement of the blacks."[19] Chase's definition of black freedom, like that of most Radicals, differed from Lincoln's. The Radicals wanted federal guarantees for black civil rights in the South, including suffrage (perhaps qualified). Lincoln, in contrast, would leave the rights of blacks in the hands of the restored state governments after emancipation.

In addition to policy concerns, a few prominent Radical Republicans—Wade, Wendell Phillips, and the brilliant Henry Winter Davis—simply disliked Lincoln and considered him a political trickster who owed his renomination to the stacking of the Union party convention with officeholders whom he had appointed. When the president, in July, vetoed a stringent Southern reconstruction bill

Benjamin F. Wade, a leading Radical Republican critic of Lincoln in the Senate and coauthor of the Wade-Davis Manifesto, which accused Lincoln of usurping congressional authority and threatened his candidacy for president in 1864.

sponsored by Wade and Davis, these two Radicals issued a blistering denunciation of him. They charged him with "dictatorial usurpation" of congressional authority and specifically castigated him for using military authority to create sham Union governments in Louisiana and elsewhere. His purpose, they claimed, was to secure the electoral votes of these bogus Southern governments. Though some Radicals quietly applauded the Wade-Davis Manifesto, as it was called, most Republicans opposed the document's publication on the grounds that it further divided the Union party on the eve of the election campaign. An outraged Lincoln wondered aloud if Wade and Davis "intend openly to oppose my election—the document looks that way."[20]

Some Radicals, particularly easterners who possessed a regional bias against westerners and had never been amused by the president's rustic jokes, privately complained that Lincoln lacked the intellectual or moral fiber to deal with the continuing crisis. They found highly inappropriate his practice of telling stories while the Union cause faltered. They attributed the military stalemate to his failure to remove incompetent generals and his refusal to enforce the Confiscation Act of 1862 against rebel property. They saw him as a weak leader, incapable of inspiring the Northern people to make the sacrifices that would save the Union. Senator Sumner of Massachusetts wrote that Lincoln had "no instinct or inspiration" for leadership. Sumner wanted Lincoln to step aside as the party's candidate in favor of "any one of 100 names." Governor John A. Andrew of Sumner's state echoed these criticisms. Andrew wrote to a sympathetic Horace Greeley of the *New York Tribune,* "Mr. Lincoln *ought* to lead the country." But, Andrew sniffed, he could not do so, because "he is essentially lacking in the quality of leadership, which is a gift of God and not a device of man."[21]

By late August the lack of confidence in Lincoln's leadership had become widespread in the Republican party. Facing what seemed almost certain defeat at the polls, Republicans blamed Lincoln for the military stalemate and for failing to take the kind of action that, they believed, was necessary to preserve the Union. Thurlow Weed, a close associate of Seward and editor of the *Albany Evening Journal,* publicly announced his intention to vote for McClellan and declared that Lincoln's emancipation policy made armed suppression of the rebellion impossible. Richard Smith, the powerful editor of the *Cincinnati Gazette,* wrote to a friend on August 27: "The people regard Mr. Lincoln's candidacy as a misfortune. His apparent strength when nominated [in June] was fictitious, and now the fiction has disappeared, and instead of confidence there is distrust." Smith clearly exaggerated for political effect when he wrote: "I do not know a Lincoln man."[22]

At the height of the political crisis, a group of New York Republicans—mostly Radicals—plotted to replace Lincoln as the party's standard-bearer. They issued a call for another Union (Republican) convention to meet in Cincinnati on September 28 to "consider the state of the nation" and to concentrate "the union strength on [a] candidate who commands the confidence of the country, even by a new nomination if necessary." The convention, they continued, should consider a plan "to secure the early return of Peace by suppressing the Rebellion" and restoring "the integrity of the American Union and the Rights and Liberties of the People." The call for the convention, which was endorsed by the influential New York editors Horace Greeley, Parke Godwin, and Theodore Tilton, did not mention emancipation. This omission was further evidence that the movement to replace Lincoln as the party's candidate had conservative Republican, as well as Radical, backing.[23]

Some disaffected conservatives sought to organize their own party and form a coalition with the Democrats in the election. The Conservative Unionists, as they called themselves, consisted mainly of devotees of the defunct Whig party who had never approved of what they considered to be the extreme tendencies of the Republican party. They included Congressman John Todd Stuart, who had parted with Lincoln, his old law partner, over war issues, Senator Edgar A. Cowan of Pennsylvania, Senator Reverdy Johnson of Maryland, Governor Thomas E. Bramlette of Kentucky, and Robert C. Winthrop, the scion of a distinguished Massachusetts family and a former Speaker of the U.S. House of Representatives. They condemned Lincoln's violation of individual rights and, even more strenuously, opposed his commitment to emancipation as a sine qua non for peace. Like the Radicals, they saw Lincoln as weak and lacking in essential leadership qualities. The conservatives, though strong advocates for the suppression of the rebellion, feared that a re-elected Lincoln would succumb to the Radical demand for the "subjugation" of the South after the war. Like the Democrats, they concluded that Lincoln's policies would prolong the war and make reunion impossible.[24]

The Conservative Unionists at first sought to persuade a former president, Millard Fillmore, to come out of retirement and accept their nomination. Fillmore, whose presidency in the early 1850s had been characterized by a policy of conciliation toward the slave South, publicly proclaimed his support for the conservative movement of 1864 as the only hope for saving the Union and the Constitution, but he refused to become a candidate. Unable to find a suitable nominee and lacking organizational strength, the Conservative Unionists announced their willingness to support McClellan, soon to be the Democratic nominee. At the same time they endorsed the former Tennessee governor and Mexican War hero William B. Campbell, an old-line Whig, for vice president. Hoping to join the Democrats on a war platform that would leave slavery and other issues to the states after reunion had been achieved, they sent a delegation to the Democratic national convention in Chicago in August.

* * *

Meeting at a time when the peace movement in the North was at its height and Lincoln's re-election already seemed doomed, the Democrats rejected the conservative platform and the suggestion of Campbell as McClellan's running mate. Instead, they adopted a platform drafted by Clement Vallandigham, a leading Copperhead, pronouncing the war a failure and demanding that "immediate efforts be made for a cessation of hostilities, with a view to an ultimate convention of states" for the restoration of the Union. The status of slavery would be left to the states to determine.

The Copperheads had gained control of the Democratic party. However, they were lukewarm in their enthusiasm for McClellan, who subsequently repudiated the party's peace resolution but not its plank affirming the states' control of their own institutions, including slavery. McClellan made it clear that he would revoke Lincoln's Emancipation Proclamation and restore the Constitution "as it was" with all civil liberties (for whites) and states' rights respected. Though disappointed with McClellan's refusal to support a cease-fire, Vallandigham and his Copperhead friends thought they could control the general after he was inaugurated, a conclusion that Lincoln had already drawn. The nomination of Congressman George H. Pendleton, an affable Vallandigham protégé, for vice president, was another sign of Copperhead strength and division among Democrats.

The work of the Chicago convention, even with the nomination of McClellan, stunned Conservative Unionists and war Democrats. At the same time, the electrifying news of Sherman's capture of Atlanta, preceded in August by Admiral David Farragut's defeat of the Confederate ironclad *Tennessee* and his seizure of Mobile Bay, turned the tables on the Copperheads. Disgusted with the Democratic platform and Copperhead defeatism, some prominent Conservative Unionists and Democrats announced their intention to vote for Lincoln rather than see the triumph of a party committed to an armistice that, they believed, would surely lead to Confederate independence. After the Chicago convention Edward Everett, New England's most influential former Whig, who had been the Constitutional Union (conservative) nominee for vice president in 1860, immediately endorsed Lincoln's candidacy and agreed to serve as an elector on the ticket. A campaign speech that Everett made in New York two weeks before the election reportedly "had a powerful effect upon a large class of cultivated and thoughtful men, whose conservative views [had] led them" to support the Constitutional Union party in 1860.[25]

Meanwhile, other Conservative Unionists, notably Robert C. Winthrop, stood by McClellan and campaigned for him while ignoring the Chicago platform. Winthrop, whom Lincoln later judged to have made the best opposition speech in the campaign, hammered on the president's failure to win the war and restore the Union. Some conservative and Democratic speakers and editors followed Winthrop's example in attacking Lincoln and avoiding the war-failure plank in the platform.[26] But many Democrats or Copperheads defended the Chicago platform as offering the only way to end the "monstrous war." They declared that only the Democratic party could save the nation from ruin and Republican despotism. Whether moved by genuine patriotic concerns, campaign strategy, or hatred of Lincoln—or perhaps all three—Copperheads went to excess in their denunciation of the president. They repeatedly referred to him as a "buffoon" who joked while sending thousands of American men to be slaughtered in the South. One Copperhead editor wrote that Lincoln's "face is a faithful chart of his soul, and his face is that of a demon, cunning, obscene, treacherous, lying and devilish." As they had done before, Copperheads appealed to racist sentiment in the North. Having introduced the word "miscegenation" into the nation's vocabulary in late 1863, they lambasted Lincoln for his "fanatical abolition" policy and charged that his purpose, as well as that of his party, was to establish black equality in America and subject the South to Negro rule.[27]

Despite the Copperheads' anti-black propaganda, the extent of the racist harangue in the 1864 election should not be exaggerated.[28] Lincoln's insistence on emancipation as a condition for reunion carried some weight in the Democratic campaign, but the extremism of the Copperhead assault, which late in the contest became a desperate ploy of a few editors, probably helped the president and his party. As the campaign entered its final stages, most conservative and Democratic spokesmen seemed to recognize the counterproductive nature of the racial tactic. Some conservatives like Winthrop, who as Speaker of the House in the 1840s had supported the Wilmot Proviso to prohibit the expansion of slavery into the Southwest, rejected outright a racist appeal, though they continued to denounce the president's insistence on federal emancipation as a prerequisite for peace. They concentrated their attacks on the Lincoln administration's violations of civil liberties and its "miserable failure" to restore the Union. Senator Reverdy Johnson, in a letter prepared for a McClellan rally, outlined the Democratic charges against Lincoln and, without mentioning slavery or blacks, predicted that reunion was certain if McClellan won the election because of "his expressed determination to make [the Union's] restoration the one condition of peace."[29] In suggesting that Southerners would agree to this requirement for peace, Johnson ignored reports that, far from being willing to accept reunion, Confederates had been encouraged by the Democratic party's cease-fire platform and believed that a McClellan victory would result in their independence. Like Lincoln, Southerners expected that a President McClellan would succumb to Copperhead pressure and agree to a cessation of hostilities.

Many Democrats, including McClellan, attempted to distance themselves from the Copperheads by repeatedly denying the Republican charge that they were disloyal and were plotting with the Confederate government and its agents in Canada.[30] When Judge Advocate General Joseph Holt on October 8 issued a lengthy report charging a Copperhead conspiracy to establish a "Northwest Confederacy" (in the Midwest) and aid the South, Copperheads and moderate Democrats joined in condemning it as an amalgam of falsehoods and political propaganda designed to secure Lincoln's election. Vallandigham attacked the Holt report as "preposterous [and] without foundation."

He declared that the purpose of Democratic militants in the campaign, specifically the Midwestern Sons of Liberty, whom Holt had accused of disloyalty, was to "promote Jeffersonian doctrine" (states' rights) and "protect individual rights" under the Constitution, not to plot treason. Despite such denials, Holt's "Conspiracy Report," which was widely distributed, created outrage among Republicans and further damaged McClellan and his party in the campaign.[31]

* * *

The Democratic party's war-failure platform and Sherman's dramatic victory at Atlanta had turned the presidential campaign in Lincoln's favor by mid-September despite remaining skepticism about his leadership. Lincoln and other Republicans, however, could not be sure that their advantage would hold until the election. A military setback might quickly reverse their gains and place the Union and emancipation in great jeopardy in the election.[32] The early autumn return to Missouri of General Sterling Price with a Confederate army of twelve thousand men, despite the simultaneous Union successes of General Philip H. Sheridan against Jubal Early in the Shenandoah Valley, gave Republicans cause for concern. Although Price was turned back in late October after a failed attempt to take St. Louis and free Missouri, a border slave state, from Union control, Democrats called his military campaign "ample proof" of the Lincoln administration's inability to pacify "even a single State under the easiest conditions." In nearby Illinois, Congressman Elihu B. Washburne wrote to Lincoln on October 17: "It is no use to deceive ourselves about this State . . . There is imminent danger of our losing" the election. Washburne insisted that "steps must be taken instantly to have every soldier home" to vote "if you would save the State from the most appalling calamity." Lincoln, though seriously worried, scribbled one word on the envelope from Washburne: "Stampeded"—referring to the irrational fears of Illinois Republicans that their state was lost to the Copperheads.[33]

Republican unity became essential as the campaign entered its final weeks. Lincoln knew that strong opposition to his candidacy within the party, culminating in a convention to replace him and perhaps change the platform, would probably irreparably divide the party and lead not only to his own defeat but also to that of other Union candidates. He foresaw a real possibility that Democrats, once in control of the country, would make an inglorious peace with the rebels. Lincoln's personal ambition, which had been a driving force in his rise to prominence as a lawyer and politician in Illinois, played a secondary role, if it figured at all, in his motivation to defeat McClellan and the Copperheads in November. The principles embedded in the Constitution, its laws, and the Declaration of Independence, ideas he had expressed in his Gettysburg Address and on other occasions, would be endangered if he lost.

Lincoln was elated when talk of a convention to replace him as the party's candidate faded. Frightened by the Democrats' war-failure platform, dissident Republicans recognized the need to drop their opposition to the president. Sherman's success at Atlanta had restored the confidence of rank-and-file Republicans in Lincoln's leadership. Conservative (or moderate) Republicans quickly fell into line. Orville H. Browning of Illinois, Senator Jacob Collamer of Vermont, Daniel S. Dickinson of New York, and a number of party editors announced their support for Lincoln in the hope of rallying conservatives to his candidacy. They ignored, however, the antislavery plank in the party's platform. In New York, Thurlow Weed, after a patronage favor from Lincoln, threw his political weight behind the president.[34]

Lincoln also reached out a hand to the Radicals in Congress when he forced from his cabinet Montgomery Blair, the intemperate postmaster general who had denounced and intrigued against administration opponents. Blair's dismissal removed an impediment to Radical support and Republican unity in the election. One day earlier, on September 22, John C. Frémont, who had been nominated for president in May by a group of disaffected Radicals including Wendell Phillips and Frederick Douglass, and whose candidacy might have siphoned off support from Lincoln, had withdrawn from the race. Whether Blair's dismissal was the result of a quid pro quo with Frémont is debatable.[35] The timing may have been coincidental.

Lincoln had been reluctant to dismiss Blair, of whom, despite their differing personalities, he was genuinely fond. Earlier, when Thaddeus Stevens and two other Radical congressmen visited the White House to demand Blair's dismissal, Lincoln angrily told them, "To have my constitutional advisers selected beforehand, to be told I must do this or leave that undone . . . would be degrading to my manhood to consent to any such bargain." He said that he would rather "refuse the office" of president "than to accept such disgraceful terms" to gain their support. After the Chicago Democratic convention, Lincoln, fearing that a Radical defection could be fatal to the Union cause, swallowed his pride and forced Blair's resignation. But he did not forget this affront to his "manhood"; furthermore, he retained Blair as one of his advisers and in early 1865 quietly supported him for a Senate seat.[36]

Despite Blair's dismissal and the critical need to avoid a Democratic victory in the presidential contest, Radical leaders still found it difficult to campaign for Lincoln. Senator Wade expressed his reluctance in a letter to Senator Chandler of Michigan: "Were it not for the country there would be a poetical justice in [Lincoln] being beaten by that stupid ass McClellan . . . I can but wish the d—l had Old Abe. But the issue is now made up and we have either got to take him, or Jeff Davis, for McClellan and all who will support him, are meaner traitors than are to be found in the Confederacy." In the campaign, Radicals like Wade, Chandler, and Henry Winter Davis emphasized the disastrous effects of a Copperhead victory and virtually ignored Lincoln as the party's standard-bearer.[37]

Francis Lieber, a friend of Senator Charles Sumner and a prominent German-American professor at Columbia University, who in early September had demanded that Lincoln withdraw from the ticket, now wrote a pamphlet emphasizing why Germans should vote for Lincoln. Many German Americans had supported Frémont because of his vigorous action to suppress rebels in Missouri and his early attempt to end slavery in that state. Believing that Lincoln had failed to act aggressively against slavery and had discriminated against their hero in appointments to military command, they seemed willing to vote for McClellan after Frémont withdrew from the race. Lieber sought to demonstrate that far more was involved in the election than the candidacy of an individual. The democratic causes that German Americans supported and the freedom from oppression that many of them had sought when they left Europe were at stake. Published in German, Dutch, and English, Lieber's pamphlet did not mention the president's name until the last three paragraphs, where it called for Germans and other immigrants to vote for Lincoln because he was the only candidate who stood for liberty and the Union.[38]

Old-line abolitionists came out almost solidly for Lincoln in the election. A notable exception was the spellbinding orator Wendell Phillips of Massachusetts. The prominent abolitionist William Lloyd Garrison had criticized Phillips for joining the Frémont movement and then, when Frémont withdrew, refusing to support Lincoln. Garrison, who applauded the president's firm opposition to slavery, also rebuked the black spokesman Frederick Douglass for his opposition to Lincoln. Douglass earlier in the year had bitterly attacked the president for not doing enough for members of his race in slavery and in the army. At that time he had unjustly charged that Lincoln in dealing with blacks had laid down a rule for his administration: "Do evil by choice, right from necessity." Nonetheless, after the "disloyal and slavery perpetuating" Democratic national convention and the rebuke from Garrison, Douglass announced his support for Lincoln's re-election. He admitted that, "while there was the slightest possibility of securing the nomination and election of a man to the Presidency of more decided anti-slavery convictions and a firmer faith in the immediate necessity and practicality of justice and equality for all men, than have been exhibited in the policy of the present Administration, I, like many other radical men, freely criticized . . . the actions and utterance of Mr. Lincoln and withheld from him my support." But, he wrote, "that possibility is no longer conceivable; it is now plain" that the election of McClellan on the Chicago platform "would be the heaviest calamity of all these years of war and blood, . . . since it would wantonly cast away everything valuable, purchased so dearly . . . on the battlefield for the perfect liberty and permanent peace of [our] common country."[39] Though he did not actively campaign, Douglass's endorsement probably contributed to the decision of reluctant abolitionists to vote for Lincoln.

Southern Unionists overwhelmingly rallied to the Lincoln-Johnson standard. Privately, some, like their political brethren in the North, had expressed displeasure with "Old Father Abraham," but after the adoption of the Democratic platform, which threatened to leave them at the mercy of the rebels, they united behind the president. Several prominent Southern Unionists, whose courageous defiance of the rebels had made them heroes in the loyal states, campaigned for Lincoln in the North. Governor Francis H. Pierpont of the Restored Government of Virginia undertook the most grueling campaign, stumping for eight weeks in the Northeast, sometimes speaking twice a day to crowds of three to four thousand. Most Southern supporters could not vote in the election: in the South, only Federal-occupied Tennessee, with its military governor, Andrew Johnson, on the Republican ticket, opened its polls. Though Lincoln easily defeated McClellan in Tennessee, Congress refused to count the state's electoral votes because Unionists there had not completed the process of reconstruction launched by Lincoln in 1863. Congress also did not recognize the Lincoln votes cast by the Unionist legislature in Louisiana. Lincoln acknowledged that the Senate and the House of Representatives had "complete power to exclude from counting all electoral votes deemed by them to be illegal." Unionists throughout the South lamented that they were not able to vote for the "vigorous, strong-minded, and conscientious man" who was in the process of suppressing the rebellion. For his part, the president would not forget the strong support he received from the Southern white Unionists.[40]

* * *

For Lincoln, the issue in the 1864 presidential campaign was clear. Even in July, before the Chicago convention, in a *"private"* letter to New York Postmaster Abram Wakeman, he delineated what he saw as the critical difference between the two parties: "The present presidential contest will almost certainly be no other than a contest between a Union and a Disunion candidate, disunion certainly following the success of the latter." Lincoln suggested that peace Democrats had become the dupes of Confederate agents in Canada who sought to undermine the Union party in the election by offering to negotiate an end to the war. Earlier in July Horace Greeley of the *New York Tribune* had attempted to arrange peace talks at Niagara Falls. Though skeptical, Lincoln had authorized his secretary John Hay and Greeley to meet with the Confederates and determine whether they had official credentials and would negotiate on the basis of reunion and the abolition of slavery. In the Niagara Falls meeting, Hay and Greeley discovered that the Confederates had no authorization from Richmond to hold talks with the Union, much less to accept Lincoln's terms. Democrats seized on the incident and charged that Lincoln had failed to negotiate in good faith. The president told Wakeman there was no doubt in his mind that the rebel emissaries had only one objective: "to assist in selecting and arranging a candidate and a platform for the Chicago convention" that would be favorable to Southern independence.

Lincoln's purpose in writing the letter was to gain the support of Wakeman's friend James Gordon Bennett, the independent owner of the influential *New York Herald* and a frequent critic of the president. Lincoln cleverly directed his last sentence to Bennett, who would assuredly see the letter. He wrote: "The issue is a mighty one for all people and all time; and whoever aids the right, will be appreciated and remembered."[41] The message was not subtle: if Bennett helped Lincoln win the election, Lincoln would reward him with a position in the administration. Lincoln rarely made direct promises of office in exchange for political support; he found such logrolling distasteful and demeaning. But his re-election was too important to the Union and antislavery cause for him to leave any political stone unturned, even the promise of office to a volatile critic like Bennett.

Later, in the fall, Lincoln told William O. Bartlett, a Bennett associate, that he had the *Herald* editor in mind for appointment as minister to France. One week before the election, Bartlett called on the president and asked him to reaffirm his promise to Bennett. The threat of withholding the *Herald*'s support if Lincoln refused was implicit. As Bartlett reported to Bennett, Lincoln, after discussing the attitude of the *Herald* toward the administration, declared that he expected to make the offer to Bennett "as certainly as I do to be re-elected myself." Bennett quickly tempered his criticism of the president. True to his promise, Lincoln after the election offered Bennett the position of minister to France; the *Herald* chief was pleased but, probably to the president's relief, turned down the appointment.[42]

* * *

The influential eastern literary establishment saw the presidential contest in the same clear light as Lincoln did. New England writers and intellectuals had earlier dismissed the president as uncouth, too inexperienced for high office, and lacking essential qualities of leadership. Though some still were skeptical of the "rail-splitter's" abilities, during the 1864 campaign eastern men of letters, motivated by Lincoln's Union and antislavery purposes in the war and shaken by the Copperhead threat, rallied to his side and used their pens to give him valuable support. No literary figure was more important to the president's cause than James Russell Lowell.[43]

Modern critics view Lowell as a second-rate poet who should not be spoken of in the same breath with Longfellow, Whittier, Holmes, Whitman, and other literary giants of the Civil War era. But in his own time, few intellectuals had a higher standing than Lowell for his multiple attainments as poet, writer of prose, editor, and commentator on public affairs.[44] Throughout the war, Lowell maintained a steadfast support for Lincoln's policies, first in the *Atlantic Monthly* and, beginning in January 1864, in the *North American Review,* which he co-edited. Though he fervently opposed slavery, Lowell came to understand the political and constitutional necessity for Lincoln's patience in acting against the institution. Like the president, Lowell believed that the preservation of the Union was paramount. In the first issue of the *North American Review* under his editorship, he defended Lincoln's policies, including his conduct of foreign affairs and his conservative reconstruction plan. After receiving a copy of the issue, Lincoln wrote to the magazine's publishers expressing his delight with the article and indicating that it "will be of value to the country."[45]

Inspired by the positive reception the article received from the president and in the Northeast, Lowell wrote three additional political essays in the *Review* before the election. In the first of these, appearing in April, he launched a blistering attack on General McClellan, the presumed Democratic candidate for president, who had twice been removed from command by Lincoln. In the second, published in July, at a time when the peace movement was growing in the North, Lowell gave a damning historical account of secession and a strong defense of the Union cause. The third, which appeared in October, aimed to win support for Lincoln in the election.

"Mr. Lincoln," Lowell declared in the third essay, "has shown from the first the considerate wisdom of a practical statesman." The president, he asserted, understood that a permanent peace, based on the restoration of the Union and the end of slavery, could only be achieved by "the complete subjugation of the rebellion." Yet his amnesty policy for Southerners was "wide enough to satisfy the demands of the most exacting humanity." Lowell deliberately stopped short of calling Lincoln "a great man, for over-hasty praise is too apt to sour at last into satire, and greatness may be trusted safely to history and the future; but an honest one we believe him to be, and with no aim save to repair the glory and greatness of his country." McClellan, meanwhile, had proven his lack of honor by accepting the Democratic nomination and then declining to run on the party's peace platform. Moreover, "McClellan's election will be understood by the South and by the whole country as an acknowledgment of the right of secession," an acknowledgment that would weaken if not destroy American nationalism. In contrast, Lincoln was "the exponent of principles vital to our peace, dignity, and renown,—of all that can save America from becoming Mexico, and insure popular freedom for centuries to come."[46]

* * *

Protestant clergymen and editors of church publications provided another powerful force for Lincoln and the Republicans in the campaign. In the beginning of Lincoln's presidency, the Protestant hierarchy, which had become increasingly antislavery and anti-Southern during the antebellum period, was lukewarm toward the Illinois railsplitter. Because Lincoln showed no disposition to move against slavery in the South, or even to repudiate the onerous Fugitive Slave Law, the clergy saw little difference between him and his Democratic opponents. But Lincoln's Emancipation Proclamation and his persistent efforts to save republican self-government and institutions produced a dramatic improvement in their attitude toward the president.[47] Democratic opposition to emancipation and the administration's measures to restore the Union persuaded Protestant leaders to support Lincoln's policies, though many continued to doubt his abilities.

The Methodist Episcopal Church, the largest denomination in the North, especially rallied the faithful to the Union cause. A general conference of Methodist bishops and ministers, meeting in Philadelphia in May 1864, in effect announced the denomination's support for Lincoln's re-election. It sent an address to the president praising his efforts to suppress "this wicked rebellion" and restore an undivided Union "founded on the Word of God, and securing in righteousness liberty and equal rights to all." Lincoln, in a carefully prepared written response, praised all of the churches for their support of the government, singling out the Methodists "as the most important of all." "The Methodist Church," he wrote, "sends more soldiers to the field, more nurses to the hospital, and more prayers to Heaven than any. God bless the Methodist Church—bless all the churches—and blessed be God, Who, in this our great trial, giveth us the churches." Lincoln's pronouncement was music to the ears of these powerful clergymen.[48]

The Methodist Church justified its support of Lincoln and the Republicans on lofty moral grounds. "The moral and religious interests of the country," the *Christian Advocate and Journal,* the leading Methodist publication, asserted, "demand the prosecution of the war to the extinction of the rebellion, and the extirpation of slavery from all parts of the nation; and as a means to these most desirable consummations, we recognize the necessity for the continuance of the present administration in power." Bishop Gilbert Haven of New England in a sermon preached in Boston on September 11 admonished all Methodists to "march to the ballot-box, an army of Christ . . . and deposit a million of votes for [the church's] true representative, and she will give the final blow to the reeling [rebel] fiend." Haven insisted that "the Church must do her duty in this hour, and that duty is, by every righteous means in her power to secure the re-election of Abraham Lincoln."[49]

Except in Kentucky, few Methodist ministers in the Union states failed to preach the pure Union gospel from their pulpits. They demanded the relentless prosecution of the war to suppress the rebellion and also the adoption of an antislavery constitutional amendment. Some pastors read from their pulpits Judge Advocate General Holt's report charging a Copperhead conspiracy to subvert the Union cause and aid the Confederacy in the election. In addition, many of the almost five hundred Methodist chaplains in the army urged their communicants to vote for "Father Abraham" and his party. Methodist tracts and periodicals supporting Lincoln and the war flooded the North and the army camps. Subscriptions to official Methodist journals alone totaled more than four hundred thousand. The Methodist Church was a militant, disciplined organization that played an important role in the election.[50]

Other Protestant denominations, perhaps with less partisan zeal or self-righteousness than the Methodists, also contributed to the Republican campaign. Some church organizations, without directly endorsing Lincoln's candidacy or the Republican platform, passed resolutions proclaiming, as the 1864 Lutheran General Synod expressed it, the necessity of the "forcible suppression" of slavery, "the righteousness of the war, [and] the duty of every Christian to support it." Baptist and Congregational ministers tended to be more explicit in their advocacy of the war party. A Congregational pastor, for example, announced from his Boston pulpit, "The man who casts his vote, in the election now pending, in favor of a peace not won by the conquests of our armies, does the rebel cause more service, if possible, than he would by joining the rebel army." Of course, not all Protestants followed the lead of their ministers; many, along with most Irish-American Catholics, supported McClellan. Still, the *Christian Advocate and Journal* accurately concluded after the ballots had been cast: "There probably never was an election in all our history into which the religious element entered so largely, and nearly all on one side." Indeed, in this critical election for the Union and the antislavery cause, civil religion, or the influence of the church on political affairs, achieved its high-water mark in American history.[51]

★ ★ ★

Lincoln himself did not campaign, though he took a keen interest in the canvass and sometimes played an active role without leaving Washington. He observed the early American tradition that presidential candidates stay at home and not engage in a direct appeal for votes. (Stephen A. Douglas, who campaigned nationally in 1860, was an exception to the rule.) If Lincoln had spoken at Republican rallies and perhaps faced heckling, as was the nineteenth-century American political custom, it could have backfired on his candidacy. As a president who took seriously the dignity of the office, he did not want to compromise it by appealing for votes.

In Washington, the president spoke to returning Union regiments, visited hospitals, and attended charitable events. On these occasions he talked about the virtues of the Union and free government, but he made no explicit appeal for support at the polls. Responding to a rally of supporters on the White House grounds on October 19, he affirmed that he would abide by the will of the people in the election even if the "immediate peace" party prevailed. "I believe, however," he added, "that [the people] are still resolved to preserve their country and their liberty." Lincoln closed his remarks with the assertion that the men in uniform supported him. "In this purpose to save the country and it's liberties," he declared, "no classes of people seem so unanamous as the soldiers in the field and seamen afloat. Do they not have the hardest of it? Who shall quail while they do not? God bless the soldiers and seamen with all their brave commanders." Lincoln probably knew that these remarks would receive wide circulation in the press and identify him with the patriotic sacrifices of the troops, and thereby appeal to voters in the army and at home.[52]

Lincoln's faith in the soldiers' support prompted him, after a frantic appeal from Governor Oliver Morton of Indiana for aid at the polls, to ask General Sherman to release his Hoosier soldiers to go back to Indiana to vote in the October state elections. The loss of Indiana in November, he told Sherman, "would go far toward losing the whole Union cause." He reminded Sherman that "Indiana is the only important State, voting in October, whose law prohibited soldiers from voting in the field. Any thing you can safely do to let her soldiers, or any part of them, go home and vote at the State election, will be greatly in point. They need not remain for the Presidential election." Lincoln made it clear that "this is, in no sense, an order, but is merely intended to impress you with the importance, to the army itself, of your doing all you safely can" to aid the Union cause in Indiana. Sherman, sufficiently impressed with the need, whether ordered or not, granted furloughs to sick and wounded Indiana soldiers so they could go to the polls.[53]

Early in the campaign a Republican club in Buffalo asked Lincoln to write a statement for delivery before a "national union mass ratification meeting." In the letter he drafted for the meeting, he claimed that only his policy could save the Union and that "any substantial departure from it insures the success of the rebellion." Writing only twelve days after the Democratic convention had called for a cease-fire, he argued that "an armistice—a cessation of hostilities—is the end of the struggle, and the insurgents would be in a peaceable possession of all that has been struggled for." He reiterated a point he had made to his Wisconsin visitors on August 19: "Any different policy in regard to the colored man, deprives us of his help, and this is more than we can bear. We can not spare the hundred and forty or fifty thousand now serving us as soldiers, seamen, and laborers. This is not a question of sentiment or taste, but one of physical force which may be measured and estimated as horse-power and Steam-power are measured and estimated. Keep it and you can save the Union. Throw it away, and the Union goes with it." Furthermore, Lincoln declared, he could not be a party to the re-enslavement of Southern blacks. "It *can* not be; and it *ought* not to be."[54]

Upon reflection, Lincoln decided not to send the letter. Instead, he told the president of the Buffalo club that "it is not best for me now to write a general letter to a political meeting" and explained that "it is not customary for one holding the office, and being a candidate for re-election," to participate in the campaign. He also noted that "a public letter must be written with some care, and at some expense of time"; otherwise, his words might be misconstrued.[55] From the beginning of his presidency, Lincoln had carefully prepared his public statements to avoid making errors that could mislead the American people and become easy targets for his critics. During the presidential campaign of 1864, when the fate of the Union and emancipation hung in the balance, he was even more careful to observe this cautious policy.

* * *

Lincoln's concern about losing the election lessened after the mid-October contests in the critical states of Indiana, Ohio, and Pennsylvania. The Union party won almost all the congressional seats in Indiana and Ohio, easily returned Indiana governor Oliver Morton to office, and won a narrow victory in Pennsylvania. (There were no gubernatorial elections in Ohio and Pennsylvania.) The adoption by

Maryland voters of a new state constitution abolishing slavery especially pleased Lincoln. Two days after these victories, while waiting at
the War Department telegraph office for military dispatches, he jotted
down his "estimated electoral vote" for each state in the November
election. He calculated that he would win 120 votes to McClellan's
114. This "estimated" vote, to be sure, represented a narrow margin,
but Lincoln conservatively gave Pennsylvania and New York to the
Copperhead party, despite indications that he probably would win
those states. After the election the Washington correspondent of the
Boston Daily Advertiser remarked that Lincoln's political "calcula-
tions were always sober," dating back to his days in Illinois: "He
never made the mistake of underestimating the enemy."[56]

By November most astute political observers expected Lincoln and
his party to win the election. But no one could be certain, and many
Democrats, including General McClellan, predicted that *they* would
win. A swing of 31,500 votes in eight states, including New York,
could have given the election to McClellan. Though McClellan won
only three states (Kentucky, New Jersey, and Delaware), 44 percent of
voters cast Democratic ballots. As in most elections, the reasons for
the voters' behavior were varied and are difficult to assess. Many in
the North who voted for McClellan had been persuaded by the barrage of Democratic propaganda and Radical Republican criticism asserting that Lincoln had failed. These disaffected voters believed that
McClellan somehow would be able to negotiate an end to the war,
followed by the restoration of the Union, even if it meant state control
of black emancipation and other concessions. With some exceptions,
Democrats were not concerned about the future of slavery or blacks
in the South.

No other political contest in American history compares with the
intensity of the 1864 presidential campaign and the conspiratorial
tone that characterized it. The political warfare in the North and the
border states over the purposes and conduct of the war and over issues of confiscation of rebel property, emancipation, civil liberties,
conscription, finance, and reconstruction policy had been intense
since the bloody battles of 1862 had failed to suppress the rebellion. It
reached a crescendo in the presidential and state campaigns of 1864.
The Holt report in October 1864 of a widespread Copperhead con-

spiracy in the Old Northwest (the Midwest) to disrupt the election, though exaggerated, frightened many Northerners and convinced some excitable Republican leaders like Salmon P. Chase that the North was on the brink of its own civil war. Rumors of rebel plots to burn Northern cities proved partly accurate in the case of New York, where Confederates operating from Canada attempted with little success to set fire to hotels.

It is remarkable that during this crisis Lincoln, despite his private fear, did not publicly charge peace Democrats with sedition and giving aid and comfort to the enemy. If Lincoln had been the despot that the Democrats repeatedly claimed he was, he would have ordered the arrest and incarceration of leading Copperheads like Clement Vallandigham and encouraged local authorities to root out other "traitors" in their communities. But Lincoln was no tyrant. His purpose was to maintain Northern support for the war with only necessary infringements on civil liberties (for example, the temporary suspension of the writ of habeas corpus). He wanted to avoid dangerous precedents for the future. Two days after the election he declared that the nation had passed the "severe test" of protecting the liberties of the people while its existence was threatened. After learning that no major disturbances had occurred on election day, Lincoln publicly admitted that most Democrats had been loyal. Still, he could not resist commenting that "he who is most devoted to the Union, and most opposed to treason, [received] most of the people's votes."[57]

The equanimity with which Lincoln handled himself during the campaign and his acknowledgment of Democratic fidelity after the election went far toward diffusing the political excitement that had prevailed in the North. Except for Radicals such as Chase and Senators Charles Sumner and Ben Wade, most Republicans followed his lead in recognizing the political legitimacy of the Democrats, a position they had refused to take after the adoption of the Copperhead platform at Chicago in August.[58]

★ ★ ★

The triumph of Lincoln and the Republicans in November produced, in addition to rallies celebrating the victory, an avalanche of commentaries on the meaning of the election. Supporters of the Union party, with good reason, proclaimed Lincoln's victory the most important in the history of the republic. To them it meant that the Union had been saved, and most (but not all) believed the election had rung the death knell for slavery everywhere in the United States. George Templeton Strong, an urbane New Yorker who once had ridiculed Lincoln's western manner of speaking and doubted the wisdom of the voters, now hailed his success. He recorded in his diary: "The crisis has been past, and the most momentous popular election ever held since ballots were invented has decided against treason and disunion. My contempt for democracy and extended suffrage is mitigated."[59]

Northeastern intellectuals, who earlier had questioned Lincoln's capacity for leadership, rejoiced in his victory. George William Curtis, editor of *Harper's Weekly,* wrote that "the grandest lesson of the [election] result is its vindication of the American system of free popular government." "No system in history," Curtis reminded his readers, "was ever exposed to such a strain directly along the fibre as that which ours has endured in the war and the political campaign . . . Thank God and the people, we are a nation which comprehends its priceless importance to human progress and civilization, and which recognizes that law is the indispensable condition of Liberty." Lincoln himself, Curtis continued, "notwithstanding his unwearied patience, perfect fidelity, and remarkable sagacity, is unimportant; but as the representative of the feeling and purpose of the American people is the most important fact in the world." The literary giant Ralph Waldo Emerson simply remarked, "Seldom in history was so much staked on a popular vote." For James Russell Lowell, "The re-election of Mr. Lincoln was a greater triumph than any military victory could be over the principles of the rebellion. The eighth of November, 1864,—the election day, will stand always as one of the most memorable days in our history." Lowell told a friend that he had "little doubt [Lincoln's] course and his character will both be estimated more highly in history than they are . . . by his contemporaries."[60]

From Europe, the American minister to Austria, John Lothrop Motley, informed Lincoln that his re-election was a stunning victory for democracy and liberty against oligarchy and privilege. William Marsh, a U.S. consul in Germany, affirmed Motley's opinion, probably with some exaggeration: "All Germany rejoices at the re-election of Mr. Lincoln. The event inspires them with a confidence in us they never felt before."[61]

Protestant leaders and editors, who had vigorously supported Lincoln during the campaign, saw the election results as a marvelous victory for God's purposes in the war. The *Christian Advocate and Journal* boasted, "In this last great peril, the Protestant Churches have proved to be the strong holds of freedom, and the sources of the power that turned back the floods of treason and disaffection." Henry Ward Beecher, a prominent abolitionist minister, exclaimed from his Brooklyn pulpit that the Republican success meant "the triumph of pure moral forces" against the Devil as represented by the Democratic party. Devout Protestants, still reflecting the prewar Know-Nothing movement's opposition to Irish Catholic immigrants that ironically had found a home in the antislavery Republican party, thought that the bulk of McClellan's vote had come from the dram shops and slums of the cities and from the "foreign born Romanist population." According to Protestant ministers, the election reaffirmed God's blessings upon American republican institutions, including its Protestant churches, and upon the Union antislavery cause. The triumph of the Union party, Beecher declared, should be a lesson for European governments, "for it shows that we, under a republican form of government, have made immense advances in civilization" and become a shining example for other nations.[62]

The idea of American exceptionalism had existed for decades. This nationalistic doctrine owed a great deal to the belief that America had been ordained by God to serve as a republican and constitutional model for the world. At times Lincoln seemed to share this view of America's role in history, as when he referred to the nation in 1862 as "the last best hope of earth." The belief in American exceptionalism reached new heights during the Civil War and would continue to be a powerful force in the growth of American nationalist sentiment.

Many Protestant reformers in Europe agreed with Beecher on the meaning of the American election. In London, the *Spectator* announced that Lincoln's re-election was a triumph of the "Christian political idea" because it had demonstrated that "the law of Christ has political bearing," designed to free and elevate the working masses. Emancipation societies in England echoed the *Spectator*'s view that Lincoln was an instrument of God in the war. The Union and Emancipation Society of Manchester informed the American president: "You have been raised up by the Providence of God to rescue your nation from anarchy, disruption and ruin."[63] European reformers believed that Lincoln's victory would provide a powerful boost to democracy in their countries. In imperial France, democratic republicans hailed the election as proof that republicanism could withstand the disruptive strains of a horrendous civil war.

Nowhere did news of Lincoln's re-election produce more relief and joy than among the Union troops in the field. General Grant himself told Lincoln's secretary John Hay, "The quiet and orderly character of the whole affair . . . proves the worthiness of free institutions, and our capability of preserving them without running into anarchy or despotism." Eight out of ten soldiers voting in the election cast ballots for "Father Abraham." To them, his victory meant that the rebellion would soon be crushed and that their sacrifices and their comrades' deaths would not have been in vain. Troops in Grant's army near Petersburg "cheered until they were hoarse" when they heard he had won.[64] Black troops also celebrated the re-election of "the man whose name was synonymous with freedom." African-American soldiers in at least one regiment in Virginia—the 5th U.S. Colored Troops, Ohio—cast absentee ballots, despite threats from white McClellan supporters. Ironically, if they had been at home these soldiers could not have voted because Ohio's constitution denied the ballot to blacks, but apparently their ballots were counted with those of the white Ohio troops.[65]

At Beaufort, South Carolina, on election day, African-American soldiers and white Unionists held a "mock" election and gave Lincoln 942 out of 1,004 votes cast. Confident that the president would win the national contest, that night black and white troops joined in a rousing Lincoln rally in Beaufort. A black soldier in Jacksonville, Florida, wrote to the *National Anti-Slavery Standard* that "the re-election of 'Uncle Abe'" would spell the doom of "Traitors, Slavery, Disunion, and all such infamy."[66] Though the soldiers' vote may not have been decisive in the election, Lincoln must have taken great pleasure in their overwhelming support for him and the Union cause against their old commander, McClellan, whom they had once idolized but now viewed as the candidate of traitors. Lincoln knew that many of them would still have to die and suffer to sustain the cause.

Radicals like Henry Winter Davis and Ben Wade, while expressing delight with their party's success and the defeat of the Copperheads, did not give Lincoln much credit for the victory. Davis sniffed: "The people now know Lincoln and voted for him to keep out worse people—keeping their hands on the pit of the stomach the while! No act of wise self-control—no such subordination of disgust to the necessities of a crisis and the dictates of cool judgment has ever before been exhibited by any people in history."[67]

Frederick Douglass, who like Davis and other Radicals had reluctantly supported the president's re-election, in an address celebrating the victory made no mention of Lincoln's role. Douglass proclaimed the election "the most momentous and solemn that ever occurred in our country or in any other," because it saved the Union, preserved self-government, and mandated the end of slavery. However, the black heroine Sojourner Truth, who had had a cordial meeting with Lincoln in the fall, noted his role in the victory and declared that "by the Grace of God" he would be "President of the United States for 4 years more."[68]

Conservative or moderate Republican spokesmen, while attributing much of their party's strength at the polls to outrage against the Democrats' war-failure platform, awarded Lincoln considerable credit as well. The *New York Times* told its readers: "The country, after four years' experience [with] it, has given an emphatic adhesion to the policy of President Lincoln." Richard J. Oglesby, the new governor of Illinois, warned the president that, though he was the "idol of the people," Republicans found fault with his "somewhat too much indulgence" of rebels. Nonetheless, Oglesby commended Lincoln for his strong leadership in the national crisis and said that honesty was the key to his success. He told Lincoln, "I am truly glad again that your wisdom exceeded all the wisdom of the scribes and Pharisees" in the Republican party who had predicted his defeat.[69]

Secretary of State Seward echoed these sentiments and provided a prophetic assessment of Lincoln now that the election was over and the president's war and antislavery policies close to being realized. "Henceforth all men will come to see him [as] a true, loyal, patient,

William H. Seward,
once a Republican rival
of Lincoln, who became
his secretary of state and
a confidant during the
Civil War.

patriotic, and benevolent man," Seward predicted two days after the election. "Having no longer any motive to malign or injure him, detractors will cease" their criticism, "and Abraham Lincoln will take his place with Washington and Franklin, and Jefferson, and Adams, and Jackson, among the benefactors of the country and of the human race."[70] Seward was correct: the election of 1864 marked the beginning of Lincoln's apotheosis as an American icon.

Crestfallen Democrats, many of whom had expected to defeat Lincoln, bitterly deplored the results. In addition to losing the presidential election, Democrats saw the Republicans capture 145 of the 185 seats in the next House of Representatives; the old party of Andrew Jackson would hold only 10 seats in the Senate. These figures, however, did not include a few conservative Unionists from the border states who could be expected to cooperate with the Democrats on some issues. A number of Democratic stalwarts charged fraud and intimidation at the polls in a few states like Indiana and Massachusetts, which probably occurred locally but not to the extent of winning any important state for the Republicans. The Democratic *Boston Courier* characterized Lincoln's victory as a "sham election" carried by "the unscrupulous and profligate agents of the administration and their besotted followers." The *Courier* promised that Democrats would continue the struggle "to recover their lost liberties, for themselves and their posterity; . . . success must eventually be theirs."[71]

McClellan himself did not charge fraud, but he claimed that "the power wielded by the Administration" had made the Republican victory inevitable. The general, with an element of self-pity in his tone, told a friend that the Democratic defeat was all "a part of a grand plan of the Almighty, who designed that the cup should be drained to the bitter dregs, that the people might be made worthy of being saved" at some future time. Samuel L. M. Barlow, a New York Democratic leader, cried out, "I see little prospect of anything but fruitless war, disgraceful peace, & ruinous bankruptcy." The *Springfield Register,* the Democratic newspaper in Lincoln's hometown, called the election result "the heaviest calamity that ever befell this nation." The Republican victory, the *Register* insisted, meant "farewell to civil liberty, to a republican form of government, and to the unity of these states." Manton Marble, editor of the *New York World,* lamented to McClellan that "the election shows that we have more reason to despair of the constitutional restoration of things at the North" than in the South, and that "the coming calamities will teach even the North their bitter lesson." In what is surely one of the cheekiest statements ever made in American political history, Marble's *World* declared that the Democratic party's mission, now that it had lost the election, would be to prevent Lincoln from making a peace that would recognize the Confederate States.[72]

Some McClellan supporters, especially conservative former Whigs like Robert C. Winthrop of Boston who had never felt comfortable cooperating with Democrats, accepted defeat with better grace. Though disappointed with the outcome, Winthrop applauded Lincoln's post-election conciliatory remarks. "I rejoice that the election is over," Winthrop said, and that the radicalism of men like Senator Charles Sumner "has not been accepted as the keynote to the policy of the victors."[73]

Like Winthrop, the conservative *National Intelligencer,* the long-time Washington organ of the Whig party, was encouraged by Lincoln's conciliatory tone after the election and predicted that his basic conservatism would resurface and guide him during his second term in office. The *Louisville Journal,* edited by George C. Prentice, an old Whig whose newspaper Lincoln had read before the war, "exhorted Constitutional Unionists everywhere to be of good cheer." The *Journal,* which during the campaign had charged Lincoln with attempting to establish a "brutal tyranny," admitted that in the past the president had faced "exigencies we may not have understood, requiring measures which, though doubtful now, shall be approved by future events . . . Throughout this struggle his Administration has been subjected to the bitterest partisan crimination. It may have been natural, but we are now convinced that it was always extravagant, and has brought no good to the country."[74]

As expected, Confederates found little solace in Lincoln's re-election. The Southern leaders and newspapers proclaimed that the success of "the Northern tyrant" meant that the Confederacy should fight harder to secure its independence. The alternative was the suppression of the people's freedom by a heartless antislavery regime. Anticipating Lincoln's victory, Jefferson Davis the day before the election informed the Confederate Congress that, though peace sentiment had risen in the North, "the authorities who control the Government of our enemies have too often and too clearly expressed their resolution to make no peace, except on terms of our unconditional submission and degradation." Davis defiantly announced that Southerners must "resolutely continue to devote our united and unimpaired energies to the defense of our homes, our lives, and our liberties." The *Savannah Republican,* only a few weeks away from a change of its management by General Sherman, asserted that the election had "accomplished one valuable purpose: it will set to rest forever all issues but one—subjugation or independence." Josiah Gorgas, Jefferson Davis's Northern-born ordnance chief, confided to his diary, "There is no use in disguising the fact that our subjugation is popular at the North, and that the war will go on until this hope is crushed out" or Southern society destroyed.[75]

The *Richmond Examiner* concluded that in the election the Northern people had renewed their vow "to destroy us, to seize our lands and homes, to beggar our children, and brand our names forever as the names of felons and traitors." The publishers of this newspaper, well aware that Federal armies under Sherman, Sheridan, and others were ripping the South apart, called on Southerners to make a determined effort to "drive back the foul invaders of our homes and make them expiate their crime with their own base blood." Such a unified effort, the *Examiner* promised, would place the Confederate States "on the safe shore from whence at our ease we may look at the absurd Yankee nation going to utter wreck in the storm it had conjured up for our destruction."[76]

Some Confederates, attempting to shore up Southern morale, sought to put the best face possible on Lincoln's re-election. The Richmond press told Southerners that the electoral victory for Lincoln's ruthless policy toward the South was a godsend because it would ensure a more vigorous Confederate resistance, leading to the triumph of peace sentiment in the North, whereas a victory for McClellan's conciliatory policy would have created division among Southerners and inspired reunion sentiment. Catherine Ann Edmondston, a member of a North Carolina planter family, sarcastically proposed that General Robert E. Lee "order a shotted salute along our whole line in honour of" Lincoln's election, the news of which should be received with exultation as well as defiance, "for there is little doubt [Lincoln] is our best antagonist; the weaker the man, the weaker the Government." Like many desperate and embittered Southerners, by late 1864 Edmondston had deluded herself into believing that the "precious mess" Lincoln had created would ultimately result in Confederate independence.[77]

* * *

In retrospect, the presidential election of 1864, as Lincoln concluded, demonstrated the strength of the nation's democratic institutions at a time of its greatest crisis. The Republican victory largely cleared away the conspiratorial political tone that had afflicted the North during the Civil War and especially in the electoral campaign. Though careful not to publicly condemn the Copperheads as traitors—and thereby risk losing important conservative support—even Lincoln for a time had been convinced that the peace Democrats plotted treason. He and other Republicans were correct in their judgment that the Democratic campaign, highlighted by the party's war-failure platform, encouraged the rebels to believe that if they persevered in the war until after the election they could yet achieve their independence.

Lincoln's electoral triumph meant the proven success of his firm war policy in contrast to the weak and vacillating approach of the Democrats and McClellan. The Northern will to prosecute the war to a successful conclusion would have been severely jeopardized by a McClellan victory, not so much because of disloyalty in the Democratic party as because of a subsequent debate over war aims, peace negotiations, and the treatment of former rebels. Without Lincoln's skillful leadership the outcome of the debate would have been in doubt. Confusion in Washington would have prolonged the battlefield carnage and the social and political disorders spawned by the war. Furthermore, though slavery was perhaps "too far mutilated and undermined to recover," a Democratic victory would have continued the life of the institution in those slave states which had not abolished it in their constitutions.[78] The initiation of the Thirteenth Amendment ending slavery in every state would have been delayed indefinitely.

Even if the war had ended in the spring of 1865, as it did, and slavery had been destroyed, the history of Southern reconstruction would have been far different had McClellan won the White House. McClellan's election would have strengthened the Democrats in Congress, giving them, if not a majority, a stronger anti-Republican minority. Congressional Democrats, joined by emboldened conservative Unionists like Senators Edgar Cowan of Pennsylvania, Reverdy Johnson of Maryland, and Garret Davis of Kentucky, would have thwarted any Republican effort after the war to prevent the quick restoration of the political rights of former Confederates. They would have denied the federal government the power to protect black freedom in the South. A McClellan administration would have drastically changed wartime federal measures relating to national banking, currency and bond issues, and tariff duties. In essence, Democratic success in the election would have prevented Lincoln from finishing the work that he had so ably crafted and would have shattered the vision for America that he had eloquently expressed at Gettysburg in November 1863.

Important challenges remained for Lincoln, not the least of which was guiding the nation to the final victory over Confederate armies led by such resourceful commanders as Robert E. Lee and Joseph E. Johnston. He had the responsibility for determining surrender terms that would be satisfactory to a North hardened by almost four years of enmity toward the South and at the same time avoiding terms so harsh that they would extend the social and political turmoil and hostility after the war. His lenient reconstruction plan of 1863, allowing for a quick restoration of the South and the rights of rebels, had not been completed for any state. It still needed the approval of Congress for the seating of the representatives and senators from the first of these states, Louisiana and Arkansas. Strengthened by his re-election, Lincoln expected the Republican Congress to seat these men and accept his control of reconstruction policy.

At the same time, he wanted quick congressional action on a constitutional amendment abolishing slavery everywhere in the United States. Despite their electoral success on a platform promising such an amendment, the Republicans did not have the necessary two-thirds of the votes in the old Congress to initiate it. This Congress would meet from December to March. If the resolution initiating the amendment was to pass without the convening of a special session of the new Congress later in the spring, several conservative Unionists and Democrats in the old Congress, who had earlier opposed emancipation, would have to be persuaded to support it. Even if the antislavery resolution won approval, Lincoln and Congress would also need to address the urgent economic and social problems of freed blacks in the postwar South as defeated Confederate soldiers returned home.

In the last months of 1864 Lincoln had overcome great adversity and skepticism about his leadership to win the election and emerge, in the minds of his contemporaries, as the savior of the Union. Faced with strong opposition from both inside and outside his party when the war stalemated and demands for peace swept the North, he remained steadfast in his refusal to negotiate with the rebels on any terms short of the restoration of the Union and immediate emancipation. Although he wisely maintained a low public profile during the electoral campaign, he made several practical political moves that contributed to his victory. These included his cultivation of Protestant leaders, his patronage concessions to conservative Republicans in New York, and, to appease Radicals, his removal of Montgomery Blair from the cabinet. Lincoln's success at the polls provided him with the political strength and confidence to face the months ahead when important decisions regarding peace and the status of white and black Southerners would have to be made. Inevitably, other challenges, not directly related to the war, would arise and require his attention. For the moment, however, Lincoln could relish his re-election and the voters' approval of the principles and war purposes that he had unswervingly supported.

CHAPTER 2

CAREWORN AND HAGGARD

As Lincoln prepared for his second term in office, those around him noted a transformation in his appearance. Noah Brooks, a newspaper correspondent who was frequently at the White House, wrote that the president's "hair is grizzled, his gait more stooping, his countenance shallow, and there is a sunken deadly look about [his] large, cavernous eyes." Lincoln's portraitist, Francis B. Carpenter, thought that his "weary air . . . was more of the mind than the body" and observed that the president knew no real rest. Congressman Isaac Arnold of Illinois reported that friends who had known him as "ever genial and sparkling with frolic and fun, . . . now saw the wrinkles on his face and forehead deepen into furrows; the laugh of old days was less frequent, and it did not seem to come from the heart." Joshua Speed, Lincoln's close friend before the war, now described him as "jaded and weary." Lincoln told Speed, "I am a little alarmed about myself; just feel my hand." Speed found his hands "cold and clammy," and he recorded that Lincoln put his feet so close to the fire that they steamed.[1]

Visitors who saw the president for the first time were shocked by his appearance. One woman wrote: "I was totally unprepared for the impression instantly made upon me. So bowed and sorrow-laden was his whole person, expressing such weariness of mind and body, as he dropped himself heavily from step to step down to the ground." For her, the worst was the president's face. "Oh, the pathos of it!—haggard, drawn into fixed lines of unutterable sadness, with a look of loneliness" that "no human sympathy could ever reach." C. B. Crane, a Protestant minister, noted: "The President looks thin and careworn. His form is bowed as by a crushing load; his flesh is wasted as by incessant solicitude; and his face is thin and furrowed and pale." A French visitor in early 1865 reported Lincoln's habit of withdrawing within himself while among company. He counted more than twenty such occasions in one evening. But the president "would shake off this mysterious weight and his generous and open disposition" would reassert itself. Despite his "painfully anxious" features, Lincoln, according to another visitor, was "quite quick in his movements, and his articulation distinct, sharp and rapid rather than slow."[2]

Lincoln had indicated to associates a strong desire to escape from the burdens of the presidency. When Postmaster General William Dennison in early 1865 remarked that the president deserved a better chair than the one he was sitting in, Lincoln, referring to the chair as a symbol of his office, expressed a wish to have someone else in it. "The responsibilities of the office [were] so oppressive," Lincoln told a visitor, and "so terrible [were] its complexities that he felt as though the moment when he could relinquish the burden and retire to private life would be the sweetest he could possibly experience." Soon after the election he told Noah Brooks, "I should have been a little mortified if I had been beaten in this canvass before the people; but that sting would have been more than compensated by the thought that the people had notified me that all my official responsibilities were soon to be lifted off my back."[3] It is conceivable that Lincoln, after having achieved his purposes of saving the Union and ending slavery, would have seriously contemplated resigning as president at war's end. If so, his estimation of Vice President Andrew Johnson's capacity to fill the office and sustain Union governments in the South would have been important in his decision.

* * *

Despite his weariness with the burdens of office, Lincoln during the winter of 1864–1865 could take great satisfaction in the successes of the Union armies in the South. After the election, General William Tecumseh Sherman left Atlanta and began his famous "March to the Sea," cutting a thirty- to fifty-mile swath of destruction through Georgia. Arriving at Savannah in mid-December, Sherman occupied the city on the twenty-first and exuberantly offered it as a "Christmas gift" to President Lincoln. Meanwhile, at Franklin and Nashville, Tennessee, Federal forces under General George H. Thomas shattered General John B. Hood's Confederate army of more than thirty thousand men, ending the last major threat to the Union in the Mississippi Valley theater. (Nathan Bedford Forrest and other Confederate commanders with small forces would continue to harass Federal troops in the region.)

One disappointment marred the joy of the holiday season in the North. An amphibious assault on Fort Fisher, the earthen Confederate stronghold on the lower Cape Fear guarding Wilmington, North Carolina, failed on Christmas Day. But the new year would bring success. General Alfred H. Terry replaced General Benjamin F. Butler, the commander of the failed assault, and on January 15 led an attack that overpowered the fort's defenders. On February 22 Terry's troops entered Wilmington, sealing off the Confederacy's last blockade-running port and a major source of supplies for Lee's army in Virginia.

On February 1, after two weeks of preparation, General Sherman left Georgia and began a destructive march through the heart of South Carolina. Sherman seemed determined to make South Carolina pay for beginning the rebellion. When his forces left Columbia, much of the capital lay in ruins. On March 1 the vanguard of the army entered North Carolina, where they continued their depredations on the countryside, despite Sherman's orders to go easy on the state because of its presumed reluctance to secede in 1861. A few days later Sherman entered Fayetteville, where he stopped in mid-March to plan to link up at Goldsboro with Federal forces from the North Carolina coast.

In Virginia, Grant's armies were finally making progress against Lee's troops entrenched around Petersburg and along the James River. Hard fighting remained, however, before Lee could be forced to surrender or flee, leaving Petersburg and Richmond open to Grant's troops. On March 2, two days before Lincoln began his second term, Federal forces at Waynesborough scattered Jubal Early's once-feared army in the Shenandoah Valley. By the end of the month, only Lee at Petersburg and Joseph E. Johnston, who had assumed command in North Carolina of the remnants of several Confederate armies, stood in the way of Union victory in the war.

After the election Lincoln eagerly wanted to complete the suppression of rebel arms. His ultimate aims were to restore loyal governments in the South and to secure a constitutional amendment ending slavery everywhere in the United States. But first he had to decide what to do about Confederate leaders and soldiers as the Confederacy collapsed. In particular, the fate of Jefferson Davis, the main villain for Unionists, had become an emotional issue in the North. Many Unionists wanted to "hang him from a sour apple tree." Lincoln had no such harsh plans for Davis or any rebel officers, but he was faced with demands to arrest and try Davis and other leading rebels for treason. In addition, he was under pressure to have rebel prison commandants and guards severely punished for the horrible treatment of Union prisoners in their camps. By late 1864 reports of the cruel conditions in these camps were flooding the North and creating powerful calls for retribution.

Lincoln, though, was clearly the master of affairs, a term he frequently used when granting authority to his army commanders and military governors in the South.[4] Even Radicals admitted that Lincoln had been greatly strengthened by the election and by the heightened prospects for the early collapse of the rebellion. At the same time they reminded him that he owed his victory to the Republican platform and not to his personal popularity. Some Radicals still fretted that Lincoln would make a compromise peace with the rebels and renege on the party's commitment to ending slavery. Despite their weakened post-election position and some important defections from their ranks, determined Radicals in Congress like Benjamin F. Wade, Charles Sumner, Zachariah Chandler, and Henry Winter Davis promised to keep Lincoln's feet to the fire. When Congress met in December, they hoped to find a way to overturn his generous reconstruction and amnesty policy and instead impose a stringent political settlement upon the South. Radicals as well as other Republicans, however, were divided on the specifics of a Southern policy and on the extent of rights to be given to blacks in freedom.

Defeated Democrats, though promising to cooperate with the president in ending the war, indicated that they also would be carefully watching his actions. If he veered from a conservative course on reconstruction, race relations, constitutional rights (for whites), and federal power, they would make political capital out of it. Democratic political leaders and editors, mainly in the Northeast, where anti-slavery sentiment had been strongest, believed the election had settled the matter of emancipation, but they warned Lincoln that any attempt to impose black rights on the South would be cause for vigorous opposition.

Thus the final stages of the war produced a host of issues and problems for Lincoln's administration. In addition to securing military victory, the issues included complications at sea with Great Britain, Confederate operations based in British Canada, the disturbing French presence in Mexico, continuing revelations of deplorable conditions in Southern prisoner-of-war camps, reports of illicit and harmful Northern trade with the rebels, management of the large war debt, and troubles on the Indian frontier. But for Lincoln the primary objectives were saving the Union and freeing the slaves. Only after achieving those objectives could he turn his energy and determination to the multitude of new problems that awaited him.

* * *

The management of the war had absorbed most of the president's attention. To a great extent he had left other important executive responsibilities to cabinet members and their subordinates. As a small-town lawyer and a state politician, Lincoln had been skillful in handling delicate political and legal matters, usually on a personal basis. Before becoming president he had never held an executive office requiring a broad range of administrative duties and experience in acting on a variety of issues. Even in his law practice Lincoln lacked system, according to his partner William H. Herndon. In the presidency the weaknesses in his experience and style became apparent to many subordinates, often driving his secretaries John G. Nicolay and John Hay and his cabinet members to distraction. Hay later wrote that Lincoln "was extremely unmethodical; it was a four-years struggle on Nicolay's part and mine to get him to adopt some systematic rules. He would break through every regulation as fast as it was made."[5]

Lincoln clearly grew in the overall management of the war and in his confidence to deal with the issues associated with the conflict. But he never learned how to administer wisely. Secretary of the Navy Gideon Welles complained in his diary that Lincoln "makes his office

Gideon Welles, the acerbic but able secretary of the navy, critical of
Lincoln but intensely loyal to him, whose diary is an important
source for the study of Lincoln's presidency.

much more laborious than he should. Does not generalize and takes upon himself questions that properly belong to the Departments, often causing derangement and irregularity." Welles also thought Lincoln too quickly yielded to requests: "The more he yields, the greater the pressure upon him" for favors.[6]

Lincoln increasingly sought respite from his burdens at the theater, at the nearby Soldiers' Home, with old Illinois friends, and in social functions at the White House. He told General James Grant Wilson, who attended a play with him in March 1865: "I have not come for the play, but for the rest. I am being hounded to death by office-seekers, who pursue me early and late, and it is simply to get two or three hours' relief that I am here." On another occasion Lincoln joked that he could reduce the number of office seekers and others demanding favors if he moved his office to the local smallpox hospital. But then, on second thought, "they'd all go and get vaccinated, and they'd come buzzing back, just the same as they do now—or worse."[7]

Located on a small hill about three miles from the White House, the Soldiers' Home, a group of buildings and surrounding grounds set aside for retired veterans and recuperating soldiers, became a frequent retreat for the president, especially during the summer and on weekends. When at the Home, he usually rose early and rode into town to be at his office by eight o'clock. He also found some solace in walking the grounds. The wooded area contained a variety of trees, and Lincoln could be seen talking to women who visited the retired soldiers and the nearby graves. On one occasion two women disagreed regarding the type of evergreens in the yard, whereupon Lincoln announced that he would enlighten them on the subject: "I know all about trees in light of being a backwoodsman. I'll show you the difference between spruce, pine, and cedar." He then gathered specimens of each kind and described their distinguishing characteristics. When his secretaries or friends visited him at the Soldiers' Home, Lincoln liked to read aloud from his favorite Shakespeare plays, the tragedies of Hamlet, Macbeth, and Richard II.[8]

Lincoln's fondness for quaint humor afforded a brief escape from his burdens. He enjoyed the stories and satire of such popular humorists as Orpheus C. Kerr (Robert N. Newell), Artemus Ward (Charles Farrar Browne), and Petroleum V. Nasby (David Ross Locke). Locke's

The Nasby Papers became the president's favorite light reading. This publication was a serial work of rustic satire, supposedly written by an uneducated and dissolute country preacher. Lincoln often read passages from *The Nasby Papers* in cabinet meetings, to White House visitors, and at the War Department while waiting for telegraphic dispatches. He felt no compunction about subjecting "grave and prominent men who came charged to the brim with important business" to such burlesque literature.

At one cabinet session in early 1865, Lincoln stopped reading from the latest installment of *The Nasby Papers* when Secretary of the Treasury William Pitt Fessenden, a humorless New Englander, protested that it was not a proper subject for a cabinet meeting. On another occasion in 1865, Lincoln interrupted a constituent's appeal by Senator Charles Sumner, another humorless New Englander, with a quotation from *The Nasby Papers*. Quickly realizing that the erudite senator lacked an appreciation of homespun literature, the president announced, "I must initiate you." He took a copy of *Nasby* from his desk and read to Sumner. After twenty minutes of this imposition, the bored and unconverted senator took advantage of a pause in the reading and excused himself. Again, a few hours before his assassination, Lincoln pulled from his desk the latest edition of *The Nasby Papers* and read four chapters to a group of surprised Illinois politicians. Clearly, Nasby provided the kind of leavening he felt politics and politicians needed. Such rural humor brought him solace and comfort in the White House.[9]

Lincoln possessed his own deep reservoir of humorous anecdotes that he had brought with him from Illinois. He did not claim that these stories originated with him, though he probably created a few and embellished others. Storytelling had become a habit with him and, more important, a way to make a point. His remarkable recall and the appropriateness of the anecdotes reveal his high intelligence and extraordinary wit. His homespun stories were almost always on target. The humorist David Ross Locke, who met Lincoln before and during the war, later wrote that the president "was a master of satire, which was at times as blunt as a meat-ax, and at others as keen as a razor; but it was always kindly except when some horrible injustice was its inspiration, and then it was terrible."[10]

Social functions, many of which Mary Todd Lincoln organized, became another way for Lincoln to escape the press of business. Mrs. Lincoln usually received guests in the Blue Room on Saturday afternoons, and the president often attended the receptions, especially during the winter of 1864–1865 when many visitors, anticipating an imminent victory in the war, were in Washington. The New Year's reception on January 2, 1865, was the largest one hosted by the Lincolns. One guest happily noted "a great contrast" between this social event and "any previous one for the past 3 years." At the earlier receptions "a solemn stillness, a burdensome weight [hung] upon the minds of all, a fearful foreboding of Evil, a dread of the future . . . Today all are in good spirits."[11]

The 1865 New Year's reception began at noon with the president and Mrs. Lincoln receiving members of the cabinet and foreign ministers. Then came members of the Supreme Court and, according to a correspondent of the *New York Herald,* several hundred army and navy officers. After the formal reception "came the rush of the people, and such a rush," this writer reported. "All classes, sexes, ages and conditions came rolling up, tumbling up, climbing up, getting up any way they could—some in order and some in great disorder, some sober, some not so sober . . . Mrs. Lincoln retired early, but the throng continued to press forward until the gates of the White House were closed and the crowd excluded." The reception ended at four o'clock. Secretary of the Navy Welles, who also left early, concluded: "The day is one which the people seem to enjoy, and one which they want, [but] a little more system at the President's would improve matters."[12]

Another large White House reception was held from eight to eleven in the evening on January 20. Eight thousand people, according to a report, attended this open house. Lincoln reportedly shook hands and said something to almost everyone, which seems an obvious exaggeration. A French visitor during this period was impressed by the president's willingness, while maintaining his dignity and good humor, to stand for two hours or more and shake hands in a receiving line. When a woman asked the president whether the repeated handshaking was not harder work than his office duties, he replied: "Oh, no-no. Of course, this is tiresome physically; but I am pretty strong, and it rests me, after all, for here nobody is cross or exacting, and no man asks me for what I can't give him."[13]

Lincoln's relationship with his wife, unfortunately, provided little relief from his presidential burdens. As is well known, by the time of the Civil War the passion in the Lincoln marriage had long since faded. Although Mary Todd Lincoln has generally been blamed for the problems in the marriage, it should be remembered that the pressures of the presidency, in addition to Lincoln's often abstracted and withdrawn nature, contributed to the couple's marital difficulties. While she recognized the tremendous public responsibilities her husband faced, Mary felt the need for his companionship in the lonely wartime atmosphere of the White House. This was especially true after the death of their son Willie in early 1862. A fair understanding of Mary's conduct requires an acknowledgment of Lincoln's shortcomings as a husband and a family man. Nonetheless, his neglect and the demands and tensions created by the war do not seem to justify Mary's irrational and hurtful outbursts, her personal extravagance, and, on occasion, her unseemly selfish behavior.

Still, the Lincolns remained devoted and dependent on each other. Mary was an excellent hostess and, as she had done in their Springfield home, assumed control of most White House social affairs, an important aspect of the presidency. Even her proverbial extravagance, which she attempted to keep secret from her husband, was partly designed to bring more beauty and style to an otherwise drab Executive Mansion that was in great need of improvements after years of neglect by miserly prewar administrations and Congresses.[14] Despite carping behind her back by Republicans in Washington, including Nicolay and Hay, it was mainly opponents of the administration who leveled public criticism against her.

Mary was an ardent supporter of the war and by 1863 a strong antislavery advocate, a stance that Lincoln probably found reassuring. At times she must have encouraged her cautious husband to take more vigorous action against slavery. Over appointments to—and removals from—office Mary had little influence, though she often attempted to have "enemies" removed and friends and relatives appointed. On one occasion she joined with others to prevent the appointment of General Nathaniel P. Banks to a cabinet position. Mary believed that Banks was not a staunch Republican, was too conservative on war issues, and would abandon her husband if the opportunity arose.[15] Though Lincoln was probably not influenced by

Mary's argument against Banks, a failed military commander in Louisiana, he did not appoint the general to his cabinet.

The old canard that Mary's Southern background and Confederate kinsmen were a major handicap and a weapon that was effectively used against her does not survive scrutiny. After all, the Radical leader Charles Sumner became her close friend. Mary also thought highly of the black spokesman Frederick Douglass, though he often criticized her husband. After Lincoln was assassinated, she gave Douglass the president's favorite walking cane.[16] Senator Sumner admired Mary's political views, her learning, and her quick wit. Although Sumner differed sharply with Lincoln on policies and questioned his leadership ability, he never broke with the president and often visited the White House. Mary clearly was influential in helping to maintain her husband's relationship with the sensitive Massachusetts senator.

* * *

With so many problems to confront and critical decisions to make, Lincoln turned increasingly to religion for solace and as a source of meaning regarding the war. Sensitive to the suffering of others and keenly aware of the tragic impact of his actions on thousands of soldiers and civilians in the South, Lincoln sought assurances of God's support for the Union. His mental health virtually depended on the spiritual comfort he found in reading the Bible and contemplating God's purposes. The religious fervor that late in the war reached its height in the North penetrated the White House as well. The president's frequent contacts with Protestant clergymen, most of whom were against slavery and agreed with him on political issues, also contributed to his deepening spiritual consciousness.

Old friends, who remembered Lincoln's early skepticism, expressed surprise at his vibrant religious feelings late in the war. Joshua Speed visited Lincoln at the Soldiers' Home during the summer of 1864 and found him reading the Bible. When Speed remarked that he himself was still a skeptic, the president replied: "You are wrong, Speed. Take all of this book upon reason that you can and the balance on faith, and you will live and die a happier and better man." Lincoln's longtime friend Orville H. Browning, who was often with the president late in the war, remembered that Lincoln read the Bible and held a pew in Dr. Phineas D. Gurley's New York Avenue Presbyterian Church in Washington. Another old friend, James H. Matheny, believed that Lincoln "was a very different man in later life" than he had been in Springfield; he had become "a firm believer in the Christian religion."[17]

Others who saw Lincoln during the war also testified to his growing spirituality. Francis B. Carpenter, the artist who spent several months at the White House, recalled the president in 1864 as saying that "a change" had come over him after the death of his son Willie and that he hoped he was now a Christian. Lincoln related a slightly different version of the "change" to a Massachusetts visitor: "When I left home to take this chair, I requested my countrymen to pray for me. I was not then a Christian. When my son died—the severest trial of my life—I was not a Christian. But when I went to Gettysburgh [sic] and looked upon the graves of our dead heroes that had fallen in defense of their country, I then and there consecrated myself to Christ." Mary Lincoln later recalled her husband's deepening spirituality after Willie died, and said he had begun reading the Bible "a good deal about 1864." Noah Brooks reported that the president had a "change of heart" or a "change of mind," which Brooks characterized as a "process of crystallization" in Lincoln's religious thought. He noted that Lincoln studied the Bible and prayed regularly. A Philadelphia Protestant minister found the president at five o'clock on Thanksgiving Day morning, 1864, reading the Bible aloud to himself. A White House servant probably exaggerated when he informed the surprised minister that the president "spends every morning from 4 o'clock to 5 in reading the Scriptures and praying."[18]

When Sojourner Truth visited the White House in October 1864, Lincoln showed the African-American heroine the beautiful Bible that Baltimore blacks had presented to him. He remarked sorrowfully that the good book had been given to the head of a government that had prohibited members of her race from learning enough to read it. The president showed Representative Henry C. Deming of Connecticut the same Bible and challenged the congressman's knowledge of obscure biblical passages. In another conversation the president told Deming that he had never joined a church because he had reservations about the complicated denominational doctrines. "When any church," Lincoln reportedly said, "will ascribe over its altar, as its sole qualification for membership the Saviour's condensed statement of the substance of both law and Gospel, 'Thou shalt love the Lord thy God with all thy heart, and with all thy soul, and with all thy mind, and thy neighbor as thyself,' that church will I join with all my heart and all my soul."[19]

Lincoln's observance of the charitable tenets of Jesus' ministry contrasted with the harsh attitudes of many Protestant leaders, ministers, and editors who as the war progressed became passionate in their denunciations of the "evil rebels" and suggested sending Southern leaders to an early Hell. Lincoln, with his caring nature, cultivated at an early age in rural Indiana and Illinois and influenced by his interest in the Bible and literature, believed that a wise national policy dictated a charitable view of the South. Thus he hoped to restore the South quickly to the Union and prevent postwar sectional strife. Lincoln's antislavery commitment, and the goodwill he demonstrated to blacks like Sojourner Truth and Frederick Douglass as well as to white Southerners, owed a great deal to his dogma-free spiritual beliefs and his inborn sensitivity to the plight of others. In 1866 William O. Stoddard, "Lincoln's third secretary," accurately summarized the late president's religion: "President Lincoln was deeply and genuinely religious, without being in any way what may be called a religionist."[20]

Lincoln's spirituality did not imply a belief in the afterlife. He seemed satisfied that God had put people on Earth for good works and for certain providential purposes that could not always be known. On September 4, 1864, he wrote to a Quaker correspondent, Eliza Gurney: "The purposes of the Almighty are perfect, and must prevail, though we erring mortals may fail to perceive them in advance . . . Meanwhile we must work earnestly in the best light He gives us, trusting that so working still conduces to the great ends He ordains." On one point Lincoln expressed confidence regarding God's purpose: he had no doubt that the Almighty was on the side of the Union, and that for this reason it would ultimately win the war.[21]

Lincoln demonstrated his ecumenical spirit and Christian charity by supporting the work of the United States Christian Commission, an organization formed in 1863 to provide religious tracts and comfort to soldiers, especially those in hospitals. The president attended at least two sessions of the commission's annual national conventions in early 1864 and 1865. He also contributed to the commission's fund. Lincoln took a special interest in the 1865 convention, which met in Washington for four days in late January. On January 27 he greeted more than a hundred convention delegates, who proclaimed themselves "representatives of the patriotism and benevolence by which the national cause was maintained at home and the national armies succored in the field." One delegate said that during the introductory remarks by George H. Stuart, the commission's chairman, Lincoln stood "with his head slightly bowed, and with an abstracted air that left his eyes lustreless." But when "he lifted himself up to reply, his whole aspect changed. All his features kindled into a most genial and attractive expression. A pleasant smile overspread his face, and his eyes were filled with a gentle, winning light." In his remarks to the delegates, the president denied any credit for advancing the work of the Christian Commission, "nor do I know that I owe you any thanks for what you have done. We have all been laboring for a common end—the preservation of our country and the welfare of its defenders." This purpose, he said, "has been our motive and joy and reward."[22]

After Lincoln's remarks, Stuart suggested that, since his group represented a broadly based Christian association, "it would be gratifying to us" if the president did not object, "to invoke the blessing of God upon our Chief Magistrate." The president, according to one delegate, "promptly and cordially responded that it would be agreeable and most fitting, and requested that prayer be offered." At the conclusion, Lincoln shook the hand of each delegate.[23]

Two days later, on Sunday, January 29, the president, along with Mrs. Lincoln and numerous national leaders, attended the final session of the Christian Commission convention. Presided over by Secretary of State Seward, the meeting was held in the House of Representatives, which was packed with hundreds of people; many others were turned away. A spirit of religious revivalism prevailed in the chamber. Lincoln, who did not speak, "joined heartily" in the chorus of "The Battle Hymn of the Republic." Moved by the music, he passed a note to Stuart requesting that the soloist Philip Phillips repeat his singing of

"Your Mission," which had brought tears to Lincoln's eyes. The request was granted.[24]

* * *

During a normal day at the White House, Lincoln found little time for spiritual contemplation. After his re-election the demands upon his time were greater than before, making for long and exacting days. He usually began his work about two hours before breakfast, frequently having spent the night in intermittent sleep and thought. In the early morning, when no one would disturb him, he did most of his reading, studying, and writing. He only glanced at the newspapers. After a light breakfast, usually consisting of an egg, a piece of toast, and a cup of coffee, he went over his mail with either Nicolay or Hay and prepared for the crush of visitors. These visitors included ordinary citizens, inventors, businessmen, military men, relatives of soldiers who sought clemency or discharges, local politicians, office seekers, persons wanting passes through army lines, delegations of various sorts, and some who simply wished to meet the president. Only cabinet members, prominent politicians, and military commanders had immediate access to him. At about nine o'clock Lincoln opened the door for a secretary, usually Nicolay, to begin ushering the waiting citizens into the room. Sitting at a table in "a common office room," he greeted his visitors and asked what he could do for them. He quickly sensed the substance of their requests and frequently interrupted them to ask a question, announce his decision, or write a note referring them to a subordinate. Lincoln often told a "little story" to illustrate a point or ease a caller out of his office.[25]

A European visitor in late 1864 was astounded by the lack of formality in gaining access to the president. He wrote that no guard was posted to protect the president from an assassin who could easily enter his office and accomplish his devilish purpose. He was also amazed that "a very large part of [Lincoln's] morning is consumed in interviews which do not in any way promote the public service"; instead, they distracted him from important business.[26] Lincoln, however, justified his open-door policy on the grounds that in a republic all citizens had a right to see the president and present their grievance or express their opinion to him. These contacts also allowed him to keep in touch with the people at the grass roots and to know what they were thinking and experiencing.

On one occasion Senator Henry Wilson of Massachusetts remonstrated with Lincoln about the swarms of visitors. "You will wear yourself out," Wilson said. Lincoln smiled and replied, "They don't want much; they get but little, and I must see them." When a visitor breached a certain decorum, though, the president showed his displeasure. The White House clerk William O. Stoddard in 1866 recalled that "nothing displeased him more than any attempt—and some fools did attempt it—at unseemly or undignified familiarity, for [the president's] nature was genuinely dignified." Lincoln became impatient when his visitors persisted in their demands, especially in requests that he intervene in petty personal disputes. When a soldier repeatedly sought presidential intervention against his commanding officer, Lincoln blurted out: "Now, my man, go away! I cannot attend to all these details. I could as easily bail out the Potomac with a spoon."[27]

Though he might express irritation with those who tried his patience, Lincoln, according to John Hay, even after four years of the burdensome practice, continued to receive hordes of callers at the White House. "Anything that kept the visitors away from him he disapproved," Hay later wrote. Nonetheless, he could only see a minority of those who waited in the antechamber. Inevitably, many of them left disappointed. Some returned to the White House daily until they obtained an interview. A journalist who witnessed the parade of petitioners into the president's office on March 21, 1865, reported that, despite the pettiness of some of their requests, Lincoln dealt with them in a "frank, cordial and candid manner." The visitors seemed "well pleased with their reception, and in most cases gratified with the decision of the president." Lincoln's unpretentiousness endeared him to many people who called at the White House.[28]

The president's willingness to accommodate people seeking pardons or sentence commutations for soldiers convicted of desertion or serious crimes became more apparent during the months after his reelection. Some requests came from cabinet members and congressmen. Lincoln searched for reasons to pardon or commute death sentences. He observed that "no man was ever yet improved by killing him," a dubious piece of logic in the minds of his generals and at least one White House clerk. But he refused to overturn the military convictions of spies and rebel marauders operating out of Canada in late 1864, despite the intervention of influential Northerners. One of these men, Robert C. Kennedy, led "a gang of desperadoes" in an unsuccessful attempt to burn the main hotels in New York City. Another "desperado" was Confederate Captain John Y. Beall, who launched a raid on Lake Erie shipping, followed by an effort to rescue prisoners in New York, before his capture in November. Both went to the gallows after Lincoln refused to commute their sentences.[29]

Lincoln had a difficult time resisting the appeals of soldiers' mothers and wives. In February 1865 Joshua Speed witnessed a touching scene in which the president not only granted the requests of two Pennsylvania women for the release of their kinsmen imprisoned for draft dodging but also ordered the release of all conscription evaders in western Pennsylvania. Lincoln explained his decision to Assistant Secretary of War Charles A. Dana, whom he called into the room to draw up the order. "These fellows," he declared, "[have] suffered long enough and I have thought so for some time, and now that my mind is on it, I believe I will turn out the flock." The women, according to Speed, rushed forward in tears and knelt before the president in thanks. Lincoln directed them to "get up thank God & go." The older woman grabbed his hand and said good-bye, sobbing, "I shall never see you again till we meet in Heaven." Leading her to the door, Lincoln replied, "I am afraid with all my troubles I shall never get there— But if I do I will find you—That you wish me to get there is the best wish you could make for me."[30]

After the women had gone, Lincoln told Speed: "That scene which you witnessed is the only thing I have done to day which has given me any pleasure. I have in that made two people happy . . . Speed, die when I may I want it said of me by those who know me best to say that I always plucked a thistle and planted a flower where I thought a flower would grow."[31] This incident reflected Lincoln's longtime habit as a lawyer in Illinois of dealing with clients on a personal level in an effort to solve their problems. He much preferred to find a way to aid unfortunate victims of the war rather than to confront office seekers and the problems of governing. His extraordinarily caring nature found a just reward in these contacts with citizens in distress.

Lincoln, however, refused to intervene when women sought the release of their sons or husbands serving in the field. On January 7, 1865, a French visitor heard the president inform a woman, "I cannot grant your request" to discharge her husband from the army. "I can disband all the Union armies, but I cannot send a single soldier home," Lincoln told her. "Only the colonel of the regiment can do that for your husband." The president said that he sympathized with her plight, but he asked her to "consider that all of us in every part of the country are today suffering what we have never suffered" before for the survival of the nation. Still, when the interview ended, Lincoln wrote a consoling note and gave it to the woman.[32]

* * *

At noon on most days Lincoln walked through the crowded corridors of the White House to the family room for lunch. His lunch usually consisted of a biscuit and a glass of milk; he ate fruit when it was in season. He relished the baskets of fruit he received from well-wishers. After lunch he returned to his office and continued to see visitors, except on Tuesdays and Fridays, which he set aside for cabinet meetings. Cabinet sessions did not always occur as scheduled and, when they did, were rarely attended by all of the department heads. Cabinet members knew that the meetings would only occasionally deal with important national issues and that few decisions would be made. Secretary of the Navy Welles complained that the meetings were "infrequent, irregular, and without system" and that three out of four times when cabinet members assembled for the scheduled meetings, the president would appear and announce "no business." Another department head wondered why the meetings were held at all. Lincoln, in his deliberative way, made decisions on his own, though often after consulting with appropriate officials. He saw no need to discuss issues in cabinet meetings about which some members had little knowledge. Confident in his own judgment after studying an issue, he disliked presiding over meetings where free-wheeling discussions could become contentious and unproductive.[33]

When meetings were held, their informality contrasted sharply with the dignified image portrayed in Francis B. Carpenter's famous painting of Lincoln and his cabinet. William O. Stoddard, a clerk who frequently entered the room with documents, recalled that cabinet members did not stiffly sit around the table discussing matters of state: "I have seen one stretched on the sofa with a cigar in his mouth, another with his heels on the table, another nursing his knee abstractly, the President with his leg over the arm of his chair, and not a man of them all in any wise sitting."[34]

In addition to the president, the most important members of the administration were Secretary of State William H. Seward and Secretary of War Edwin M. Stanton. Much to the dismay of Welles and other department heads, Seward and Stanton could often be seen conferring with Lincoln in a corner of the room, both before and after cabinet meetings. This secretive practice contributed to the distrust and rivalries among cabinet members. Furthermore, some members had never completely rid themselves of their prewar political animosities. Welles and Montgomery Blair (before his forced resignation in September), old Democrats, maintained a "courtly distrust" of Seward and William Pitt Fessenden, both former Whigs.[35] Most cabinet members resented Stanton, more because of his abrasive personality and secretive nature than because of his past political affiliation with the Democratic party.

Lincoln rose above these partisan and personality differences. Though opponents charged that the cabinet lacked unity, he brought the members together on important issues involving the war and emancipation. In view of their differing personalities, political backgrounds, and constitutional views, Lincoln's success in managing his key subordinates was a remarkable achievement. His ego rarely intruded into his relationship with his cabinet or with his small White House staff. His secretaries, John G. Nicolay and John Hay, were devoted and loyal to their boss. Edward D. Neill, a Minnesota minister and writer who served in the White House late in the war, recalled the president's lack of self-importance and the republican simplicity and quiet dignity with which he conducted himself. Neill wrote that, while Lincoln wanted to be esteemed, "he was never puffed up, nor used great, swelling words. In conversation I never knew him to speak of himself as President, but when necessary to allude to his position, he would use circumlocution, and say, 'Before I came here,' or something equivalent."[36]

By late 1864 all members of the cabinet, whatever their views and suspicions of one another, had come to respect this Illinois lawyer who, against tremendous odds, had led the Union to the verge of victory in its most terrible war. The summer departure from the cabinet of the Radical Salmon P. Chase and the conservative Montgomery Blair, both extreme partisans, made it easier for Lincoln to establish harmony in his administration and gain the support of those who worked with him.

In the afternoons, after the cabinet meetings, Lincoln often slipped out of the White House and visited the nearby state, war, and navy departments to confer with officials and receive the latest war reports. Later he frequently rode out "for an hour's airing." At about six o'clock he ate a frugal dinner, which rarely if ever included wine and never hard liquor. At any time during the day he could expect to be interrupted by his rambunctious eleven-year-old son, Tad, who after Willie's death in 1862 became the apple of Lincoln's eye and was "perfectly lawless." John Hay remembered that Tad "would lie around the office until he fell asleep & Lincoln would shoulder him and take him off to bed." Tad usually slept with his father.[37]

Lincoln spent most evenings in his office. He enjoyed having old friends like Orville H. Browning, Joshua Speed, Leonard Swett, Joseph Gillespie, Isaac Arnold, Dr. Anson G. Henry, and even John Todd Stuart, his first law partner and a member of Congress who had opposed him in the 1864 election, come by and talk. He did not seem to mind the fact that some of them also pestered him for favors. The company of his Illinois friends gave Lincoln an opportunity to unwind and drop his official pose. He became one of them again and was sometimes able to unburden himself. He rarely revealed all of his thoughts or purposes, however, even to his close Illinois associates.

* * *

Though the voters in November 1864 had sustained his policies and Federal arms had made dramatic progress in suppressing the rebellion, Lincoln feared that months of hard fighting with costly casualties remained before victory could be achieved. By late 1864 the war had taken a terrible toll on him. His acute awareness of the impact of his actions on others and on the Union cause had contributed to his physical decline. Always subject to periods of melancholy or depression, Lincoln during the last months of his life fretted more than usual about his burdens and about the difficult conditions created by the war and emancipation. Increasingly he found solace in religion and in the assurance that somehow God's purpose for America was involved in the war. He also found sporadic relief in humorous anecdotes, evenings at the theater, and visits with his Illinois friends. But, as he admitted, no relief could ever "reach the tired spot" in his body. His energy had been sapped by the demands of the war, by the political conflict associated with it, and by his own powerful sense of responsibility. Though only fifty-five years of age when re-elected, Lincoln was worn down and unable to shake his feeling of dread at the prospect of four more years of the presidency.

CHAPTER 3

THE BURDEN OF PATRONAGE

Lincoln's first priority after the November election was to secure peace based on the restoration of the Union and the ending of slavery. But a great deal of his time and energy in late 1864 and early 1865 would be consumed by factious disputes over office and preferment in his new administration. Rivalries within the Republican party had been exacerbated by the war and the divisive electoral campaign. These were reflected immediately after the election in a struggle over federal patronage. The competition for office and political favors had the potential to undermine Lincoln's efforts to end the war on his terms, to obtain approval of the antislavery amendment, and to implement his liberal amnesty and reconstruction policies. Lincoln's skill at managing intraparty divisions dated back to his experience in Illinois. His understanding of the importance of state and local politics and his practicality, candor, and good humor enabled him to negotiate and compromise to get what he wanted without conceding his main purposes. Still, matters involving political patronage were disagreeable and depressing tasks facing Lincoln as he prepared for his second term as president.

★ ★ ★

After the election, office seekers and their champions crowded the corridors of the Executive Mansion and flooded the mail with applications and solicitations. A steady stream of Republican senators and representatives entered Lincoln's office with petitions and letters from their constituents seeking local appointments. Some sought to turn out incumbents on the dubious grounds that they either had done little for the party in the fall election or, even worse, had supported the Copperheads.[1] Others, including the president's wife, pressed him to appoint relatives or friends. Elizabeth Grimsley, a cousin of Mary Lincoln's, was especially persistent in seeking the postmistress position in Springfield with Mary's support. Balancing these pressures at the office and at home took its toll, especially when Lincoln resisted, as he did in the case of Mrs. Lincoln's cousin.[2]

Anticipating the pressure from office seekers, Lincoln decided to make few changes in the more than fifteen hundred positions at his disposal. He confided to Senator John B. Clark of New Hampshire that "the bare thought of going through again what I did the first year here, would crush me." To another person he said: "I think now that I will not remove a single man, except for delinquency. To remove a man is very easy, but when I go to fill his place, there are *twenty* applicants, and of these I must make *nineteen* enemies."[3] By this time almost all federal offices from local postmasters to cabinet members were held either by Republican party activists or by strong conservative supporters of the president's war policies. Removals and replacements would be likely to intensify intraparty conflict. Nonetheless, vacancies created by resignations and deaths had to be filled, and the president, of necessity, confronted the challenge.

No appointment loomed larger—or threatened to be more controversial—for Lincoln than that of chief justice of the Supreme Court. On October 12, 1864, Chief Justice Roger B. Taney had died. Lincoln had earlier filled three vacancies on the court with virtually unknown conservative Republicans from border states. In 1863 he had selected another member, Stephen J. Field, a California judge from a famous northeastern family, when a tenth justice position was authorized for the court. The president probably had a personal acquaintance with only one of these four appointments: David Davis, a native of Maryland and a judge of the Eighth Illinois Circuit where Lincoln had practiced law. Davis had been his manager at the Republican national convention in 1860 and was supported by many of his Illinois friends. All four appointments had been easily approved by Republicans and quickly confirmed by the Senate. Now, however, the appointment of a chief justice at a time of sharp divisions over the war and emancipation promised to be considerably more contentious.[4]

The selection of a replacement for Taney raised a host of concerns.

With the war ending, constitutional questions regarding reconstruction and the place of blacks in Southern society meant that the Supreme Court would have an important role in shaping the future. Along with his predecessor John Marshall, Taney, the author of the infamous Dred Scott decision which ruled that blacks were not citizens and an obstructionist to Republican war measures, had demonstrated the powerful influence of the chief justice on the decisions of the court. Republicans, after their experience with Taney, wanted a chief justice who would unequivocally validate their antislavery and war policies, including the controversial financial measures that were certain to arouse Democratic opposition after the war. Lincoln himself believed that, until the adoption of an antislavery amendment to the Constitution, his Emancipation Proclamation stood on shaky legal ground and might be struck down by the federal courts. He knew that he must select a strong and earnest Republican to replace Taney, even if it meant alienating conservative Unionists. The man he had chosen was Salmon P. Chase, a Radical Republican, whose resignation as secretary of the treasury he had forced in late June. However, to avoid losing conservative support at the polls, he waited until after the November election to make the appointment. It was not until Congress met in early December that the president submitted Chase's name to the Senate for confirmation.

The choice of Chase as chief justice caused Lincoln considerable anguish. Chase's own ambition to be president had been temporarily stymied by Lincoln's ascendancy, and he had let it be known that he would rather be chief justice of the Supreme Court than hold any other position. To assuage several disaffected Republicans before the election, Lincoln during the summer of 1864 assured them that if the chief justice position became vacant (Taney was eighty-six years old and in failing health), Chase would be his choice to fill it. Chase's friends soon informed him of the president's promise.[5]

If Lincoln thought that leaking his promise to Chase would immediately gain Radical support for his candidacy, he was wrong. Though Chase had important supporters like Senator Charles Sumner, other powerful congressional Republicans had been unhappy with him. His failure to stand up to Lincoln in a cabinet crisis of December 1862 had antagonized some Radicals. Chase had precipitated the crisis by

Salmon P. Chase, an ambitious Republican rival of Lincoln, who resigned as secretary of the treasury in June 1864 over a patronage dispute, but, for political reasons, was appointed chief justice of the U.S. Supreme Court in December.

complaining to his friends in Congress that Secretary of State Seward was the evil genius behind the president and the cause of disharmony in the cabinet. In a meeting that Lincoln arranged with congressional leaders and the cabinet on the issue, however, Chase, when confronted by the president, denied that problems existed in the administration and was silent regarding Seward's influence. Radicals left the meeting muttering that Chase had betrayed them. Some Radicals also found Chase's ego and ambition insufferable. Senator Benjamin F. Wade quipped that "Chase is a good man" in terms of the war and emancipation, "but his theology is unsound. He thinks there is a fourth person in the [Holy] Trinity," himself. Lincoln told a Massachusetts congressman: "Chase is, on the whole, a pretty good fellow and a very able man. His only trouble is that he has 'the White House fever' a little too bad, but I hope [the chief justice position] may cure him and that he will be satisfied."[6]

During the summer of 1864, as the president's political prospects plummeted, disaffected Republicans had mentioned Chase as a replacement for him on the party's ticket. Chase had discreetly cultivated the opposition to Lincoln, but, knowing he had been promised the position of chief justice, and uncertain about Lincoln's strength in the party, he had remained noncommittal regarding a presidential draft. In September, when Lincoln's position improved dramatically as a result of Union military successes and the reactionary Democratic platform adopted at Chicago, the effort to replace him on the ticket collapsed. Chase rushed to Washington in mid-September to consult with Republican leaders. On three consecutive days he talked to the president. After two of these meetings, at which third persons were present, Chase wrote to his daughter that Lincoln's "manner was evidently intended to be cordial & so were his words: and I hear of nothing but good will from him. But you know he is not at all demonstrative either in Speech or Manner—not at all in these respects what I like. I feel that I do not know him, & I found no action on what he says or does." However, he had concluded that "the cause I love & the general public interests will be best promoted by his election, and I have resolved to join my efforts to the whole body of my friends in securing it." The president in these conversations apparently did not renew his promise to make Chase chief justice: a few days later Chase wrote a friend that in giving Lincoln "my active support, . . . it is not probable that my action will be appreciated, as I would wish."[7]

Nevertheless, Chase left for Ohio to campaign for Lincoln and the party. He spoke in several lower Northern states and in Kentucky, remaining away from Washington to avoid the appearance of seeking Taney's seat on the court, but he did encourage his friends to increase their lobbying on his behalf.[8] Several Radical Republican newspapers, having received reports (perhaps from Chase or his friends) of the president's earlier promise to appoint him to the Supreme Court, appealed to Lincoln to make the appointment soon. But Lincoln was in no hurry to act; indeed, he had developed second thoughts about choosing his old rival. He found Chase's lobbying for the position inappropriate. On one occasion, when a secretary brought the president a letter from Chase, Lincoln asked: "What is it about?" The secretary answered that it simply was "a kind and friendly letter." The president, without reading it, smilingly replied, "File it with [Chase's] other recommendations for the appointment."[9]

Lincoln also wavered because after the election conservative Republicans launched a vigorous campaign to block Chase's nomination. They reminded Lincoln that Chase had long intrigued against him and would be a thorn in his side as chief justice. Furthermore, they predicted, Chase's ambition would not be satisfied by the appointment.[10] The anti-Chase forces, however, could not agree on an alternative candidate. Several names were mentioned to the president, including William M. Evarts, a prominent New York lawyer, Associate Justice Noah H. Swayne, Secretary of War Edwin M. Stanton, former cabinet member Montgomery Blair, and Attorney General Edward Bates, who personally asked Lincoln to appoint him. In the case of Bates, who had earlier informed the president that he wanted to retire from the cabinet after the election, Lincoln exhibited his practice of occasionally dissembling to avoid unnecessary offense. Although he had no intention of appointing Bates, he told a friend of the attorney general that "if not overborne by others, [he] would gladly make" Bates chief justice. Bates left the cabinet in late November with expressions of goodwill toward the president.[11]

Blair soon attracted the most attention as the alternative to Chase, making Lincoln's decision even more difficult. The scion of a powerful political family, Blair, who had taken a political fall for Lincoln and the Union party in September when he resigned as postmaster general, believed the president owed him the top place on the Supreme Court. A number of prominent conservative supporters of Lincoln agreed. Edward Everett, citing Blair's sterling court arguments in behalf of Dred Scott in the 1850s and his moral courage in supporting the Republican party in a slave state, wrote the president a long letter advocating the Marylander's appointment. Even William H. Seward, an old Blair foe who desperately wanted to prevent Chase's selection, sought Blair's appointment as the lesser of two evils. Mary Todd Lincoln, who also had little love for Blair but less for Chase, appealed to her husband to name Blair to the bench rather than the Ohioan. Francis P. Blair Sr. spoke to Lincoln in mid-November on behalf of his son, and came away from the meeting believing that Montgomery would be chosen. Secretary of the Navy Gideon Welles also appealed to the president to choose Blair, insisting that "it was all-important that [Lincoln] should have a judge who would be a correct and faithful expositor of the principles of his administration and policy." Welles recorded in his diary that "the President at different points expressed his concurrence in my views, and spoke kindly and complimentarily of Mr. Blair," but refused to commit himself regarding the appointment. Welles did not expect Lincoln to choose Chase. "The President," he wrote, "sometimes does strange things, but this would be a singular mistake . . . for one who is so shrewd and honest,—an appointment that he would soon regret."[12]

But a few days later Lincoln, without informing his cabinet or anyone else beforehand, did precisely what Welles thought he would not do. He sent his nomination of Chase to the Senate. The decision was obviously a tortured one. When a New England friend protested against the selection, the president told him that he "would rather have swallowed his buckhorn chair" than to have chosen Chase. Lincoln, however, told Senator Lafayette S. Foster of Connecticut, "Mr. Chase will make a very excellent judge if he devotes himself exclusively to the duties of his office and don't meddle with politics."[13]

In view of his misgivings and the important opposition to Chase, why did Lincoln choose him for chief justice? Though he hoped to bury Chase's presidential ambitions by appointing him to the Supreme Court, Lincoln had a more fundamental reason to select his old rival. He knew that with Chase on the court he would have a strong supporter of his emancipation policy, a policy he believed would be in jeopardy once the war was over and presidential authority regarding slavery ended. Until the proposed antislavery amendment could be initiated by Congress and ratified by the required three-fourths of the states, the Emancipation Proclamation was vulnerable in the federal courts, which might strike it down and conceivably return to slavery those who had been freed by it. Despite his obvious dislike of Chase and opposition to his radical tendencies, Lincoln could rest assured that Chase would be a bulwark on the Supreme Court against efforts to invalidate emancipation. In addition, as the president told Congressman George S. Boutwell of Massachusetts, he knew that Chase would uphold other war measures of the administration, specifically its financial policies. Lincoln informed a delegation of Maryland supporters that, with the appointment of Chase, all holders of government securities in the United States and in Europe would be assured of their value because "Judge Chase would only be sustaining himself, for he was the author" of these issues.[14]

Montgomery Blair, Chase's chief rival for the position, had become too extreme in his views for Lincoln to appoint him to the Supreme Court. After listening to one of the former postmaster general's harangues, John Hay wrote in his diary, "Blair denounces nearly everybody as Lincoln's malignant enemies." Blair also falsely claimed that Seward and Stanton had conspired against Lincoln in the election.[15] Though the president personally liked Blair, it would have been foolhardy to appoint such an intemperate person to the country's highest judicial position. Also, Lincoln's earlier promise to nominate Chase carried a great deal of weight in the decision. As both his prewar career and his presidency had demonstrated, Lincoln took promises seriously.

Reaction to the selection of Chase for chief justice proved surprisingly mild. Many Radical Republicans expressed delight with the appointment; they concluded that Lincoln would now reshuffle his cabinet and include members of their faction in it. They would soon be disappointed, but the nomination of Chase, along with Lincoln's triumph in the fall election, temporarily quieted their opposition to the president. Congressman Henry L. Dawes, who earlier had identified with the Radicals, believed the appointment had done much to establish harmony in the Republican party.[16] Not surprisingly, the Blair family, Welles, and other conservative Republicans close to Lincoln were upset about the nomination, but they held their peace and made no public statements criticizing it. Frank Blair, a general in Sherman's army and a former congressman who had denounced Chase on the floor of the House of Representatives, wrote to his brother Montgomery that the "appointment shakes my confidence in the President's integrity. He must know that Chase is dishonest as well as an enemy to him and the Government." Democrats, demoralized by their defeat at the polls and believing that one Republican was about as bad as another, largely ignored Chase's elevation to the Supreme Court. Former president James Buchanan, who had no love for the Republicans but opposed the peace wing of the Democratic party, told a friend: "Mr. Lincoln made the best selection from his party for the office of Chief Justice. Mr. Chase is a gentleman; and although extreme in his views on the abolition question, I have no doubt he will worthily fill the place of his eminent predecessors."[17]

Chase was effusive in his expressions of gratitude. Returning to his Washington home on the day Lincoln sent the nomination to the Senate, Chase immediately wrote to him: "I cannot sleep before I thank [you] for this mark of your confidence, & especially for the manner in which the nomination was made. I shall never forget either and trust that you will never regret either. Be assured that I prize your confidence & good will more than nomination or office." The next morning Chase visited the president and accepted the nomination, which the Senate quickly—and unanimously—approved.[18]

The new chief justice, as Lincoln had suspected, continued to dabble in politics and government affairs, pressing his views on Lincoln and members of Congress; on one occasion he briefly attended a cabinet meeting. Chase especially sought support for civil and political rights for Southern freedmen.[19] On April 11, after consulting with Henry Winter Davis and other Maryland Radicals in Baltimore, he wrote to Lincoln that the extension of black suffrage in the South was "essential to the future tranquility of the country" and to the freedom of the race. He argued that it would be "a crime & a folly if the colored loyalists of the rebel states shall be left to the control of restored rebels," who would perpetuate "new calamities" upon them and upon white Unionists. Lincoln, however, had already determined that he would not force black suffrage upon the restored Southern governments, though, as he indicated in his last public address—on the day Chase penned his letter—he preferred the enfranchisement of "the very intelligent" blacks and "those who serve our cause as soldiers."[20]

The appointment of Chase revealed Lincoln's pragmatic willingness to put aside his dislike of an individual for the good of the Union. The president believed that Chase not only would sustain his administration's wartime policies but would provide a more positive leadership to a Supreme Court that for years had suffered under Taney's obstructionism. Lincoln also sought to heal the divisions in his party by selecting a Radical as chief justice. Having given the Radicals this important judicial plum, he felt free to choose men for other vacancies in the administration who were more personally and politically compatible with him.

* * *

After appointing Chase, Lincoln set out to smooth the ruffled feathers of conservative Republicans. He regretted the way Montgomery Blair, once an influential and able member of the cabinet, had been treated. The Blair family had been instrumental in the rise of the Republican party to power and had been a major contributor to the success of the Union in the border states. Lincoln did not want to appear ungrateful to the Blairs for their support, nor did he want to alienate a political clan that had its roots in the Jacksonian period and was still fondly thought of by Democrats and border-state Unionists. But Lincoln could go only so far in his efforts to restore the political standing of the hot-blooded Montgomery Blair. What Blair wanted more than anything was the annihilation of the Radical faction in his home state of Maryland, a faction headed by his bitter rival Henry Winter Davis, who also had been Lincoln's political enemy. Blair expected Lincoln to give him control of federal patronage in Maryland and to use his influence to secure a senatorial seat for him or one of his allies.

In early December Blair approached the president about removing Henry W. Hoffman, a Davis associate, as collector of the port of Baltimore, and replacing him with Blair's friend Senator Thomas H. Hicks. Appointing Hicks would open his Senate seat, to which Blair hoped to be elected by the Maryland legislature. But Lincoln, believing (incorrectly) that Davis, after the election, had decided to cease his attacks on the administration, did not want a renewal of strife with him or his Radical friends, nor did he want a quarrel with treasury officials who supported Hoffman. The collector owed his appointment to the former treasury secretary, Chase. The president attempted a ploy that he hoped would satisfy Blair without offending the Davis faction. He said he would place an opening at the Spanish mission in Madrid at Blair's disposal so he could offer it to Hoffman. If Hoffman agreed to vacate the collectorship and accept the position, Blair could then secure Hicks's appointment as collector and his own elevation to the Senate.

Blair immediately saw through this Lincolnesque maneuver, realizing that Hoffman, with the encouragement of the Davis faction, would not voluntarily surrender the office. He stormed into his friend Gideon Welles's office and charged that the president had succumbed to his enemies. He also expressed a fear that, because Lincoln had failed to support him, Hicks and Governor Thomas Swann would make their peace with the Davis "malcontents" in Maryland. Welles advised Blair to speak sternly to the president and demand Hoffman's removal, advice that the intemperate Blair was certain to follow.[21]

Two days later Blair went to the White House. When the president arrived, he summoned both Blair and General Nathaniel P. Banks, who were waiting in the antechamber, to follow him into his office. Lincoln attempted to deflect Blair's anger by asking the two men's advice on the Ashley reconstruction bill, a Radical proposal under consideration by the House of Representatives. Blair, momentarily forgetting the main purpose of his visit, lashed out at the Radicals in Congress, accusing them of underhanded motives and hostility to the president. Taken aback by Blair's vitriolic tone, Lincoln admonished him: "It is much better not to be led from the region of reason into that of hot blood, by imputing to public men motives which they do not avow."[22]

At this meeting Blair received no satisfaction from the president regarding affairs in Maryland. Lincoln wanted to help Blair, not only out of gratitude for his support but also because of his prominence as a conservative Republican. Nonetheless, Lincoln routinely refused to give ground to anyone, even the likeable Blair, who acted in "hot blood" in his presence. For Lincoln, the dignity of the presidency mattered.

In Maryland and elsewhere, Lincoln moved slowly, if at all, to replace Radicals or reputed Radicals for whom Chase as treasury secretary had secured appointments. Many of these men had intrigued against Lincoln in the presidential contest. Lincoln's friends, in addition to Blair and Welles, expressed dismay when he did not act quickly after the election to "decapitate" these "disloyal" officials. Even John Hay found Lincoln's reluctance to remove his political enemies hard to accept. "It seems utterly impossible," Hay wrote in his diary, "for the President to conceive of . . . any good resulting from a vigorous and exemplary course of punishing political dereliction. His favorite expression is 'I am in favor of short statutes of limitations in politics.'"[23]

The bitter Blair-Davis conflict in Maryland, however, would not go away, and shortly before his death Lincoln finally gave Blair some hope that his enemies in the state Radical faction would be punished. The death of Senator Hicks set in motion events that ultimately led to the Blair faction's political resurrection. Lincoln privately favored Blair in the election to replace Hicks, but he refused to make known his position because, as Welles believed, powerful influences "control him against his will." These influences included not only the Davis faction but also Treasury Department officials in Maryland and Washington and, perhaps more important, Secretary of War Stanton, who had frequently crossed swords with Blair in the cabinet. With "the purse and the sword" on the side of the Davis forces, the Maryland legislature elected Congressman John A. J. Creswell to the Senate.[24]

Davis, who was still in the House of Representatives (his term would expire at the end of the session), was emboldened by Creswell's election and renewed his attacks on the Lincoln administration. The brilliant, sharp-tongued Maryland Radical particularly denounced the president's reconstruction policy and the management of the Navy Department. Irritated by Davis's conduct and probably feeling guilty that he had not aided Blair in the senatorial contest, Lincoln finally in early April removed Hoffman as collector of the lucrative Baltimore port. He also asked Creswell to meet with Governor Swann, a Blair associate, and submit a slate of appointments for collector and other important federal offices in Maryland. Creswell, now that he had been elected to the Senate, indicated a willingness to cooperate with Lincoln and the Blair wing of the Maryland party. On April 14, the last day of his life, Lincoln accepted the Swann-Creswell list of appointees.[25]

* * *

Contention over patronage among New York Republicans proved as troublesome for Lincoln as the Maryland imbroglio. The New York factionalism had deep roots in the state's Whig party, the mother party of most Republicans. The division occurred between the William H. Seward–Thurlow Weed faction and those Republicans, generally of the Radical persuasion, who took their cues from Horace Greeley of the *New York Tribune*, William Cullen Bryant of the *New York Evening Post*, and Salmon P. Chase. The Seward-Weed faction, whose main newspaper organ was Henry J. Raymond's *New York Times*, emerged during the war as a conservative (or moderate) force in support of Lincoln's policies. In the 1864 presidential campaign, Lincoln came under strong pressure from both factions to extend patronage to their side as a quid pro quo for their active support of him. Influence in appointments to office had great symbolic prestige as well as practical significance for party activists. Federal patronage in New York, including control of the lucrative U.S. Custom House, had become a major bone of contention among Empire State Republicans.

After Chase resigned as secretary of the treasury in mid-1864, the Seward-Weed faction demanded the removal of his Radical Custom House appointees. Lincoln at first resisted, but during the bleak days of August when faced with a revolt by Weed, who was editor of the influential *Albany Evening Journal,* and the possibility that he might lose the election, the president acted. He removed Collector Hiram Barney and other pro-Chase activists, replacing them with men acceptable to Seward and Weed. In doing so he gained the active support of New York conservatives. Weed placed himself in charge of the Lincoln forces in the state and shook down officeholders for contributions to the campaign.[26] Nevertheless, the president refused the Weed faction's requests to replace minor federal clerks and General McClellan's supporters in the large Brooklyn Navy Yard. Secretary of the Navy Welles, who had battled the Weed junto when he was a Democratic leader in Connecticut, applauded Lincoln's "good sense and sagacity" in preventing the "abuse of power and patronage" in New York. The ouster of New York Radicals continued after Lincoln's inauguration on March 4. The president, two days before his death, replaced the Radical U.S. district attorney for southern New York with the conservative Daniel S. Dickinson, who supported his administration's policies.[27]

★ ★ ★

After the 1864 election, northeastern Radicals demanded that Lincoln reorganize his administration in keeping with the Republican platform's declaration that it was "essential to the general welfare that harmony should prevail in the national councils." Radicals interpreted this statement to mean that the president should dismiss the conservatives Seward, Welles, and Attorney General Edward Bates from the cabinet and appoint more "earnest" and capable Republicans in their places.[28] But Lincoln rejected this interpretation of his party's platform; he viewed the Radicals, along with the Democrats, as the main perpetrators of disharmony in Washington, though the Radicals, he believed, were more clearly on the side of the angels. In his first administration Lincoln had sought to appoint men from all factions of his party in order to achieve Northern and border-state unity as the nation faced the secession crisis. The conflict over war policies and emancipation within his cabinet, however, had led to backbiting among its members and the division into factions. Lincoln did not want this problem in his second administration.

The removals in 1864 of Chase and Blair, both lightning rods for their factions, had gone far to bring harmony to the cabinet. When replacements were necessary, Lincoln was determined to appoint men who were congenial to his personal and political tastes. He certainly had no intention of forcing out Seward and Welles. The *New York Herald* was on target when it reported that northeastern Radicals "may point as much as they like to the broad hints of the Baltimore [Republican] platform" regarding the dismissal of Seward and others from the cabinet, but "it is all moonshine to Old Abe." Lincoln had earlier told a Missouri Radical, who grumbled about a lack of unity in his administration, that he would not make changes based on complaints. He explained that each member of the cabinet was responsible "for the manner of conducting the affairs of his particular department; that there was no centralization of responsibility for the action of the cabinet anywhere." Yet Lincoln admitted that he reserved final authority over cabinet members; presumably he meant in important matters of national concern.[29]

Characteristically, Lincoln did not publicly reveal his intentions regarding cabinet changes. As a result Washington was awash in late 1864 with rumors and speculations about appointments. Names of presumed candidates for positions were reported in the newspapers. Seward reportedly would be replaced by Charles Francis Adams, the American minister in London; Stanton would give way to General

Nathaniel P. Banks or General Benjamin F. Butler; Welles would be succeeded by Senator James W. Grimes of Iowa; outgoing Vice President Hannibal Hamlin would replace Treasury Secretary William P. Fessenden, his rival in the Maine Republican party; and so on.[30]

Governor John A. Andrew of Massachusetts emerged as a candidate for several cabinet positions. He soon became a symbol of New England Radical hopes for an influential place in Lincoln's administration. Andrew's friends believed that the governor could bring "intelligent unity of purpose" to an administration lacking in "coherence, method, purpose, and consistency."[31] Andrew agreed with his friends. But Lincoln never seriously considered him (or any New England Radical) for a cabinet position because, like Chase, he might use his influence to undercut the administration's policies. Lincoln also had geographic considerations in mind. The Northeast was already well represented in the cabinet, with Fessenden of Maine, Welles of Connecticut, and Seward of upstate New York. Lincoln remarked to Assistant Attorney General Titian J. Coffey that his "cabinet has shrunk up North," and, in seeking a replacement for Bates, he admitted that he "must find a southern man. I suppose if the twelve apostles were to be chosen nowadays the shrieks of locality would have to be heeded." Trans-Mississippi Republicans had let Lincoln know that their section should have a seat in the cabinet, particularly if the position of secretary of the interior, as rumored, became vacant. The *St. Louis Missouri Democrat* (a Republican paper) argued that, with the war ending, Indian affairs, public land issues, western mining development, and the continental extension of the railroads would assume great importance, and these matters would require a knowledgeable westerner as secretary of the interior.[32]

Repeated rumors and Lincoln's refusal to reveal whether he intended to make any changes in his cabinet, except for replacing Bates, who had resigned as attorney general, contributed to a feeling of uncertainty among high-level officials in the administration. Gideon Welles recorded in his diary on December 9 an incident that illustrated the confusion. After an unproductive cabinet meeting, Seward took Welles and Secretary of the Interior John P. Usher aside and remarked "that Congress and the country were full of speculations about appointments; that he did not care a damn about himself,—if the President wanted him he would remain, and would go if he did not . . . Usher said it was important that he should know, for he had to depend on his salary or income for his support." According to Welles, Usher asked Seward to talk to the president about his status, but Welles himself "gave no thought to the rumors, manufactured by correspondents and quidnuncs." Lincoln, Welles concluded, would know how to deal with "quidnuncs" (busybodies) who attempted to dictate to him on patronage matters.[33] Despite such fears and pressures, Lincoln waited to make changes in his administration.

Bates's resignation created the first vacancy in the cabinet after the election. Since the new attorney general would need to be sensitive to issues growing out of the war in the South, Lincoln quickly decided to select someone from the Southern border states. At the suggestion of John Hay, he offered the position to the army's judge advocate general, Joseph Holt, a Kentuckian. Holt, a proslavery man until Lincoln issued the Emancipation Proclamation, was not considered a member of the Radical faction, despite his severe October 8 report charging a vast Copperhead conspiracy against the Union in the Midwest. As judge advocate general he had worked closely with Lincoln on numerous military cases requiring presidential action. Lincoln had come to have great respect for Holt and remarked that his selection as attorney general "would be an excellent appointment."[34] The Kentuckian also could be expected to support the constitutionality of the Emancipation Proclamation and, unlike the increasingly conservative Bates, vigorously enforce other war measures.

Holt, however, declined the appointment, citing "embarrassments" that would occur if he became attorney general. Lincoln reportedly told an associate that Holt refused the office because "he was unwilling to undertake the Supreme Court work." Holt might also have declined because his brother was a Mississippi slaveholder and his nephew a rebel soldier. Conceivably, after the war, Holt, if he had become attorney general, would have been in the difficult position of having to prosecute his Mississippi relatives.[35]

Whatever Holt's reasons for rejecting the appointment, Lincoln had to renew his efforts to fill the position. With the office vacant, he could not be deliberate in choosing a replacement for Bates, as was his usual practice in making an important decision. He again looked to the border states for someone with whom he would be comfortable and who would also support his policies. On the day after Holt turned down the position, Lincoln selected James Speed of Kentucky, the older brother of his close friend Joshua Speed. The president's cryptic telegram gave Speed no opportunity to decline: "I appoint you to be Attorney General. Please come on at once." Speed obeyed the summons and was in Washington by December 6, but he refused to be sworn in until the Senate had confirmed his appointment, as it did a few days later. On December 16 the new attorney general attended his first cabinet meeting, where Lincoln introduced him to the other members, most of whom apparently had not met him before.[36]

The appointment of an unknown Kentuckian, from a former slave-holding family, to the top legal position in the administration surprised the country. Many "earnest" Republicans saw it as another "indication of [Lincoln's] increasing tendencies toward the 'Border State Policy,'" meaning his conservative approach to Southern reconstruction and federal policy regarding the rights of freed slaves. Some disappointed Republicans, however, put the best face possible upon Lincoln's decision. The Washington correspondent of the *Boston Commonwealth* wrote that though "Mr. Speed's hankering after conservatism" was "well-authenticated," he supported Republican war policies, had Holt's warm endorsement, and was a firm enemy of rebels and Copperheads. This correspondent concluded that Lincoln, without regard to politics, had selected the Kentuckian simply because of his "old-time friendship for and back woods familiarity with the Speed family."[37]

James Speed, a successful Louisville lawyer, had met Lincoln when the Illinoisan had visited his brother Joshua before the war. Though Speed opposed Lincoln in the 1860 election, he later became a staunch Unionist and played a key role in raising and arming loyal troops in Kentucky. He also advised the president on Kentucky affairs, including the explosive issue of emancipation. As early as December 1861, Speed called for the destruction of slavery, but only through state action, not federal intervention. In 1862 he favored Lincoln's compensation scheme for the border states, which Kentucky defiantly rejected as a federal infringement on the rights of the states to control the institution of slavery. Later Speed endorsed the Emancipation Proclamation and also a constitutional amendment to end slavery everywhere in the United States.[38] Though a conservative and a strong supporter of the president's mild reconstruction policy when he became attorney general, after Lincoln's assassination Speed cooperated with the Radical Republicans in their opposition to Andrew Johnson's flawed Southern policy. The Speed appointment, which the Democrats and some Radicals labeled cronyism, actually proved to be one of Lincoln's best.

★ ★ ★

The new year, 1865, brought two more changes in Lincoln's cabinet, the first involving the resignation of Secretary of the Treasury William Pitt Fessenden. During the summer of 1864 Fessenden, an influential Maine senator, had reluctantly agreed to replace Chase as treasury secretary. Immediately after the election, however, he began intriguing with his friends in Maine to return to the Senate. Fessenden was partly motivated by the desire to prevent retiring Vice President Hamlin from securing the vacant Maine seat. When it became apparent that Fessenden would win the seat, Hamlin sought to replace his rival as secretary of the treasury. Thurlow Weed, who asked Lincoln to appoint Hamlin to the office, later wrote that the president dismissed the suggestion and commented, "Hamlin has the Senate on the brain, and nothing more or less will cure him."[39] Lincoln had another and more important reason for refusing to select Hamlin—the opposition of Fessenden. According to Hamlin's son, Fessenden "threatened war if he should appoint [Hamlin] to the Cabinet." The president reportedly told Hamlin: "You have not been treated right. It is too bad, too bad. But what can I do? I am tied hands and feet."[40] Lincoln's desire to maintain harmony in the Republican party as he began his second term was the main reason he refused to appoint Hamlin. He could not afford to alienate the more powerful New England Republican, Fessenden; he perhaps could placate Hamlin with the excuse that his hands were tied.

Fessenden waited until the Maine legislature had elected him to the Senate in early 1865 before resigning as secretary of the treasury, to be effective on March 3. In his letter of resignation, Fessenden, who had been a critic of Lincoln before becoming a part of his administration, profusely thanked the president for his "kindness and consideration." "In retiring," he wrote, "I carry with me great and increased respect for your patriotic character, and for the ability which has marked your administration of the government." Though Lincoln appreciated the praise from Fessenden, he had the problem of finding a replacement in the highly charged political atmosphere of the nation's capital. Pennsylvania Republicans sought the appointment of Thaddeus Stevens, chairman of the House Appropriations Committee, but Lincoln did not seriously consider the acid-tongued Radical.[41] Others were recommended, including John W. Forney, who had consistently supported Lincoln's policies in his newspapers, the *Washington Chronicle* and the *Philadelphia Press*. Lincoln focused on a prominent New Yorker who had the confidence of eastern bankers and merchants (as Stevens and Forney did not) and who would support the administration's financial policies: the senator and former governor Edwin D. Morgan, an erstwhile political associate of Seward and Weed. The problem was that if Morgan entered the cabinet, New Yorkers—and members of the Seward-Weed faction at that—would hold the two top offices in the cabinet. Nevertheless, after talking to Weed, Lincoln decided to offer the position to Morgan.

In an attempt to forestall criticism, Lincoln pledged Weed to secrecy and dispatched him to Morgan's home in Washington to inform him that he might be called upon to perform "other duties" in the government. Morgan, kept in the dark as to what the "other duties" would be, made no commitment to accept a position. Lincoln, however, was confident that Morgan, a successful merchant with a keen interest in financial matters, would agree to become treasury secretary. On February 13 he submitted Morgan's name to the Senate for approval. Taken by surprise when his name was presented on the Senate floor, Morgan immediately secured the postponement of the matter, then rushed to the White House to inform Lincoln that he could not accept the appointment. An effort by Lincoln and Weed to change his mind failed. Probably Morgan's main reason for rejecting the post was that if he resigned from the Senate, New York governor Reuben Fenton, a political opponent, would probably succeed him. Morgan may have believed that the election of Fenton to the Senate would damage his position and further divide the party in New York, where Republicans held a razor-thin advantage over the Democrats.[42]

Lincoln's secretiveness in dealing with Morgan had backfired, and he now found himself in the embarrassing situation of having to dispatch John Hay to the Senate to withdraw the nomination. He lamented to Weed, the middleman in the affair, that Morgan's refusal "is very awkward, but we must look elsewhere for a secretary." Before giving Weed an opportunity to suggest another candidate, Lincoln indicated that, through the process of elimination, he had narrowed his choices to Hugh McCulloch, a banker then serving as comptroller of the currency, and Congressman Samuel Hooper of Massachusetts. Weed expressed a preference for Hooper and a mild opposition to McCulloch, whom Chase had brought from Indiana to Washington and who, Weed argued, might favor his former boss's political views. Lincoln laughingly reminded Weed that Hooper had "disappointed" Seward's friends, including Weed, at the Republican national convention in 1860 when he supported "a new man"—Lincoln—for president. Weed quickly understood that the president had selected the virtually unknown McCulloch for the position. To ensure the support of the Seward-Weed faction and their friends on Wall Street, Lincoln sent Weed to break the news to McCulloch at his residence and discuss the implications of the appointment. Weed warmed to McCulloch when he discovered that the Indianan had been affiliated with the Whig party before the war and had not imbibed Chase's radicalism.[43]

As with the Speed appointment in December, Republican newspapers reacted cautiously to McCulloch's selection as secretary of the treasury. The *St. Louis Missouri Democrat* remarked that McCulloch was a "thoroughgoing business man," known by financiers and bankers, and active in the Union cause, though not a politician. The paper's editor also noted, however, that "it appears strange" that Lincoln did not fill the position with "a notable public man" in the mold of McCulloch's predecessors Chase and Fessenden. Assuming office on March 4, McCulloch would serve under Lincoln and Andrew Johnson for four years, ably managing the bewildering array of financial matters created by the war. In appointing McCulloch, Lincoln had made a wise choice. He had selected a treasury secretary who understood financial matters and had no political handicaps that could cause trouble for his administration.[44]

* * *

Lincoln had one more cabinet change to make as he began his second term. The selection of McCulloch of Indiana gave him an excuse for replacing Secretary of the Interior John P. Usher, also a Hoosier. According to Lincoln, no state should have two representatives in the cabinet, though he had been willing to break this rule if Morgan had accepted the treasury office.[45] Furthermore, powerful western Republicans complained of Usher's ineffectiveness as an administrator. Some of them, particularly the Iowa delegation in Congress, opposed Usher because of his support of the Kansas route for the Union Pacific Railroad, which competed with Iowa for the eastern terminus of the first transcontinental line. The Iowa forces, along with other groups that had been denied favors by Usher, spread false reports that he was corrupt. Probably the strongest charge that could be made against him was that he had selected (with Lincoln's approval) too many subordinates and agents from Indiana and Illinois, some of whom were incompetent and, in the tradition of the Interior Department, corrupt. In early 1865 a group of Usher's western opponents visited Lincoln and demanded that he find another interior secretary. By late February the president had talked to Usher, and, apparently without directly asking him to resign, had obtained his resignation. Lincoln, perhaps feeling guilty that Usher had been forced from the cabinet, suggested that the resignation not take effect until May 15, when Usher would take a position on the Union Pacific Railroad.[46]

Even before Usher submitted his resignation, Lincoln had someone in mind to fill the position. His choice was Senator James Harlan, an Iowa Republican, a former Methodist minister, and a splendid orator. Late in the war Lincoln and Harlan had become friends. An even closer relationship had developed between the president's son Robert and the senator's daughter Mary; after the war they would marry. An advocate in the Senate for the confiscation of rebel property, which Lincoln opposed, Harlan nonetheless consistently defended Lincoln during the 1864 presidential campaign. Like many congressional Republicans by early 1865, Harlan could not be clearly identified with any particular faction of the party. As chair of the Senate Committee on Public Lands, he had helped secure the enactment of the Homestead and Pacific Railroad bills, two measures dear to Lincoln. He had led the Iowa forces in their efforts, which were ultimately successful, to undercut Usher and the supporters of the Kansas route for the Union Pacific Railroad. Harlan also was a member of the Committee on Indian Affairs and had protested vigorously against the violation of Indian rights and land. Familiar with public land issues, western railroad developments, and Indian affairs, and hailing from an important trans-Mississippi state, Harlan was a logical choice for secretary of the interior, even without a personal connection to Lincoln.[47]

Still, Harlan hesitated to accept the appointment, confiding to a friend that he would prefer to remain in the Senate. "Nothing but a sense of public duty would induce me to change," he declared. "A pressing necessity for a renovation in the Interior department . . . may possibly control my decision, contrary to my own personal wishes." In late March Harlan wrote to Iowa congressman James F. Wilson that he would accept the office "if I find I can get the pack of thieves now preying on the Govt. under its auspices out of power, otherwise I will not." He admitted that "the prospect of effecting this is not very good, for it happens that some of the worst of these people have the President's confidence." Harlan finally agreed to serve, though he did not take office until after Lincoln's death. He failed, however, to "get the pack of thieves" out of the Interior Department or to reform Indian affairs, which was virtually an impossible task in late nineteenth-century America. After clashing with President Johnson over reconstruction policy, Harlan resigned as secretary of the interior in July 1866.[48]

★ ★ ★

The new appointees in Lincoln's cabinet—Speed, McCulloch, Harlan, and William Dennison, who had replaced Blair in the fall—had proven themselves during the war. All were from the rapidly developing and politically emerging Mississippi-Ohio basin and reflected western values similar to those of Lincoln. They had consistently supported the president's war and emancipation policies and agreed with his conservative border-state strategy. Harlan's earlier endorsement of the confiscation of rebel property was in line with many middle-of-the-road Republicans who saw it as a means to punish secessionists and a source of funds to finance the war. As governor of Ohio, Dennison had supported Chase, but by the time of his appointment to the cabinet he had turned against the Radical leader and had become a firm Lincoln supporter.[49] Unlike the men they replaced—Usher, Fessenden, Blair and, to a lesser extent, Bates—the new cabinet members did not have troublesome political or ideological agendas to promote. They fitted in nicely with the conservative holdovers in the cabinet—Seward, Welles, and even the volatile Stanton, all of whom, despite their petty differences with one another, were personally attached to the president. By the time of his second inaugural, Lincoln had welded together a strong cabinet, one that promised to be second to none in American history had its master lived to maintain its unity through the next four years.

On March 3, the day Lincoln informed his cabinet of Usher's resignation and the day before he began his second term in office, he announced to the cabinet that he contemplated no further changes in personnel. "The continuing swarms of contending applicants for his patronage," a report indicated, were affecting his health and were a cause of concern for both Lincoln and Mary.[50] Since his re-election, difficult patronage issues had taken up too much of the president's time. He had more important matters to consider and act on, none more important than a quest for peace now that the election had demonstrated the determination of the Northern people to persevere until reunion and emancipation had been achieved. He intensely wanted an early end to the fighting and suffering, though he believed the carnage might continue into the summer or even later.[51] The Southern people, Lincoln fervently hoped, would realize that the rebellion had failed and that he would restore all of their rights, except property in slaves, as soon as they had laid down their arms and agreed to return, as he expressed it, to their "proper practical relation with the Union."[52]

CHAPTER 4

THE SEARCH FOR PEACE

Encouraged by his victory in the November election, Lincoln set to work preparing his annual message to Congress, which was scheduled to assemble on December 5. In late November he read a draft of the message to the cabinet. In the discussion that followed, he dealt at length with the issue of ending the war. On the military front, General Sherman had broken away from his base at Atlanta and was marching toward Savannah; General Thomas was confidently awaiting Hood's army at Nashville; and Grant was gradually wearing down Lee's forces in Virginia. Lincoln hoped that the Confederates would recognize the inevitability of defeat and, to avoid further bloodshed and ruin at home, would agree to peace on his terms. The Republican victory at the polls should have convinced Southerners that they could not expect a compromise peace short of reunion and emancipation.

Indicating that he could not "treat" with Jefferson Davis's government because he had never recognized its legitimacy, Lincoln expressed uncertainty as to whom he should approach in the South and how peace negotiations should begin. Secretary of the Navy Gideon Welles said that he should deal only with the states, which the administration had always recognized as "entities" and not outside the Union. Secretary of War Edwin Stanton agreed with Welles and advised Lincoln to make no new offer to the rebels but to "bring forward his former policy and maintain it, to hold open the doors of conciliation and invite the people to return to their duty."[1] In view of Stanton's later reputation as a Radical Republican and his postwar hard-line policy toward former rebels, his advocacy of Lincoln's lenient or conservative policy at this time is remarkable. It reflects Lincoln's success in establishing himself as master of his administration and in gaining by late 1864 a cabinet consensus for his policies.

* * *

On December 6 Lincoln, as was the custom, sent his annual message to Congress, where the clerks read it aloud in both chambers. The message did not rise to the high standards of the president's other public addresses, though its preparation had weighed "heavy on [Lincoln's] mind," according to Welles. Much of the document was a summary of department reports. It conveyed to Congress and the public a positive if not optimistic view that ignored or obscured problems facing the administration. The long section on foreign affairs (five pages), for example, devoted only two sentences to the presence of the French in Mexico, which by late 1864 was giving Lincoln and Northerners considerable concern. Lincoln glossed over the strained relations with Great Britain caused by the construction of Confederate sea raiders in British shipyards and the Confederate use of Canadian soil to plot against the Union. He euphemistically referred to the troubles with France and Britain as "unforeseen political difficulties" and reassured Americans that "the condition of our foreign affairs is reasonably satisfactory." He particularly noted that "official correspondence has been freely opened with Liberia, and it gives us a pleasing view of social and political progress in that Republic." Lincoln expected that Liberia, which had been founded in the 1820s by the American Colonization Society for freed slaves, would "derive new vigor [from] the rapid disappearance of slavery in the United States."[2]

The president also summarized western territorial, mining, and railroad developments. He happily reported that "the great enterprise of connecting the Atlantic with the Pacific States by railways and telegraph lines has been entered upon with a vigor that gives assurance of success." He referred Congress to the secretary of the interior's report for specific recommendations regarding changes in the federal government's management of the western Indians. These reforms, Lincoln said, should provide for "the welfare of the Indian" and also protect "the advancing settler."[3] But he ignored the November massacre of more than one hundred Cheyenne Indians at Sand Creek by Colorado territorial troops, which had followed Indian raids in the area. Overall, Lincoln made few recommendations for congressional action, preferring instead "to invite your attention to the subject" as outlined by each department head.

Finally, two-thirds of the way through his annual message, the president focused on the rebellion and emancipation. "The war continues" with important successes, he reported. But except for Sherman's "march of three hundred miles directly through the insurgent region," he did not mention specific military operations but rather referred Congress to the secretary of war's report. He described political movements in the South, including the border states, "to the effect of moulding society for durability in the Union" and said that, though "short of complete success," they "were much in the right direction." He applauded border-state efforts to end slavery, specifically praising Maryland for its "complete success" in securing "Liberty and Union for all the future." "The genius of rebellion will no more claim Maryland," he announced.[4]

The president called on Congress to reconsider and approve for state action the constitutional amendment abolishing slavery everywhere in the United States. Earlier in the year the proposed amendment had failed to secure the necessary two-thirds congressional vote to send it to the states for ratification. Though the same members still sat in Congress, Lincoln told them that the voice of the people, as expressed in the election, had demanded that they approve it. If they did not act, he said, the next Congress, which had been elected in the fall, would certainly pass it. He suggested that it would be better if the old Congress approved the amendment and thereby speeded up the process of eradicating slavery in America. He reminded Congress that one of the means to preserve the Union was the destruction of slavery, which the proposed amendment would swiftly advance.[5] He did not mention his fear that without the constitutional amendment the Emancipation Proclamation, the legal justification of which had been military necessity, might be declared invalid by the courts after the war.

Next Lincoln reiterated the importance of "our popular elections." The 1864 election, he said, had revealed that "the purpose of the people, within the loyal States, to maintain the integrity of the Union, was never more firm, nor more nearly unanimous, than now." During the campaign "much impugning of motives, and much heated controversy as to the proper means and best mode of advancing the Union cause" had occurred; "but on the distinct issue of Union or no Union, the politicians have shown their instinctive knowledge that there is no diversity among the people. In affording the people the fair opportunity of showing, one to another and to the world, this firmness and unanimity of purpose, the election has been of vast value to the national cause." With a Southern audience in mind, the president announced that "we are not exhausted, nor in process of exhaustion; that we are *gaining* strength, and may, if need be, maintain the contest indefinitely."[6]

Then he turned to the issue closest to his heart—ending the war: "On careful consideration of all the evidence accessible it seems to me that no attempt at negotiation with the insurgent leader [Jefferson Davis] could result in any good. He would accept nothing short of severance of the Union—precisely what we will not and cannot give . . . Between him and us the issue is distinct, simple, and inflexible. It is an issue which can only be tried by war, and decided by victory." The president expressed hope that the Southern people would seek an end to their rebellion. He announced that "some of them, we know, already desire peace and reunion," and that their numbers should soon increase as Union forces continued to advance. Southerners, he said, "can, at any moment, have peace simply by laying down their arms and submitting to the national authority under the Constitution . . . If questions should remain, we would adjust them by the peaceful means of legislation, conference, courts, and votes, operating only in constitutional and lawful channels." However, he reaffirmed his commitment to emancipation: "While I remain in my present position I shall not attempt to retract or modify the emancipation proclamation, nor shall I return to slavery any person who is free by the terms of that proclamation, or by any of the Acts of Congress."[7]

The president acknowledged that some "questions are, and would be, beyond the Executive power to adjust; as for instance, the admission of members into Congress, and whatever might require the appropriation of money." He also noted that his power "would be greatly diminished by the cessation of actual war. Pardons and remissions of [property] forfeitures, however, would still be within Executive control." "In what spirit and temper this control would be exercised," he continued, "can be fairly judged of by the past." Many repentant rebels had already received amnesty, and no application for a special pardon of individuals of the excepted classes (mainly leaders) had been denied. Clemency was still open to all. "But the time may come—probably will come—when public duty shall demand that it be closed; and that, in lieu, more rigorous measures than heretofore shall be adopted." Nothing in Lincoln's message indicated that he had changed his fundamental policy, announced in December 1863, of permitting a large measure of self-reconstruction controlled by Southern white Unionists, with former rebels participating after they had taken the loyalty oath.[8]

Lincoln concluded with a simple declaration: "In stating a single condition of peace, I mean simply to say that the war will cease on the part of the government, whenever it shall have ceased on the part of those who began it."[9] This hardly constituted a demand for "unconditional surrender" by the South. Lincoln's peace terms, except for the addition of the emancipation requirement, had not fundamentally changed since 1861 when, in his July 4 message to Congress, he promised that the government would restore the constitutional rights of Southerners once they had ceased their rebellion.

The annual message to Congress of December 1864, though its tone lacked inspiration, clearly established Lincoln's immediate objectives for his new term as president. In effect, his second term began with his re-election, not with the inauguration on March 4. Except for his urging Congress to initiate a constitutional amendment abolishing slavery, the annual message was more a report than a recommendation for congressional action. Largely directed to the Southern people, the message revealed Lincoln's strong desire for an early peace now that his authority had been sustained at the polls. He elaborated on the strength of the "national cause" and the determination of the Northern people in the war. He carefully explained his terms for peace—the end of the rebellion and slavery—and indicated that these requirements had not changed, but he now warned that the door for individual Southerners to obtain amnesty might soon close. Southerners must end their rebellion soon or risk unknown consequences. Lincoln, who had always overestimated the strength of Unionism in the South, naively assumed, or perhaps hoped, that a large body of Confederates would respond favorably to his terms and seek an end to the war. Since most people in the Union states were well aware of the course of the war, Lincoln saw no need to provide an extended report on it. How the war should end, not past military campaigns, was his main interest.

* * *

Republicans and Unionists generally praised the president's message. The *Washington National Republican* pronounced it "one of the clearest, firmest, and most able and important State papers that has ever emanated from the Chief Executive of this nation." The *New York Evening Post*, which had frequently doubted Lincoln's capacity for leadership, exclaimed, "God bless Abraham Lincoln" and declared his message "the best that has yet been written; calm and dignified in tone, clear in statement, and bold and magnanimous in spirit." The *Pittsburgh Gazette* echoed this praise: "No true American can rise from the perusal of President Lincoln's message without a feeling of enhanced national pride, and a more joyful assurance that all is well, and that we have a man at the head of our Government who is as genuine a type of the American character, as viewed on its best and brightest side, as ever occupied the Executive chair."[10]

Radical Republicans in Congress, who had just received the good news of Chase's appointment as chief justice, breathed a sigh of relief that Lincoln had stood firm on emancipation and the suppression of the rebellion—though they had had little reason to expect otherwise. Even Congressman Thaddeus Stevens of Pennsylvania praised "the most important and best message that has been communicated to Congress for the last sixty years." Stevens applauded Lincoln's moral courage in opposing those high in the Republican party—he probably meant Henry J. Raymond and Thurlow Weed—who during the summer had wanted a compromise peace with the rebels, including a retreat on emancipation. Though pleased with Lincoln's strong stand behind an antislavery amendment, Radicals fretted that he would agree to a gradual emancipation scheme similar to the halfway station between slavery and freedom that General Nathaniel P. Banks had established in Louisiana. Outside Congress, the abolitionist *New York Independent*, whose editor Theodore Tilton had intrigued in August to replace Lincoln on the Republican ticket, praised the president's call for an antislavery amendment and declared the annual message "more full of sound sense, high-toned patriotism, fidelity to moral principle, Christian courage in the Good Cause [than] has ever come from his homely pen."[11]

★ ★ ★

Lincoln, however, parted company with the Radicals on reconstruction policy. His liberal "restoration" plan was intended to spare the nation further bloodshed and restore "a Union of hearts and hands as well as of States."[12] Since the beginning of the war, he had encouraged a nucleus of Unionists, with the aid of Federal forces, to form loyal governments and send representatives to Congress, even if large areas of their states remained in rebel hands. Under this policy, the Restored Government of Virginia had been organized in 1861 at Wheeling and military governors had been sent to eastern North Carolina, Tennessee, Louisiana, Arkansas, and Texas in 1862. The results had soon disappointed the president. In December 1863 he had issued a Proclamation of Amnesty and Reconstruction designed to provide a uniform and conservative plan of reorganization and spur Unionist sentiment in the South. Though again disappointed with the pace of reconstruction, he had continued to support Union governments in Virginia (now at Alexandria), Louisiana, Arkansas, and Tennessee and to view his policy as a blueprint for the future reorganization of the other rebel states. But by late 1864, with the rebellion still not completely suppressed in any of the Confederate states, Radical Republicans and other critics saw the policy as a case of putting the cart before the horse. Complete military success, they contended, was essential before state governments controlled by true Unionists and guaranteeing black freedom could be established.

After the election, Lincoln agreed that he should wait for the suppression of the armed insurrection before proceeding with civil reorganization in the Southern states, except for the nascent Union governments in Louisiana, Arkansas, Virginia, and Tennessee. (Congress in 1861 had endorsed Virginia's rump Union government, and a Tennessee state convention in early 1865 adopted a new constitution abolishing slavery and providing for early elections to a restored government.) He believed that the reestablishment of civil governments in the remaining rebel states, after a brief period of military control, would quickly follow. The states then would regain all of their rights in the Union.

Lincoln's insistence that Congress recognize the Union governments established in Louisiana and Arkansas and his willingness to pardon rebel leaders, thereby enabling them to retain their property and regain their political rights, caused serious concern among "earnest" Republicans. The *Boston Commonwealth,* the leading Radical newspaper in New England, found disconcerting Lincoln's statement in the message to Congress that "if questions should remain" after the war, "we would adjust them by . . . legislation, conference, courts, and votes, operating only in constitutional and lawful channels." Such a policy, the African-American correspondent of the *New Orleans Tribune* contended, was "fraught with evils of great magnitude" for black freedom and for the Union. This writer, however, praised Lincoln's firm support for the antislavery amendment and his "good wishes for Liberia" as a sovereign nation, suggesting that "the president is now alive to the absurdity of [black] 'Colonization,' and that we shall hear no more of that suicidal folly."[13] The prediction proved accurate. Lincoln, having witnessed the impracticality and inhumanity of colonization in 1863, when he had supported a failed federal effort to establish a black settlement in the Caribbean, never mentioned it again.

★ ★ ★

Soon after Congress convened in December 1864, the issue of seating senators and representatives from Louisiana (later joined by those from Arkansas) took center stage at the Capitol. These men had been elected by Unionists in those states. A loyal government, initiated by General Banks and headed by Governor Michael Hahn, had drawn up a state constitution in Louisiana that Lincoln pronounced "an excellent new constitution—better for the poor black man than we have in Illinois," though it stopped short of extending the ballot or other important civil rights to African Americans.[14] The Louisiana government, however, was severely criticized by disaffected Unionists in the state, many of whom had been supporters of Salmon P. Chase for president. Northern Radicals condemned the "half-abolitionist" Hahn administration in Louisiana and charged that, because it owed its existence to the military authority of General Banks, it did not meet the national constitutional requirement for a republican form of government.

Led by Benjamin F. Wade in the Senate and Henry Winter Davis in the House, authors of the stringent reconstruction bill that the president had pocket vetoed in July, Radicals announced their determination to prevent the seating of the Louisiana delegation. But other Republicans understood that the political equation in the nation had changed with the president's re-election and that Lincoln was now master of affairs. More confident of his own authority since the election, Lincoln believed he had the primary responsibility for ending the war, as he had had for conducting the war, and for reconstruction policy. Republicans in Congress knew, as an observer in Washington reported, that "Mr. Lincoln is likely to use all his power to secure the recognition of [his] State Governments" in the South. "His feelings," this writer noted, "are very much enlisted in the matter." As an indication of his resolve, Lincoln directed Banks to come to Washington and lead the lobbying effort for the seating of the Louisiana representatives, though he conceded the constitutional authority of Congress to judge the credentials of its own members. The president did not personally lobby congressional leaders.[15]

Most Republicans, including some erstwhile Radicals but not Wade, Davis, or Senator Charles Sumner, sought a compromise with the president that would permit Congress to play a role in reconstruction policy. They hoped that Lincoln's wish to secure congressional approval of his Louisiana and Arkansas governments would influence him to accept legislation on reconstruction for the unorganized Southern states. With this purpose in mind, Representative James M. Ashley on December 15 introduced in the House a bill "to guarantee to certain States whose governments have been usurped or overthrown, a republican form of government." The measure, similar to the Wade-Davis bill in most of its features, outlined a procedure for the reorganization of loyal governments in the South and their recognition by the president and Congress. The bill required the abolition of slavery by the restored states. It also provided that only "loyal male citizens" who could take the ironclad oath (swearing to unstinting loyalty during the war) would be eligible to vote in reconstruction elections. Though its wording was vague, this provision probably meant black suffrage as well as the temporary disfranchisement of former rebels. As an inducement for Lincoln to approve the measure, Congress would immediately recognize the Union government in Louisiana and seat its representatives (Arkansas was later added).

After studying and making marginal notations on a printed copy of the Ashley bill, Lincoln told General Banks that the provision for a federally imposed suffrage "would be a fatal objection to the Bill." Furthermore, the Ashley proposal resembled too closely the vetoed Wade-Davis bill. Both violated Lincoln's policy of self-reconstruction by Southern whites who willingly subscribed to his amnesty oath and thereby regained all of their political rights, as set forth in his 1863 Proclamation of Amnesty and Reconstruction. The president quietly indicated to Republican leaders in Congress that he could not accept the Ashley bill.[16]

A number of Republicans, including Wade and Davis, who objected to any compromise recognizing the Louisiana and Arkansas governments, also opposed the bill. Ashley repeatedly revised the bill in a futile effort to secure a majority in Congress. Finally, on February 21, by an overwhelming vote, the House tabled it. Other congressional attempts to pass reconstruction legislation met a similar fate.[17] The disagreements among Republicans on reconstruction and on how far they should go in challenging the president's control had stymied congressional action. Lincoln, though he had not secured recognition for his Louisiana and Arkansas governments, still had the upper hand in reconstruction policy.

Meanwhile, during the winter, revelations of deplorable conditions in prisoner-of-war camps in Richmond and elsewhere outraged Northerners and threatened to undermine Lincoln's lenient policy toward the South. When Lincoln refused to retaliate against the rebels in January, Senator Wade, chair of the Joint Committee on the Conduct of the War, introduced a resolution ordering him to do so. Wade exclaimed that he would "make the South a desolation, and every traitor shall lose his life, unless they treat our men with humanity." During the two-week Senate debate on the resolution in late January and early February, the Ohio Radical charged that "the President has not the nerve to come up to the mark" and demand better treatment for Union prisoners. "I wish to God he had more courage," Wade declared, "but I must confess that he has been perfectly reckless of his duty for a long time."[18]

The vehemence of Wade's attack hardly concealed his political agenda. He saw an opportunity to embarrass Lincoln and weaken his control over reconstruction policy and the Republican party. However, Wade soon discovered that though his Radical colleagues were deeply disturbed about conditions among Union prisoners, not all of them were willing to dictate to Lincoln on the issue. Charles Sumner and Henry Wilson of Massachusetts engaged in a shrill exchange on the Senate floor with Wade and Zachariah Chandler of Michigan over the principle of retaliation. Sumner argued that retaliation went against "the sacred landmarks of Christian civilization." Wade and Chandler attacked Sumner for his "sublimated specimen of humanitarianism that does not apply to these accursed rebels" and threatened to hold him responsible before his constituents. Wilson snapped back that the two midwestern senators had revived the "insolent" style of "the old slave masters" in the debate. Faced with defeat, Wade agreed to a compromise resolution requesting only that the president appoint commissioners to meet with rebel authorities and secure their approval for visits to the camps and humane treatment of the prisoners. The compromise measure passed the Senate, but the House refused to consider it. Mitigating the urgency for action was an arrangement in January for an exchange of prisoners, including black soldiers held by the Confederates.[19]

Wade and Davis, joined by Sumner and a handful of other Radical Republicans, still had one trick up their sleeves in their effort to derail Lincoln's reconstruction policy. They planned a filibuster to prevent the seating of the Louisiana and Arkansas senators and representatives. In late February, when the congressional session was about to expire, committee reports in both houses had recommended seating the two delegations. However, as a sop to vocal Radicals who wanted to retain a semblance of congressional authority in reconstruction policy and also to avoid a bruising floor debate, the Senate committee concluded that the Louisiana claimants should not be seated "till by some joint action of both Houses there shall be some recognition of an existing State government acting in harmony with the government of the United States."[20] Inexplicably, the Senate committee omitted the Arkansas representatives from its report.

"Bluff Ben" Wade worried, with good reason, that the Senate's acceptance of the committee report would lead to the recognition of the Louisiana government, followed by the seating of its representatives. Before the report had been voted on, Wade moved in the Senate to postpone the issue until the next regular session of Congress. His motion failed by a vote of twelve to seventeen, which observers concluded was a true indication of the division on the Louisiana question.[21] Having failed to table the issue, the Wade and Sumner Radicals launched their filibuster to prevent its further consideration during the final days of the congressional session. A few Democrats and border-state Unionists at the other end of the political spectrum joined the Radicals in the filibuster. The main motive of the ultraconservatives was clear: they feared that if the Louisiana and Arkansas governments were recognized, the votes of these two states would be counted toward the ratification of the antislavery amendment, which they opposed. Faced with the defeat of important appropriations measures as the session expired, the Senate agreed to postpone the question of seating the Southern representatives until December. The House immediately concurred.[22]

Lincoln quietly accepted the postponement and expressed confidence that the representatives would be seated by Congress in December. According to Senator-elect R. King Cutler of Louisiana, the president in "a long and very satisfactory interview" with the state's delegation reaffirmed his support for the restored Louisiana constitution and government.[23] Both Lincoln and the Republican majority in Congress believed that once the rebellion had been suppressed the president's reconstruction plan would be fully implemented.

★ ★ ★

The ending of the war on the terms outlined in the president's annual message to Congress—cessation of armed rebellion, reunion, and the end of slavery—had to take place before the Southern states could be completely restored to their "proper practical relation with the Union." Northern opinion in late 1864 and early 1865 generally supported Lincoln's peace terms. *Harper's Weekly,* arguably the most influential periodical in the Northeast, told its readers: "The prospects of peace as set forth by the President are exactly what every faithful citizen supposed them to be. When the men who began this war upon the Government lay down their arms, and yield to the Constitution and the laws and acts in accordance with it, the war will end" and rights would be restored. John W. Forney, the proprietor-editor of the *Washington Chronicle* and the *Philadelphia Press,* wrote, "It is not, and never has been, the policy of the Administration to degrade the seceded States." Lincoln's sole purpose, Forney declared, was to bring Southerners "back to the embraces of the Government of their fathers." Meanwhile, until white Southerners ended the tyranny of their leaders and submitted to Union authority, the war would continue.[24]

Lincoln had indicated in his message to Congress that, though he could not "treat" with Jefferson Davis, he could with the Southern people, who he confidently believed were willing to end the rebellion. Reports from the South in December and January seemed to confirm Lincoln's belief that the people would accept his terms as the only way to avoid complete ruin. "Disaffection at the South [was] becoming more and more manifest," the *Washington Chronicle* reported on January 4, 1865. The Southern masses were rapidly "recovering from the folly and infatuation into which they were plunged by wily leaders, [and] they were now finding out that . . . we neither seek to oppress nor to pull [them] down." The Northern press reported that even some prominent Confederates like Senator William A. Graham of North Carolina and Representative Henry S. Foote of Tennessee had declared the war for Southern independence a failure.[25]

North Carolina seemed especially receptive to Lincoln's peace terms. On November 26 Representative James T. Leach of North Carolina offered a resolution in the Confederate Congress proposing the end of hostilities and the restoration of the Southern states to the Union whenever the government of the United States indicated its willingness to recognize the reserved rights of the states and the property rights of the citizens as provided by the Constitution and the laws of Congress.[26] The Leach motion met a resounding defeat in the Confederate Congress. A resolution was introduced in the North Carolina General Assembly, also in late November, demanding that the Confederate government initiate peace negotiations with Lincoln. Introduced by State Senator John Pool, it proposed that President Davis appoint commissioners to meet with Lincoln or his representatives. These commissioners would be free to seek the best terms possible under the circumstances and would not be bound by any instructions from Davis. Implicit in the measure was the notion that reunion would result. The resolution, however, was tabled. When it reappeared in January, it was changed to provide for a delegation, including Pool, to visit President Davis and encourage him to seek an end to the war. Davis, who remained adamant that the war should continue until Lincoln conceded Confederate independence, gave the North Carolina delegation no hope for an early peace.[27]

In addition to the peace movement in North Carolina, Lincoln learned that the Confederate assistant secretary of war, John A. Campbell, a former associate justice of the United States Supreme Court, had written to Justice Samuel Nelson proposing that talks be opened on the basis of "an honorable peace [to] relieve the country from evils, possibly more permanent and more aggravated than those which have befallen it." Indicating his willingness to serve as an intermediary, a role he had played (unsuccessfully) with Seward during the Fort Sumter crisis of 1861, Campbell asked Nelson to show his letter to authorities in the North.[28] But nothing came of Campbell's effort except to reinforce Lincoln's belief that widespread discontent existed in the South.

The president found no rebel state government, and no large body of armed insurgents, willing to negotiate with him regarding peace. Rebel armies, despite their losses and heavy desertions, continued to fight and on occasion administer embarrassing setbacks to Federal forces (for example, General Benjamin F. Butler's failed attempt in late December to take Fort Fisher, which guarded Wilmington harbor). Though peace sentiment was strong in the Confederacy, most Southern political and military leaders still recognized Davis's authority to negotiate with the enemy. Even Governor Zebulon B. Vance of North Carolina, a constant thorn in Davis's side and a man Lincoln once thought was leaning toward reunion, opposed negotiations outside the regular channels in Richmond.[29]

* * *

In the North, several "amateur peace negotiators," as the *New York Herald* called them, sought passes to go south, test peace sentiment there, and attempt to open the door for negotiations. Some of these self-styled mediators had more than peace in mind: they wanted to purchase and bring out precious cotton, tobacco, and other much-desired Southern products and sell them to Northern merchants or to the United States Treasury at a handsome profit.

No one better combined patriotic and pecuniary motives than James W. Singleton, an old Illinois Whig associate of Lincoln who, nonetheless, had supported the Democratic party's peace movement during the war. In Orville H. Browning, Lincoln's close friend and a former U.S. senator, Singleton found a well-placed champion in the administration who also hoped for financial gain from Singleton's schemes. Browning, having completed the senatorial term of the deceased Stephen A. Douglas in 1863, remained in Washington to aid clients like Singleton who sought influence with Lincoln. Singleton, whom the *New York Tribune* labeled "a semi-Secesh Western politician of the Copperhead persuasion," arrived in Washington in late November 1864 and told Browning that he had visited "Rebel Commissioners" in Canada. According to Singleton, these Southerners, including Clement C. Clay, a former U.S. senator and a friend of Jefferson Davis, admitted that the Confederacy was sinking fast and said the people would agree to peace on the basis of reunion and amnesty. Singleton concocted a scheme in which he would go to Richmond, confer with Confederate authorities about peace, and purchase cotton and tobacco to sell in the North.[30] He believed that his cousin Otho Robards Singleton, a member of the Confederate Congress, would provide him with access to rebel leaders.

To initiate his scheme, Singleton needed a pass through the Union military lines from Lincoln. Browning went to the White House on Christmas Eve and outlined Singleton's plan to the president. Lincoln declined to commit himself, but three days later he asked Browning to return and continue the discussion. Having been embarrassed earlier

Orville H. Browning, a conservative Republican and an old friend of Lincoln, who often visited the White House and recorded in his diary accounts of his conversations with the president.

by private peace initiatives, mainly the Horace Greeley–inspired conference at Niagara Falls in July 1864, Lincoln did not want to risk another diplomatic debacle. Instead, he questioned Browning about the commercial aspects of Singleton's mission. This meeting also ended without a pass for Singleton. On January 5 Lincoln again sent for Browning; this time he authorized Singleton to go through the Federal lines and return "with any Southern products" that he chose to purchase. The president made it clear that Singleton's commercial transactions must conform to the regulations of the Treasury Department prohibiting trade in goods that could be used by Lee's army.[31]

Lincoln reportedly remarked at this time that he had "no objection to any man trying his hand at a job of pacification," provided he did not claim to represent the government.[32] According to Singleton, Lincoln, with rebel ears in mind, declared that he "did not desire to subjugate the South"; indeed, he wanted Southerners to feel that they were returning to the Union of their own free will. The president also said he opposed "governing the South by military satraps" because it would violate the American principle of self-government and would "cost an already burdened country too much" money. Singleton later claimed that Lincoln gave him "a memorandum on what he would do" to achieve peace.[33] The document, if it ever existed, has not been found.

Arriving in Richmond on January 15, Singleton, according to his account, met with several Confederate leaders, including General Lee. The Confederate commander told him that he desired, "above all things, to stop the carnage," but that he "was in the hands of Providence" and could not act on his own.[34] After a visit of two weeks in which he also arranged to purchase tobacco, Singleton returned to Washington on January 30. Accompanied by the omnipresent Browning, Singleton told the president that he had found "a large and influential party in favor of peace" in Richmond, but that Davis and other Confederate leaders refused to abandon their cause and had expressed confidence in the South's ultimate success. Singleton then showed Lincoln the tobacco contracts he had made in the rebel capital. The contracts called for him to pay for the tobacco in greenbacks—currency issued by the government during the war that had no gold or silver backing. Singleton indicated that he could obtain the money from New York merchants and exchange it for Confederate notes at a rate of one dollar in greenbacks to twenty in rebel currency. This arrangement, he said, would provide his Richmond associates with a profit of one-third. He asked the president for "protection in getting out" two hundred thousand pounds of the valuable weed at a cost of $250,000 in greenbacks. He also apparently mentioned that additional contracts for tobacco, cotton, rosin, and turpentine, totaling $7 million, could be made with Virginia merchants. Lincoln, according to Browning, "expressed himself pleased with what was done" by Singleton. He commented that "he wanted to get out all he could, and send in all the Green backs he could in exchange." Such a trade, Lincoln explained, would benefit economically strapped Southerners, increase their desire for reunion, and put pressure on them to end the war. He instructed Browning to get a pass for Singleton from a U.S. Treasury official, H. A. Risley; and Browning immediately did so.[35]

Lincoln also notified General-in-Chief U. S. Grant that Singleton had made arrangements "to bring a large amount of Southern produce through your lines. For its bearing on our finances I would be glad for this to be done if it can be without injuriously disturbing your military operations, or supplying the enemy."[36] Lincoln clearly had more interest in Singleton's trade mission and the influence it might have on Southern loyalties than in Singleton's self-proclaimed diplomatic mission. While the president did not object to peace efforts by private citizens as long as they did not claim to represent him, he had little confidence that such efforts would succeed. Still, these amateur diplomats might plant a few seeds of peace in the South and, upon their return to Washington, provide important intelligence about rebel morale.

Singleton's greenbacks-for-tobacco deal soon ran into trouble. Rumors circulated in the North that the transaction involved bacon for Lee's army rather than money for tobacco, a charge that Browning and Singleton angrily denied. Grant, who had never approved of trade through the lines, heard the rumors and wired Secretary of War Stanton asking that Singleton's trade permit be canceled. Grant told Stanton: "I believe there is a deep laid plan for making millions and [Singleton] will sacrifice every interest of the country to succeed."

When a train arrived at Fredericksburg carrying tobacco from the South, he ordered the shipment seized and destroyed, assuming it was Singleton's tobacco. This news caused Singleton's Confederate associates, who were playing a dangerous game in trading with the enemy, to lose their confidence in him, and they refused to ship their tobacco under the terms of the contract. Browning, upon hearing of the tobacco's destruction, rushed to the White House, where he found Lincoln "troubled and perplexed" by Grant's action and distressed that Singleton had suffered such a loss.[37]

As it turned out, the tobacco destroyed at Fredericksburg was not Singleton's. The intrepid entrepreneur, with Lincoln's blessing and Grant's reluctant assent, soon departed for Richmond to salvage what he could from his venture and to secure additional contracts for trade in Southern products. Having abandoned any notion of being a peacemaker, Singleton contracted for a large shipment of tobacco and other products to be paid for with greenbacks. Grant, however, prohibited all trade through the lines, regardless of permits, an authority that Lincoln had given him in early March.[38]

The fulfillment of Singleton's financial schemes had to await the fall of Richmond and the end of the war. Singleton claimed that he talked to Lincoln on the fateful Friday, April 14, before the president left for Ford's Theatre. The discussion, he said, focused on Lincoln's reconstruction plan for the South. The meeting actually occurred on April 13 and probably dealt more with Singleton's commercial ventures than with reconstruction. At any rate, the president granted Singleton a pass to go to Richmond. After the war, Singleton quickly sank into oblivion, along with many other Northern adventurers who flooded the defeated South seeking their fortunes in the lucrative cotton and tobacco trade.[39]

* * *

Singleton's first visit to Richmond and his report in January served to reinforce Lincoln's belief that many rebel leaders, along with rank-and-file Southerners, were demoralized and anxious for peace. This belief made him more receptive to the peace effort in January of Francis Preston Blair Sr., who, unlike Singleton, was not motivated by commercial interests. Blair, a prominent political editor of the Jacksonian period and the father of Montgomery and General Frank Blair, aspired to stop the carnage and social decay that threatened to produce radical changes in his beloved Union. Long an advocate of southwestern expansion, Blair saw an opportunity to end the war by combining reunion with a joint North-South expedition to enforce the Monroe Doctrine against the French in Mexico.

Blair's undertaking began after he received a letter from an old political foe, Horace Greeley of the *New York Tribune*, urging him to go to North Carolina as a special envoy of the Lincoln administration to persuade the leaders of that state to abandon the Confederacy. Greeley, who never seemed to give up on his ambition to be a peacemaker, even after the failure of the Niagara Falls conference in July, admitted that he was not "a favorite with our great ones" in Washington and presumed that any peace initiative on his part would be opposed by Lincoln. "I believe you, if at Raleigh, with large powers," he told Blair, "could pull North Carolina out of the Rebellion in a month," followed by other Southern states within three months.[40]

Inspired as well as flattered by Greeley's letter, Blair agreed that "events are at hand which will probably make successful new attempts to bring about peace." On December 20 he wrote to Greeley that he would "tender to the President a plan . . . to deliver our country from [this war]." He did not tell Greeley what the plan was.[41]

Blair approached Lincoln for a pass to go south. The president refused, but advised him to ask again after Savannah fell to Sherman's troops, an event that was expected to occur before the end of the month. On December 28, after the news of the capture of Savannah reached Washington, Blair, a resident of nearby Silver Spring, Maryland, again approached the president about a pass through Federal lines, specifically to visit Richmond, not Raleigh. Ostensibly he would be making the trip to retrieve personal papers seized by General Jubal Early's forces in their July raid on the outskirts of Washington. Lincoln granted the pass but abruptly stopped Blair when he attempted to describe the peace proposal he planned to present to Jefferson Davis. If the mission failed, Lincoln did not want to find himself in the embarrassing position of having sanctioned a fruitless peace attempt, as he had after the failure of the Niagara Falls peace conference.[42]

Two days later Blair wrote to Davis that, though "wholly unaccredited" by his government, he had some ideas "to submit to your consideration . . . which in my opinion you may turn to good and possibly bring to practical results, [repairing] all the ruin the war has brought upon the nation." Davis, believing he could turn the meeting to his advantage, invited Blair to Richmond. Blair arrived on January 12 and immediately outlined his peace proposal to Davis. The plan called for the cessation of hostilities between the North and the South and the uniting of forces against the French in Mexico. Davis rejected the joint expedition but, hoping for a cease-fire that could result in Confederate independence, cleverly informed Blair that he was willing "to enter into negotiations for the restoration of Peace" on the basis of *"two countries."*[43]

Blair returned to Washington on January 16 and two days later reported to Lincoln on his visit. The president expressed satisfaction with the part of Blair's report describing the despondency in the rebel capital and Davis's apparent willingness to begin peace talks.[44] But Lincoln could not agree to the "two countries" condition for negotiations because he did not recognize the Confederacy as a separate nation. However, he believed that the fall of the Confederate "Goliath," Fort Fisher, on January 15 and pressure from the Southern public to end the war might force Davis to ignore the "two countries" stipulation and open negotiations that could lead to peace and reunion. With that in mind, the president asked Blair to return to Richmond, this time carrying a carefully crafted letter for Davis. He addressed the letter, dated January 18, to Blair rather than to Davis, whom he could not recognize directly. "You may say to [Davis]," Lincoln wrote, "that I have constantly been, am now, and shall continue, ready to receive any agent whom he, or any other influential person now resisting the national authority, may informally send to me, with the view to securing peace to the people of *our one common country.*"[45]

★ ★ ★

News of Blair's mission ignited wild peace speculation and excitement throughout the North. However, Republican leaders and editors, including friends of Lincoln, questioned whether the time was ripe for peace overtures, particularly negotiations with those the *Boston Daily*

Advertiser called "Jeff. Davis and his confederates in despotic government." They also questioned whether the initiation of talks should be entrusted to an unofficial envoy such as Blair, whom many Republicans did not trust. The *New York Times* issued a warning, evidently with Lincoln in mind: "None but national authorities can wage war or make for peace, and the moment we enter into negotiations with the rebel Government for terms of peace, that moment we have actually and legally conceded everything for which they have been making war."[46]

Questions regarding the propriety of Blair's mission surfaced within Lincoln's administration as well. Secretary of War Stanton expressed strong opposition to a policy of holding peace talks with rebels before their armies had surrendered. The Union, Stanton and other cabinet members reasoned, held all the cards now, and it would be foolish to sit down at the table with the rebels and deal them a hand in the settlement. Gideon Welles confided to his diary regarding the mission: "The President, with much shrewdness and much good sense, has often strange and incomprehensible whims; takes sometimes singular and unaccountable freaks. It would hardly surprise me were he to undertake to arrange terms of peace without consulting anyone."[47]

The most vigorous opposition to Blair's mission came from Radical Republicans. Radicals like Wade, Sumner, and Thaddeus Stevens assumed that Lincoln, in sending Blair to Richmond, planned to negotiate a compromise peace that would grant universal amnesty to the rebels, return confiscated property, and abandon immediate emancipation. Stevens declared on the floor of the House of Representatives that if the country could vote again for president it would choose General Benjamin F. Butler, not Lincoln. Senator Zachariah Chandler wrote of the Blair trip, "Nothing but evil can come of this nonsense." Radicals told the president that the only way to end the war was to pound the rebels into submission.[48]

Meanwhile, Blair returned to Richmond and delivered Lincoln's message to Davis. Disregarding Lincoln's "one common country" condition and hoping to negotiate a cease-fire, Davis dispatched a three-member commission to meet with Lincoln or his representatives. The commission, headed by Confederate Vice President Alexander H. Stephens, arrived at Petersburg, Virginia, on January 29 and asked for permission to enter Federal lines, a request that General Edward O. C. Ord, in Grant's absence, relayed to Lincoln. The president sent Major Thomas T. Eckert, head of the telegraph office in the War Department, to ascertain the commissioners' purpose in seeking a pass. Lincoln's carefully worded instructions directed Eckert to interview the commissioners, show them his letter of January 18 regarding the one-country stipulation for peace talks, and "receive their answer in writing."[49]

The next day, January 31, Lincoln, in anticipation of Eckert's success, sent Secretary of State Seward to Fort Monroe, Virginia, to be available to meet with the Confederate commissioners. The president, citing his January 18 letter, instructed Seward to inform the Confederates that "three things are indispensable" to peace. First, "the restoration of the national authority throughout all the States"; second, "no receding, by the Executive of the United States on the Slavery question" as set forth in his last annual message to Congress "and in preceding documents"; third, "no cessation of hostilities short of an end of the war, and the disbanding of all forces hostile to the government." He directed Seward to assure the commissioners that "all propositions of theirs not inconsistent with the above, will be considered and passed upon in a spirit of sincere liberality." However, he told Seward not "to definitely consummate anything" but to report to him what the commissioners "may choose to say."[50]

On February 1 Eckert arrived at Grant's headquarters at City Point, Virginia, and held several conversations with the Confederate commissioners. Concluding that they did not accept the "one country" condition for peace talks, Eckert told the Confederates that they could not proceed further, and he notified Lincoln of his mission's failure. The disappointed president prepared to recall Seward from Fort Monroe. He changed his mind early the next morning, February 2, when Stanton brought him a message from Grant encouraging him to meet with the Confederate delegation because, Grant wrote, "I am convinced, upon conversation with Messrs. Stevens [sic] & [Robert M. T.] Hunter that their intentions are good and their desire sincere to restore peace and union . . . I fear now their going back without any expression from any one in authority will have a bad influence."[51]

Lincoln, immediately and without consulting any member of his cabinet, authorized the passage of the Confederate commissioners to Fort Monroe. Not wanting to entrust the negotiations solely to Seward, he decided to join the secretary of state for the talks. Within two hours of receiving Grant's message, he departed Washington for Fort Monroe. For the moment, he left his fatigue and other problems behind him. Upon leaving the capital, he reportedly expressed confidence that peace could soon be achieved.[52] On February 3 Lincoln and Seward met with the Confederate commissioners for four hours aboard the *River Queen* at Hampton Roads, Virginia, about one mile off Fort Monroe. It was the first time an American president had met with enemy emissaries to negotiate peace.

★ ★ ★

The two parties at Hampton Roads greeted each other cordially. Lincoln and Stephens had served together as Whigs in Congress, though the Confederate vice president probably had only a vague recollection of the tall but unimpressive freshman representative from Illinois. Stephens began by asking Lincoln, "Is there no way of putting an end to the present trouble?" The president bluntly replied that it could be done only if those resisting the Union ceased their resistance. The commissioners, following their instructions from Jefferson Davis, could not accept this condition. Instead, Stephens suggested that a foreign diversion might be found that would bring the two sides together and permit "an amicable and proper adjustment of those points of differences out of which the present lamentable collision of arms has arisen." Lincoln quickly realized that Stephens was referring to Blair's fanciful Mexican proposal. He dismissed the scheme with the comment that Blair had no authority in making such a proposal and reminded the Confederate commissioners that "the restoration of the Union [was] a sine qua non" for ending the war.[53]

Remarkably, after Lincoln's emphatic rejection of the Mexican scheme, Seward asked Stephens to say more about it. Stephens seized the opportunity and maneuvered the discussion to what the Confederate commissioners really sought in the conference—a cease-fire agreement that would lead to Southern independence. But Lincoln would have no part of it. He repeated that the federal government

Alexander H. Stephens, vice president of the Confederate States, who headed the Southern commission that met with Lincoln and Seward in February 1865 in an effort to end the war.

would not suspend military operations until the national authority was reestablished throughout the South.[54]

The commissioners asked Lincoln about his reconstruction policy. After the president made a perfunctory reply about Southerners resuming their place in the Union, Seward interjected that the Confederates should read Lincoln's 1864 annual message to Congress. He told them what the message said regarding the president's liberality toward the South, and he gave particular attention to the administration's emancipation policy and the fact that Lincoln would not retract any of it. This discussion led to the issue of black freedom and rights in the South. Lincoln admitted that opinions in Washington differed about the "operation" of the Emancipation Proclamation and especially about its legality once the war had ended. At this point Seward produced a copy of the proposed Thirteenth Amendment and implied that if the Southern states quickly rejoined the Union they could assist in voting it down. Lincoln, who sometimes became abstracted in meetings, ignored this comment and may not have heard it. Otherwise he would probably have corrected Seward, as he had done when the Mexican scheme was raised, and reminded the Confederates that the abolition of slavery was another sine qua non for peace. Seward, again with Lincoln silent, informed the commissioners that property issues would be settled by the courts after the war and that Congress would be "liberal in making restitution of confiscated property . . . after the excitement of the times had passed off."[55]

When the issue of emancipation came up again, according to Stephens's later account, Lincoln gave a lengthy history of his own antislavery views, beginning with his opposition to the expansion of slavery and concluding with his reasons for acting against the institution during the war. He maintained that he had always favored the emancipation of the slaves but not immediate freedom, because of the "many evils attending" it. Lincoln, Stephens wrote, said that if he were Stephens he would go home to Georgia, have the state legislature recall its troops from the war, elect senators and representatives to Congress, and ratify the Thirteenth Amendment "*prospectively,* so as to take effect—say in five years." "Such a ratification," Lincoln reportedly said, "would be valid in my opinion." Georgia thereby would "avoid, as far as possible, the evils of immediate emancipation."[56]

But Lincoln could hardly have advised the commissioners to go home and seek delayed ratification of the Thirteenth Amendment. Such a course would have been a repudiation of his vigorous efforts to secure immediate approval of the amendment. Two days earlier, when the initiating resolution passed Congress, he had pronounced the amendment "a King's cure for all the evils" of slavery, and he clearly hoped for its quick ratification by the states.[57] The fact that an account of the Hampton Roads conference written by another Confederate commissioner, John A. Campbell, does not mention what would have been an important declaration by the president provides further evidence that Lincoln did not make the suggestion that Stephens attributed to him.[58]

At Hampton Roads Lincoln did, however, prove willing to revive the idea of federal compensation for slaveholders as a means to secure an early peace and obtain Southern approval of the Thirteenth Amendment. Declaring that the North bore some responsibility for slavery, he remarkably—and unrealistically—expressed the belief that the Northern people would be in favor of "paying a fair indemnity for the loss to [slave] owners." He mentioned $400 million as a fair amount that Congress might appropriate for this purpose. Seward objected, insisting that the nation had already spent enough money and suffered enough losses on the battlefield in the effort to destroy slavery and save the Union. The president, according to one of the Confederate commissioners, Robert M. T. Hunter, rebuked Seward and argued that the North had profited from slavery, especially the slave trade, and thus should share some of the guilt for the institution. Lincoln said, as Hunter recalled, "It was wrong in the North to carry on the slave trade and sell [blacks] to the South, . . . and to have held on to the money thus procured without compensation, if the slaves were to be taken by them again."[59] Whether Lincoln said these exact words is problematic, but clearly, as he suggested on other occasions, including his second inaugural address four weeks later, he accepted the whole country's guilt for slavery.

When no agreement could be reached on peace, Hunter declared that the talks left nothing for the South but "unconditional submission" to the North. Seward replied that this was not the case: that returning to the Union and "yielding to the execution of the laws under the constitution of the United States, with all its guarantees and securities for personal and political rights, . . . could [not] be considered as unconditional submission to conquerors, or having anything humiliating in it." When Hunter expressed doubts, Lincoln informed him that he, as president, had sole power to pardon and restore property, and that he would exercise that power "with the utmost liberality." He said he could not determine what Congress would do regarding the readmission of Southern senators and representatives, but "they ought to be seated."[60] It was probably during this exchange that Hunter remarked that even Charles I of England had been willing to compromise with the parliamentary forces in arms against him, and Lincoln should do likewise with the Confederates. Lincoln laughingly responded: "I do not profess to be posted in history. On all such matters I will turn you over to Seward. All I distinctly recollect about the case of Charles I, is, that he lost his head in the end."[61]

* * *

Lincoln and Seward returned to Washington amid intense public speculation regarding the secret peace negotiations at Hampton Roads. Though the conference had failed and President Davis and other diehard Confederates hurled defiance at Lincoln's conditions for peace, Southern debate over continuing the war had widened. Many realistic Southerners understood that Lincoln's liberal amnesty and reconstruction terms did not constitute "unconditional surrender," as Davis charged. But these Southerners were in no position to initiate negotiations with Washington. Lincoln, however, continued to hope that the Confederates, having talked to him directly, would accept his terms and take action to disband their armies.[62] With this in mind, he drafted a proposal, in the form of a joint resolution for congressional approval, to compensate the slave states, including the border states, for the loss of slave property. As he had suggested at Hampton Roads, the amount would be $400 million in United States bonds to be distributed to the states in proportion to their 1860 slave populations. Half of the bonds were to be distributed if by April 1 "all resistance to the national authority" had ceased. The remaining half would be given if by July 1 the Thirteenth Amendment had become a part of the Constitution. Lincoln promised that when these conditions had been met he would declare the rebellion ended, all political offenses pardoned, and confiscated property, except for slaves, to be returned to owners.[63]

When presented to the cabinet, the compensation proposal received a cold reception. With victory in sight thanks to Grant's progress around Petersburg, the fall of Fort Fisher, and Sherman's virtually unimpeded march in South Carolina, the cabinet unanimously rejected any plan to compensate slaveholders for the loss of their slaves. (Congress also would have overwhelmingly opposed appropriating money for this purpose.) Though dismayed and evidently surprised at the cabinet's strong opposition to his proposal, Lincoln abandoned the scheme. Secretary of the Navy Welles observed after the meeting that "the earnest desire of the President to conciliate and effect peace was manifest" in the proposal, "but there may be such a thing as so over-doing as to cause a distrust or adverse feeling."[64]

The president's willingness to extend lenient terms to the South and compensate slaveholders revealed his fervent desire to end the war and avoid further bloodshed and suffering. Lincoln wanted white Southerners to accept the abolition of slavery and help give it con-stitutional validity by ratifying the Thirteenth Amendment. He also believed that unless a conciliatory hand was extended, die-hard Con-federates would resort to guerrilla tactics after their armies had sur-rendered. He had long feared that the war might degenerate into "a remorseless and violent revolutionary struggle," culminating in anar-chy.[65] Welles later reported that in the early months of 1865 Lincoln "frequently expressed his opinion that the condition of affairs in the rebel states was deplorable, and did not conceal his apprehension that, unless immediately attended to, . . . civil, social, and industrial relations [would] be worse after the rebellion was suppressed." Simi-larly, the journalist Alexander K. McClure recalled that the president "feared almost universal anarchy in the South" after the war, and that "it was this grave apprehension that made Lincoln desire to close the war upon such terms as would make the Southern people and South-ern soldiers think somewhat kindly of the Union to which they were brought back by force of arms."[66]

* * *

Republicans in Congress and elsewhere, perhaps with relief that Lin-coln had not compromised on the suppression of the rebellion or im-mediate emancipation, praised his handling of the Hampton Roads conference. When the clerk in the House of Representatives read aloud the president's report on the conference, "an instant and irre-pressible storm of applause" erupted from the floor and in the gallery. Thaddeus Stevens, the Radical Republican leader in the House and one of Lincoln's harshest critics, admitted that he had been wrong in opposing the peace effort. He approvingly cited the president's "mas-terly style, upon such a firm basis and principle," in conducting the negotiations. And not all of the tribute came from Republicans. The Democratic leader of the House, Samuel S. Cox, praised Lincoln's "laudable efforts" at Hampton Roads and predicted that the talks would be the first step toward peace and reunion. Even Fernando Wood, New York's notorious Copperhead, while ignoring the president's antislavery commitment, expressed approval of his firmness in preserving "the integrity of the American Union."[67]

Outside Washington, both Radical and conservative Republican newspapers praised Lincoln's performance in the peace talks and, by implication, his conduct of the war. Horace Greeley's *New York Tribune* announced that the president "has made plain to the impartial world, as it will be made plain to the Southern masses, that [they] can have peace on the simple condition of fidelity to their country and obedience to her laws." The *Tribune* predicted that the people of the loyal states would now "rally with enthusiastic energy to the support of their Government," and that, thanks to Lincoln's efforts, "we shall very soon have achieved a substantial, honorable and enduring Peace." The *New York Herald,* a sometime critic of the administration, declared that Lincoln's handling of the Hampton Roads conference marked him as "one of the shrewdest diplomats of the day." The *Herald* editor predicted that Lincoln's liberality regarding the restoration of constitutional rights in the South, combined with his firm commitment to reunion, "will operate to widen the distractions, dissensions, demoralizations and confusion existing throughout the rebellious States," and that the next rebel "military disaster will inevitably precipitate a Southern popular revolution in behalf of peace, on the inevitable basis of submission to the Union."[68]

The Abolitionist William Lloyd Garrison, who late in the war had come to appreciate Lincoln's leadership qualities and especially his antislavery commitment, also found cause to praise the president's peace effort. Garrison maintained that the country was indebted to Lincoln's uncompromising stand for freedom and Union at Hampton Roads. "In spite of all the wiles of all the so-called Peace Commissioners," he told an enthusiastic audience in Boston, Lincoln had been "true to his word" in the negotiations. "You may rely upon his honesty and integrity."[69]

By the time of his second inauguration, Lincoln had gained the admiration of a broad spectrum of Northerners, as well as many Unionists in the border states who had vehemently opposed his antislavery policies. Except for a small minority of Radicals and, at the other extreme, die-hard Copperheads, by the spring of 1865 Northerners and Unionists realized that the imminent Union victory owed a great deal to Lincoln's skillful management of the war and emancipation. Thousands of African Americans also recognized the critical role Lincoln had played in breaking the chains of slavery, and at his public appearances they expressed deep affection for him, referring to him, as the white soldiers did, as "Father Abraham." A few black leaders like Frederick Douglass worried that Lincoln might be unwilling to take the steps necessary to guarantee genuine freedom in the South. But their voices of concern were largely muted in early 1865 by African Americans' euphoria over emancipation and praise for the man who had made it possible.

★ ★ ★

Abraham Lincoln had undergone a remarkable public transformation since the bleak summer of 1864 when the war was stalemated and the Union purposes in the conflict, as well as his re-election, were in serious jeopardy. The overwhelming support of the troops in the election resonated favorably for Lincoln with the people at home. Federal military successes also raised the people's confidence in Lincoln's leadership. The support he received no longer depended only on the fact that, as head of the government, he symbolized the Union cause. He had achieved preeminence as a war leader.

Despite his weariness and a yearning to escape his presidential burdens, Lincoln had been invigorated by the dramatic progress in the war and by his electoral victory. In late 1864 he set out to reduce the destructive partisanship that had plagued the North and the border states during the war, and to unite the nation behind a peace and reconstruction policy designed to produce an early end to the rebellion. Though the Hampton Roads peace conference had failed to end the fighting, he was not discouraged and hoped the Confederates would soon recognize that a continuation of the rebellion was futile. In his efforts to unite the nation, he could claim impressive successes, further enhancing his political position in the North as he began his second term in office. His new political strength enabled him to make appointments to his cabinet that were designed to create harmony in his administration and end the factionalism in the Republican party. By early 1865 Lincoln clearly had become master of affairs in Washington and had gained an influence with the Northern public that would have been unimaginable six months earlier.

An observation by the venerable General Ethan Allen Hitchcock, soon after the Hampton Roads conference, indicates the stature that Lincoln had attained as the war entered its final weeks. Hitchcock told a New England friend that Lincoln's "abilities are very great—& his integrity & love of country most profound" and that "we have had no greater President—& depend upon it, . . . bye and bye this will be seen & acknowledged" by all people.[70]

CHAPTER 5

THE HUMBLE INSTRUMENT
OF GOD

The new year, 1865, brought great promise for the cessation of the rebellion and the end of slavery. In his annual message to Congress in December, the president had called for a constitutional amendment that would validate his Emancipation Proclamation. This proposed amendment read: "Neither slavery nor involuntary servitude . . . shall exist within the United States." Its approval would remove the fundamental cause of the sectional conflict and war. The destruction of slavery everywhere in the United States, Lincoln believed, would also serve God's transcendent purpose for republican America as a land of freedom and opportunity for all.

The president had informed Congress that his victory in the election on a platform calling for the end of slavery had expressed the will of the people in favor of emancipation. He knew that Northern Democrats and conservative Unionists from the border states could not be persuaded to vote for the amendment on moral or any other grounds except constitutional ones to save the republic. "In this case the common end is the maintenance of the Union; and, among the ends to secure that end" was a constitutional amendment abolishing slavery.[1]

Nonetheless, Lincoln's antislavery policy was based upon the fundamental idea that human bondage was immoral and a violation of the Declaration of Independence creed; the war provided the constitutional and political justification for him to act against the institution. Since the 1850s he had repeatedly pronounced slavery a great moral wrong. "I am naturally antislavery," he wrote to a Kentucky newspaper editor, Albert G. Hodges of the *Frankfort Commonwealth,* in April 1864. "If slavery is not wrong, nothing is wrong. I can not remember when I did not so think, and feel." At the same time, Lincoln told Hodges, his oath of office to "preserve, protect, and defend the Constitution of the United States" did not confer upon him "an unrestricted right to act officially upon this judgment and feeling." But, he went on, his efforts in 1862 to end the rebellion through a compensated emancipation scheme had been rejected by the states. Rather than surrender the Union, he had issued his Emancipation Proclamation on the constitutional grounds of military necessity. The oath he had taken as president "to preserve the constitution to the best of my ability, imposed upon me the duty of preserving, by every indispensable means, that government—that nation—of which that constitution was the organic law." "Was it possible," he asked Hodges rhetorically, "to lose the nation, and yet preserve the constitution?" By initiating emancipation and authorizing the recruitment of black troops, he had sought to save both the nation and the Constitution.[2]

Lincoln's moral antislavery fervor, along with pressure from Radical Republicans, had given him a strong impetus to act against slavery. Although the Emancipation Proclamation, issued on January 1, 1863, exempted Union states and certain Federal-occupied regions in the South, it had freed thousands of African Americans—perhaps as many as fifty thousand—in occupied or adjacent areas. These areas included districts along the Mississippi River, eastern North Carolina, the Sea Islands of Georgia and South Carolina, the Atlantic coast of north Florida, and a few counties in and near the Shenandoah Valley of northern Virginia. In many cases, slaves in nearby Confederate-held areas, upon learning of the Emancipation Proclamation, fled to Federal military posts where they gained freedom.[3] With a constitutional amendment, freedom would be extended to all slaves, including those in the border states of Missouri, Kentucky, and Delaware whose laws still protected the institution.

* * *

Achieving the required two-thirds vote in both houses of Congress to send the antislavery amendment to the states for ratification would not be easy. Republicans, who unanimously favored the amendment, constituted a majority but not two-thirds of the Congress whose term would end on March 3, 1865. The Democratic minority and a handful of border-state conservative Unionists in the House could block the approval of the resolution initiating the amendment. The new Congress, which had been elected in November, would be more than two-thirds Republican, and if necessary the president could call it into special session to pass the resolution. But Lincoln did not want to wait. He knew that the end of the war would bring new political complications that might undermine immediate emancipation. He also thought that approval and ratification of the amendment would shorten the war by demonstrating to the rebels that they could no longer hope for support from Union slave states like Kentucky and Missouri. Since the passage of the amendment was "only a question of time," he asked Congress, "may we not agree that the sooner the better?"[4]

Lincoln assumed the task of lobbying moderate Democrats and border-state conservatives to support the amendment. (Most border-state conservatives were old-line Whigs and Constitutional Unionists.) The critical vote would occur in the House of Representatives, where in June 1864 sixty-five of the sixty-eight Democrats had opposed the amendment.[5] Their party's electoral disaster in November caused some Democrats to reassess their opposition to the antislavery amendment. Moderate Democrats, both inside and outside Congress, began to see the issue as an albatross around the party's neck. The prominent historian George Bancroft, a longtime Democrat, wrote to Samuel S. ("Sunset") Cox, the moderate party leader in Congress, urging him to support the amendment. Bancroft argued that peace and the restoration of the Southern economy could occur only after slave labor had been destroyed. The financial problems arising out of the war, he predicted, would be the crucial issue facing the country in the future: "We Democrats are right on the coming financial question, and the country knows it." Bancroft told Cox, and by extension the Democratic minority in Congress: "You cannot present the issue of the finances till the slavery question is settled, and that question can be settled but one way. Do away with slavery and the Democrats will be borne into power on the wings of their sound principles of finance."[6]

Manton Marble, the influential editor of the *New York World,* gave similar advice to Democrats in Congress. In his newspaper Marble called on congressional Democrats to divorce the party "from the dead issue" of the past, slavery. Several leading Democratic newspapers took their cue from the *World* and also from Democrats in the Senate who endorsed, though reluctantly, the amendment. The *New York Atlas,* whose proprietor was Representative Anson Herrick, claimed that the Democratic party, "freed from its present embarrassment" over slavery, "will be able to meet on equal terms the many-headed hydra of Federalism which is again threatening the republic, and fight the battle of democracy upon the vital questions of State rights, personal liberty, and a sound financial policy." Despite these urgent pleas, the overwhelming majority of House Democrats rejected the advice and followed the lead of the Copperhead George H. Pendleton, who had been McClellan's silver-tongued running mate in 1864. Pendleton's speech against the amendment "dazzled" wavering Democratic members and privately even received the praise of some Republicans.[7] About twelve Democrats and conservative Unionists were needed to carry the amendment; the precise number depended upon how many members absented themselves when the vote occurred.[8] A few Democrats like W. C. Kerr and Anson Herrick of New York early announced their support for the amendment and required no nudge from the president.

* * *

On January 6 James M. Ashley introduced the amendment resolution in the House of Representatives. The debate flared immediately, with as many as one-third of the members demanding time on the floor. As the debate proceeded, Democratic party lines against the amendment became firmer, and it appeared that it would be defeated. On January 13 Ashley concluded that he lacked six votes for passage, and he wisely had the issue postponed.[9]

At this juncture, Lincoln launched an intensive lobbying campaign. He even sought the support of "Sunset" Cox, who had crossed swords with his administration throughout the war and whom he did not trust. Lincoln had once told a visitor that Cox claimed to be a good friend of his and a good Democrat at the same time. "Sunny" was "like Jacob Straus's old sow," Lincoln had said. "The old hog was down the creek somewhere," and Jacob and his two boys went looking for her. Jacob instructed the boys to go down one side of the creek, and he would go down the other side, "and we'll find her, for I believe she is on both sides of the creek." "Sunny," Lincoln had concluded, "is trying to be on both sides of the creek." Cox told the president that he would vote for the amendment if Lincoln made a major effort to negotiate a peace with the rebels. Then, true to what Lincoln believed about him, Cox reneged on his promise—ironically, because he learned that Confederate peace commissioners had entered Union lines, and he concluded that the approval of the antislavery amendment would jeopardize negotiations.[10]

An effort by Ashley and other Republicans to secure the votes of two moderate New Jersey Democrats collapsed when Senator Charles Sumner refused to support a local railroad concession that they sought. Lincoln was furious. When John G. Nicolay, his secretary, told him that congressional champions of the antislavery amendment wanted him to intercede with Sumner, he snapped back: "I can do nothing with Mr. Sumner in these matters. While Mr. Sumner is very cordial with me, he is making his history in an issue with me on this very point. He hopes to succeed in beating the President so as to change this Government from its original form and make it a strong centralized power."[11] Lincoln's ire was probably caused by the Massachusetts senator's attempt to defeat his self-reconstruction plan for Louisiana and other Southern states and to establish congressional or central control of reconstruction.

William N. Bilbo, a Tennessee adventurer and entrepreneur who had the ear of Secretary of State Seward, offered his lobbying services to the president on behalf of the antislavery amendment. Though professing to be an old-line Whig, Bilbo told Seward that he had influential Democratic friends in New York and would seek their support. With Seward's blessing and after seeing the president, Bilbo went to New York.[12] Upon arriving in New York, however, he was arrested as a spy by General John A. Dix, who, after the failed rebel attempt to burn the city's hotels, was clamping down on newly arrived and suspicious Southerners. Lincoln ordered his release on parole. The intrepid Tennessean, through his "friends," contacted Manton Marble of the

New York World, Governor Horatio Seymour, the Copperhead congressman Fernando Wood, and other Democratic leaders. In his reports to Lincoln and Seward, Bilbo invariably exaggerated his progress. In the end, he failed in his self-proclaimed mission to change New York Democrats' minds about the amendment.[13] His true objective seems to have been to ingratiate himself with Seward and Lincoln in hopes of receiving either a political office or a trade permit in the South.

Lincoln's efforts to secure support for the antislavery amendment proved more successful with border-state conservatives than with Democrats. The president called James S. Rollins of Missouri to the White House and, as Rollins later remembered, began by reminding him that "you and I were old whigs, both of us followers of that great statesman, Henry Clay, and I tell you I never had an opinion upon the subject of slavery in my life that I did not get from him." Lincoln said he was "very anxious that the war should be brought to a close at the earliest possible date, and I don't believe this can be accomplished as long as those fellows down South can rely upon the border states to help them; but if the members from the border states would unite, at least enough of them to pass the thirteenth amendment to the Constitution, they would soon see that they could not expect much help from that quarter." As a result, he claimed, the rebels would "give up their opposition and quit their war upon the government." The president told Rollins that the vote in the House would be extremely close: "a few votes one way or the other will decide it."[14]

When Rollins indicated that he would support the amendment, Lincoln rose from his chair, gave the Missourian a hearty handshake, and exclaimed, "I am most delighted to hear that." Then he obtained Rollins's promise to talk to other conservative border-state representatives and let him know if they agreed to vote for the amendment. In closing, Lincoln repeated his belief that "the passage of this amendment will clinch the whole subject; it will bring the war, I have no doubt, rapidly to a close."[15]

True to his word, Rollins lobbied his conservative colleagues and spoke on the floor of the House in support of the amendment. He succeeded, along with Lincoln, in persuading some border-state congressmen who had earlier opposed federal emancipation to vote for it. Actually, the border-state conservatives knew that slavery was collapsing in their states. In Maryland, Union voters, by a narrow margin, had abolished slavery in their state constitution. In Missouri, radical Unionists had gained control of the state constitutional convention and approved an ordinance ending slavery in their state. Kentucky and Delaware Unionists seemed to realize that they were fighting a losing battle in their attempt to retain slavery. By this time, their main concern was that the adoption of the Thirteenth Amendment would lead to federal control of race relations, even to the imposition of black political equality, the great bugbear of many Southern whites. Lincoln evidently had a hand in convincing them that loyal state governments would not be interfered with in such matters. He promised at least one border-state congressman that in return for support of the antislavery amendment he would continue to press hard for peace on the basis of his lenient amnesty and reconstruction plan.[16]

* * *

By late January it appeared that Ashley and the Republicans had gained enough Democratic and conservative Unionist support to carry the amendment, though only by a razor-thin margin. However, on the morning of the scheduled House vote, January 31, a serious complication arose. The report that Confederate peace negotiators had entered Federal lines with the purpose of going to Washington caused pro-amendment Democrats to waver in their support. These Democrats, along with staunch anti-amendment members of their party, believed that an early peace could not be achieved if the North insisted on an emancipation amendment as a condition for negotiations.[17]

Earlier in the day Lincoln had decided to send Secretary of State Seward to Fort Monroe for an anticipated meeting with the Confederate commissioners. While writing his instructions to Seward, he received an urgent note from Ashley indicating that a "report is in circulation in the House that Peace Commissioners are on their way or are in the city [Washington], and is being used against us. If it is true, I fear we shall lose the bill. Please authorize me to contradict it, if not true." Momentarily putting aside his letter to Seward, Lincoln, as he later told a visitor, "took sheets of paper" and wrote the message that Ashley wanted. "So far as I know," he wrote disingenuously, "there are no peace commissioners in the city, or likely to be in it."[18] Lincoln knew that Confederate Vice President Alexander H. Stephens and his commission were waiting to be admitted through the lines in Virginia and would probably soon meet with Seward—but at Fort Monroe, not Washington. Despite his well-deserved reputation for honesty, Lincoln occasionally stretched the truth when much was at stake, as he did in his note to Ashley to avoid jeopardizing the passage of the Thirteenth Amendment.

According to Ashley, Lincoln's reply had the desired effect in the House; "the proposed amendment would have failed" if not for the president's reassurance. Ashley recalled that "a number who voted for it could easily have been prevailed upon to vote against it, on the ground that the passage of such a proposition" on the eve of the peace conference "would have been offensive to the Commissioners," shattering any hope that the talks could succeed. Ashley marveled at Lincoln's shrewd handling of the situation, a quality, he said, that had become "characteristic of Mr. Lincoln."[19]

The vote in the House of Representatives, 119 in favor to 56 opposed, barely attained the two-thirds majority needed to pass the amendment and refer it to the states for ratification. A switch of only five supporters to the opposition would have defeated it. However, the amendment probably would have been revived and passed after the failure of the Hampton Roads peace conference three days later. As the roll call proceeded and it became increasingly clear that the resolution would pass, excitement grew on the floor and in the crowded galleries. When Speaker Schuyler Colfax announced the vote, cheers burst forth in the chamber. The journalist Noah Brooks described the scene: "Strong men embraced each other with tears. The galleries and spaces stood bristling with cheering crowds; the air was stirred with a cloud of women's handkerchiefs waving and floating" to the floor.[20] If ratified by three-fourths of the states, as expected, the amendment would abolish slavery everywhere in the United States.

★ ★ ★

News of the historic victory spread rapidly. The War Department ordered the firing of a one-hundred-gun salute. "Everywhere on the streets there were congratulations and rejoicings," a newspaper correspondent reported. "Many a glass of champagne" was consumed, and celebrations extended into the night. Washington blacks quickly gathered in their churches to sing, hear speeches, and thank God for this day. Though Frederick Douglass was not in Washington when the amendment passed, his son Charles participated in the celebration and wrote to his father: "Such rejoicing I never before witnessed, cannons firing, people hugging and shaking hands, white people I mean, flags flying . . . [Now] if only they will give us the elective franchise." A group of Republican congressmen, led by Isaac Arnold, an old Lincoln friend, rushed to the White House to give the good news to the president. "The passage of the resolution filled his heart with joy," Arnold later recalled. "He saw in it the complete consummation of his own work, the emancipation proclamation."[21]

The next day Lincoln signed the congressional resolution, though his approval was unnecessary. Even before the official document arrived at the state capitals, several legislatures had ratified the amendment. Lincoln expressed delight that his home state of Illinois was the first to act—on the same day, February 1, that he sent the amendment to the states. That night a crowd gathered at the White House to celebrate the occasion. The president told the celebrants that the amendment removed "all causes of disturbance in the future" for the Union. "This measure," he declared, "was a very fitting if not an indispensable adjunct to the winding up of the great difficulty" over the legality of his Emancipation Proclamation. He called the amendment "a King's cure for all the evils" created by slavery, and he congratulated "the country and the whole world upon this great moral victory."[22] Lincoln's optimism in proclaiming the Thirteenth Amendment "a King's cure" for the institution's evils is understandable. Along with many of his antislavery contemporaries, the president now saw a hopeful future for blacks in America.

Lincoln believed that the end of slavery would allow African Americans to benefit from their own labor and, in time, rise in life. Reflecting his long-held Whig commitment to economic progress and his belief in the inherent equality of people, he viewed freedom of opportunity as an essential ingredient for success in America. Though the former slaves might not soon achieve an equality of condition, he thought that white opposition to black rights, including the ballot, would fade as the former slaves by means of education and work became part of the free economic system. Although he was overly optimistic, Lincoln's faith in emancipation was critical to the congressional passage and ultimate ratification of the Thirteenth Amendment.

* * *

For staunch antislavery men and women, including old abolitionists, the passage of the amendment was a dramatic victory in the struggle for freedom that had begun during the 1830s and culminated in a war to save the Union. Before the war, the Constitution had been the bulwark for the protection of slavery; but under the careful, step-by-step management of Abraham Lincoln, the Constitution had been changed to a document of freedom. Throughout the Union and especially in the East, antislavery crusaders, who had sharply criticized the president early in the war for his failure to act against slavery, now praised his leadership in ending the cruel institution.

No praise attracted more attention than that of William Lloyd Garrison, the most famous—and strident—of the Northern abolitionists. In a celebratory speech at Boston on February 4, Garrison proclaimed the end of the Constitution's and the Union's "covenant with death," a highly inflammatory label he had once used to condemn the constitutional provisions protecting slavery. "Liberty and Union are one and inseparable," he exclaimed. "And to whom is the country more immediately indebted for this vital and saving amendment of the Constitution?" he asked. "I may confidently answer—to the Presidential chain-breaker for millions of the oppressed—to ABRAHAM LINCOLN." The audience responded with "immense and long continued applause, ending with three cheers for the President." Garrison, who two years earlier had denounced the president's weak approach to emancipation, closed his encomium with the assurance that "Abraham Lincoln can be trusted to the end . . . He will never consent under any circumstances to the re-enslavement of any one of the millions whose yokes he has broken."[23]

Though neither Lincoln, Garrison, nor most Republicans confronted the issue, the question of how black freedom would be protected in the postwar South was raised in early 1865 by Charles Sumner and other Radical Republicans. Sumner believed that only federally imposed civil and political rights could ensure bona fide liberty for blacks and true loyalty in the South once hostile rebels had returned from the war.[24] Black leaders like Frederick Douglass feared that freedom for the ex-slaves would be a broken reed unless President Lincoln and Congress took action to guarantee their rights. And indeed, after the war it would become apparent that without a national commitment to true black freedom, the ratification of the amendment fell short of the intentions of its supporters.

At the time, however, Republicans and old abolitionists like Garrison basked in the afterglow of the amendment's passage. The *Cincinnati Daily Gazette* exuberantly announced: "Henceforth the Constitution is to be the security of freedom instead of the guarantee of slavery. No man shall be deprived of liberty without due process of law." Furthermore, the amendment would be "the direct road to permanent peace [and] the end of sectional agitation."[25] Its passage had broken the shackles of four million black Americans and destroyed the inhumane institution that had scarred the republic and produced a terrible war.

* * *

Despite his faith in the curative powers of the Thirteenth Amendment, Lincoln, along with Republican members of Congress, became increasingly concerned about the poverty and social disarray in the South as the war entered its final stages. The Southern economy lay in ruins, vast areas suffered from a breakdown of law and order, and tens of thousands of people, mostly blacks, were displaced and lacked adequate food and shelter. In addition to feeling compassion for the victims of the war, the president feared the situation would lead to anarchy and guerrilla warfare unless something was done to aid displaced people. He praised the Herculean efforts of the Reverend Thomas W. Conway, the superintendent of freedmen in Louisiana, to assist blacks, particularly his "success in the work of [their] moral and physical elevation." The president told Conway that "the blessing of God and the efforts of good and faithful men will bring us an earlier and happier consummation than the most sanguine friends of the freedmen could reasonably expect."[26]

Meanwhile, Republicans in Congress were hammering out a measure that would establish a bureau in the War Department to aid freed slaves and displaced white Southerners (Democrats opposed any government agency for this purpose). On March 3, the last day of the congressional session, the bill creating the Bureau of Refugees, Freedmen, and Abandoned Lands passed Congress and received Lincoln's signature. The Freedmen's Bureau, as it became known, would provide food, transportation, educational facilities, and other assistance to Southern blacks and whites. It also could assign and rent for three years abandoned lands to loyal refugees and former slaves. The bill provided that at the end of the three-year period "the occupants of any parcels so assigned may purchase the land and receive such title thereto as the United States can convey." Despite his reservations regarding the extension of federal power, the bill met Lincoln's constitutional concerns, because the Freedmen's Bureau would have a temporary existence of only one year after the war and would exercise no political authority in the South. In addition, the bill's tenuous land provision would not conflict with his opposition to the permanent confiscation of property. Whatever concerns he might have had about extending federal authority, the unprecedented social problems facing the South, combined with his own fear of anarchy there, caused Lincoln to support the Freedmen's Bureau bill.[27]

The president would not live to see the day when the antislavery amendment, having been duly ratified, became part of the Constitution and the last slaves—those in his native Kentucky and in tiny Delaware—became free. But the epithet "the Great Emancipator" is truly deserved. Lincoln's Emancipation Proclamation, his support of the recruitment of black troops, his pressure on border states and restored Union governments in the South to end slavery, and, finally, his efforts to secure congressional passage of the Thirteenth Amendment were critical in the abolition of slavery and the ultimate granting of citizenship to black Americans. Lincoln eventually saw himself as a humble instrument to fulfill God's purpose for America by purifying the country from the evils of slavery and the sectionalism the institution had caused. He made this point clearly and passionately in his classic second inaugural address on March 4, 1865.

* * *

Inauguration day dawned dark and rainy. Thousands of people had thronged to the city and would stand in the cold and the mud to participate in the day's historic events. Unlike the somber mood and uncertainty four years earlier, a feeling of relief and celebration prevailed among those gathering for the second inauguration. They had reason to celebrate. Union army and naval forces everywhere were producing victories. In the Mississippi Valley, only remnants of Confederate forces remained in the field since George H. Thomas had shattered John B. Hood's army in Middle Tennessee. In the South Atlantic area, both Charleston and Wilmington had fallen to Federal forces; Sherman occupied the heartland of South Carolina; and Grant continued to make progress against Lee in Virginia.

Union people throughout the nation viewed Lincoln's second inauguration as a fitting occasion for thanksgiving and sober reflection. One midwestern editor told his readers that the inauguration should be a "cause for deep thankfulness and great reason" for the continued progress of a united America. In New York City, Albany, Providence, and elsewhere, the event was celebrated with parades, speeches, and fireworks. Watched by an immense crowd, the New York parade took more than three hours to pass any point. Horace Greeley of the *New York Tribune*, still smarting from Lincoln's refusal to dismiss Secretary of State Seward and appoint Ben Butler and other Radicals to his cabinet, announced that inauguration day should not be celebrated "as an ovation to the President" but should be a time for the people to renew their "fidelity to the country, her rights and liberties."[28]

But many Americans disagreed with Greeley, seeing the inauguration as a chance to reflect on Lincoln's achievement in guiding the ship of state through the nation's greatest crisis. To them, Lincoln's success put him on the same plane as Washington and other Founding Fathers. James Doolittle, a son of the Wisconsin Republican senator of the same name, wrote on inauguration day that Lincoln "rivals the greatest statesmen of our country; he is surpassed by none, not even by Washington." "Mr. Lincoln is possessed of great dignity," Doolittle continued. "It is not that selfish, conceited, proud, imperial dignity which Mr. [Salmon P.] Chase assumes, but is kind, approachable and winning." Furthermore, "he is great mentally, and no less morally."[29]

The *New York Times,* which had supported Lincoln's policies, led the press in praising his leadership in the war. The *Times* editor expressed the view that his administration had been "superlatively successful. But for the great practical wisdom of Mr. Lincoln, not only in shaping his action, but in recognizing the appropriate time for his action, the result [of the war] would have been very different." The errors Lincoln had made, this editor noted, had been quickly corrected. He predicted that the historian of the war "will be astonished as he scans Mr. Lincoln's path through all the immense difficulties of his Presidential term, that he has traversed it with such forecast, such firmness and such success." William Lloyd Garrison declared in *The Liberator* on the eve of the second inauguration: "There is no man in our history who has shown a more felicitous combination of temperament, conviction, and ability to grapple with a complication like that in which this country is involved than Abraham Lincoln."[30]

Even journals that had been hostile or lukewarm to Lincoln during the war now praised him for his leadership, though there were exceptions such as the Copperhead *Cincinnati Daily Enquirer,* which claimed that "Mr. Lincoln commences a second term unfettered by constitutional restraint as if he were the Czar of Russia." Conservative Unionists like George C. Prentice of the *Louisville Journal,* whose two sons fought for the Confederacy, emphasized Lincoln's role in saving the Union while downplaying the success of his antislavery policies. James Gordon Bennett's *New York Herald,* a frequent critic of the administration, proclaimed Lincoln "a most remarkable man. He may seem to be the most credulous, docile and pliable of backwoodsmen, [but] he has proved himself, in his quiet way, the keenest of politicians, and more than a match for his wiliest antagonists in the arts of diplomacy." The *Herald,* in particular, lauded Lincoln's "plain common sense, kindly disposition, straightforward purpose, and shrewd perception of the ins and outs of poor weak human nature." These marvelous qualities, the *Herald* maintained, "have enabled him to master difficulties which would have swamped any other man. Thus to-day, with the most cheering prospects before him, this extraordinary rail-splitter enters upon his second term the unquestioned master [of] American affairs, at home and abroad."[31]

★　★　★

The night before the inauguration found the president, along with cabinet members, at the Capitol reviewing bills passed as the congressional session came to an end. The next morning a procession was planned to escort him to the ceremony. However, while the procession was forming, Lincoln, with bills still to be acted on, rode ahead to the Capitol, escorted by a small military unit. Shortly before noon the inaugural ceremony began in the Senate chamber with the swearing in of new senators and Vice President Andrew Johnson. Several hundred women, including Mary Lincoln, and members of the press had been issued admission tickets and were seated in the gallery. Dignitaries occupied seats on the floor of the chamber. Lincoln, delayed by the need to act on congressional bills, arrived during the ceremony inaugurating the new vice president.[32]

The ceremony in the Senate chamber soon became "a jumble," as Secretary of the Navy Gideon Welles recorded in his diary. After the outgoing vice president, Hannibal Hamlin, delivered a few farewell remarks, the new vice president took the floor and made a rambling, largely incoherent speech. It became clear that Johnson was drunk. He had taken three shots of whiskey to overcome the effects of an illness that he had contracted before his arrival for the inauguration. During Johnson's harangue Lincoln, who disliked any intemperate or improper conduct in public, sat unflinchingly but with his eyes closed to avoid the stares of those who sought his reaction to Johnson's humiliating performance.[33]

In departing the chamber, Lincoln told the marshal of the ceremony, "Don't let Johnson speak outside." The president had earlier referred to Johnson as "the Andrew Jackson of the war" because, like his fellow Tennessean Jackson, he had made a bold stand for the Union. Now Lincoln became cool toward his vice president; he did not talk to him again until the last day of his life. Even so, he told Secretary of the Treasury Hugh McCulloch that he had known Johnson for many years, and, although the vice president "had made a bad slip the other day, . . . you need not be scared; Andy ain't a drunkard."[34]

Others seemed to agree, and Republicans downplayed the incident, though at the inauguration ball on March 6 one Republican senator was heard to remark that he did not regret Johnson's disgraceful performance, "for he has no chance now for the Presidency. He has killed himself off." Soon after the inauguration "a large number of Senators," according to the *Washington Chronicle,* called at Francis P. Blair Sr.'s Washington residence "to pay their respects" to the vice president; "they were pleased to see him well."[35] Johnson's behavior on inauguration day, however, would come back to haunt him after he became president, when he crossed swords with his wartime Republican friends on reconstruction policy. Senator Ben Wade and other Radicals repeatedly used the incident to portray Johnson as a drunkard.

When the ceremony in the Senate chamber had ended, the spectators inside the Capitol moved toward the east portico for the presidential inauguration. Unfortunately, only one door was opened for them to leave the building. "The crush was terrible," the *New York Times* reported. "The stair-cases and corridors became a mass of surging humanity" as the crowd sought alternative exits. "Ladies were lifted off their feet and carried down stair-cases." Meanwhile, the Capitol police were escorting Lincoln to the inauguration platform. After the president had passed the crowd, "a bibulous lunatic" attempted to break through the police lines, perhaps with the intent to assault Lincoln. The man was apprehended after a brief scuffle, but was released the next day after authorities determined that he was harmless. Reportedly in the crowd that day was a man who would prove to be a more dangerous threat, the actor John Wilkes Booth, who was biding his time to strike at the president.[36]

* * *

Before an estimated crowd of fifty thousand people, including hundreds of blacks, Lincoln read his inaugural address, which he had carefully prepared, probably in more than one draft. The text from which he read had been fashioned out of galley proofs of his manuscript and pasted, by Lincoln himself, in two broad columns on a large sheet of paper.[37] The speech had been printed in advance as a three-page leaflet for release to the press. Because of the commotion as people pushed to leave the Capitol, not one in fifty in the immense audience, according to an observer, "got within hearing distance of the President, and very many only got on the ground just as he closed his address." The speech, delivered in Lincoln's high-pitched voice, is the second shortest in the history of American inaugural orations; it is also the most memorable.[38]

The listeners did not get the inaugural address they expected. They wanted a spirited oration heralding the Union's triumph in the war and outlining future policies. Instead, the president told his audience that after four years "during which public declarations have been constantly called forth on every point and phase of the great contest . . . , little that is new could be presented. The progress of our arms, upon which all else chiefly depends, is as well known to the public as to myself, and it is, I trust, reasonably satisfactory and en-

Lincoln delivering his classic second inaugural address on March 4, 1865, the first time a president was photographed while making his inaugural speech. To his right, the inebriated vice president, Andrew Johnson, covers his face with his hat.

couraging to all." Despite the victories on the battlefield, however, Lincoln remained cautious and did not venture to predict when the war might end.

He devoted most of the brief address to a profound and pointed explanation of the cause and meaning of the war and God's role in it. Slavery "constituted a peculiar and powerful interest," and this interest was "the cause of the war." This view was not new for Lincoln or Northerners; indeed, many Confederates, including Vice President Stephens, had announced a similar reason for the war. Lincoln explained: "To strengthen, perpetuate, and extend this interest was the object for which the insurgents would rend the Union, even by war; while the government claimed no right to do more than to restrict the territorial enlargement of it." The president declared: "Neither party expected for the war, the magnitude, or the duration, which it has already attained. Neither anticipated that the cause of the conflict [slavery] might cease with, or even before, the conflict itself should cease. Each looked for an easier triumph, and a result less fundamental and astounding."

This version of the history of the conflict was accurate. Certainly, when the war began, both sides had expected a brief and relatively bloodless struggle. Even Lincoln in 1861 had believed that a determined federal stand against secession would lead to the reassertion of Unionism in the South and the early collapse of the rebellion. He had continued to believe that dedicated Unionists in the South would aid in the restoration of their states to the Union. The ferocity with which the Confederates fought had convinced him by mid-1862 that only a hard war, coupled with emancipation, could save the republic.

Lincoln then turned to a theological explanation of the war, primarily as it related to slavery. So passionate did he become in his allusions to the Bible and God that Frederick Douglass, who was present at the inauguration, called the address "more like a sermon than a state paper." Although some have minimized the religious significance of the speech, others have placed Lincoln's thought within the broader context of religion during the Civil War era, specifically the Northern Protestant idea of a higher moral order and the belief that God's purpose was at work in history.[39] Lincoln in this section of the address referred to God, or a synonym for God (the Almighty, Lord), on eight occasions. He began with an irony. Both sides in the conflict, he said, "read the same Bible, and pray to the same God; and each invokes His aid against the other." "It may seem strange," he continued, "that any men should dare to ask a just God's assistance in wringing their bread from the sweat of other men's faces," as did the slaveholders. However, he cautioned: "Let us judge not that we be not judged. The prayers of both [sides] could not be answered; that of neither has been answered fully. The Almighty has His own purposes."

At this point Lincoln increased the intensity of his language and invoked biblical authority for the war on slavery. He quoted Jesus: "Woe unto the world because of offences" against God. "American Slavery is one of those offences which, in the providence of God, must needs come, but which, having continued through His appointed time, He now wills to remove, and that He gives to both North and South, this terrible war, as the woe due to those by whom the offence came." "Fondly do we hope," Lincoln continued, "fervently do we pray, that this mighty scourge of war may speedily pass away. Yet, if God wills that it continue, until all the wealth piled by the bond-man's two hundred and fifty years of unrequited toil shall be sunk, and until every drop of blood drawn with the lash, shall be paid by another drawn with the sword, . . . so still it must be said 'the judgments of the Lord, are true and righteous altogether.'" This strident passage can be seen as the culmination of Lincoln's spiritual awakening and the growth of his moral and political opposition to slavery during the last part of the war.

The president concluded his speech in a softer tone, much more characteristic of his temperament and spirit and directed toward both Northerners and Southerners. He chose his words for the moment, but they have echoed through the ages: "With malice toward none; with charity for all; with firmness in the right, as God gives us to see the right, let us strive on to finish the work we are in; to bind up the nation's wounds; to care for him who shall have borne the battle, and for his widow, and his orphan—to do all which may achieve and cherish a just, and a lasting peace, among ourselves, and with all nations."

For Lincoln, who had faith in the providence of God and the progress of America toward a higher temporal order that would serve as a model for the world, these words expressed achievable ideals. From the beginning of his administration, he had wanted to believe that God had chosen him to be his instrument toward the fulfillment of these purposes. In February 1861, as president-elect, he had told the New Jersey Senate that he would be "most happy indeed if I shall be an humble instrument in the hands of the Almighty and of this, his almost chosen people," for the perpetuation of the Union.[40] The Union's impending success in the war tended to confirm in Lincoln's mind that he had indeed been the instrument of Providence in the conflict and that right and justice were on his side. In his inaugural address he sought to impress on Americans that, although the war had begun only to save the Union, God's purpose from the beginning had been to purify the country by ending slavery and thereby to make possible the nation's future greatness. In destroying slavery, the war to save the Union had been worth the heavy cost. God in his wisdom had made it so.

As Lincoln finished the address, the last clouds rolled away, sunshine flooded the platform, and Chief Justice Salmon P. Chase stepped forward to administer the oath of office. Lincoln repeated the oath and sealed it with a kiss on the Bible. He sat down to the sound of "cheer upon cheer" from the crowd and the booming of artillery guns in the background. Later that day Chase wrote to Mrs. Lincoln that "the beautiful sunshine" breaking through the clouds was "an auspicious omen of the dispersion of the clouds of war and the restoration of the clear sunlight of prosperous peace under the wise & just administration of him who took" the oath of office. Even Chase was beginning to appreciate the statesmanship qualities of the man he had earlier considered unfit for the presidency. Lincoln too saw the appearance of the sun as a providential sign for the future. The next day he remarked to a friend that he was "just superstitious enough to consider it a happy omen."[41]

* * *

After the ceremony Lincoln, accompanied by his son Tad and escorted by parade marshals wearing yellow scarves over their shoulders, rode in an open barouche back along muddy Pennsylvania Avenue to the White House. A military detachment, consisting of both white and black troops, followed his carriage. Behind them were bands, fire companies, floats depicting war scenes, and carriages. The great poet Walt Whitman, a volunteer nurse assistant in the Washington military hospitals, observed the procession. Whitman wrote that the president as he rode by "looked very much worn and tired; the lines indeed, of vast responsibilities, intricate questions, and demands of life and death cut deeper than ever upon his dark brown face; yet all the old goodness, tenderness, sadness and canny shrewdness underneath the furrows" could be seen.[42]

That evening the Lincolns gave a public reception at the White House. When the doors opened at eight o'clock, a repetition of the crush at the Capitol earlier in the day occurred. Two thousand people stampeded through the doors, which were opened and closed at intervals to prevent overcrowding in the Blue Room where the weary but good-natured president, wearing white gloves, shook the hands of well-wishers. Whitman noted that Lincoln, though "receiving, as in duty bound," looked "very disconsolate and as if he would give anything to be somewhere else." Hundreds of carriages had to wait from one to two hours before delivering their riders at the reception. Some well-wishers, hearing of the "jam" inside, angrily went away without seeking entrance. Before the reception ended at midnight, Lincoln reportedly had shaken the hands of five thousand people—at an astounding rate of one hundred every four minutes. His hand was still quivering the next day.[43]

Frederick Douglass, in the company of a Republican congressman, got through the crush at the White House door and, after a brief confrontation with two policemen, entered an area adjacent to the reception room. The congressman worked his way through the crowd to the president and asked permission to introduce the black leader to him. Lincoln, who had already met Douglass, agreed, and when the former slave approached, he held out his hand in welcome and announced, "Here comes my friend Douglass." They chatted briefly while others waited in line. The next day, as the White House seamstress Elizabeth Keckly recalled, Mary Lincoln asked her husband, "Why was not Mr. Douglass introduced to me?" "I do not know," the president replied. "I thought he was presented . . . It must have been an oversight then, mother. I am sorry you did not meet him."[44]

On March 6 the inauguration ball was held at the United States

Patent Office building, where partitions were removed to provide a room that could accommodate eight hundred dancers. Several thousand tickets to the ball had been sold at ten dollars each. No African Americans had received tickets, an omission by the Republican managers that the Democratic press gleefully seized upon, charging Lincoln's party with hypocrisy in their policy toward blacks.[45] Many affluent "strangers" arrived by train to attend the celebration; they joined members of Congress, government officials, military officers, and Washington citizens at the ball. The women came wearing elegant silk and lace dresses and adorned with jewelry. The sumptuous menu included oysters, beef, veal, poultry, game, pastries, salads, and desserts. In deference to Lincoln, who did not drink, the caterers did not serve wine at the tables. Church leaders and many of their followers did not attend; they found such partying morally wrong while men were struggling and dying to save the Union less than two hundred miles away. The inauguration ball, however, had become a tradition, and to some extent the 1865 affair was designed to celebrate the impending success of the Union in the war. Republican managers had rejected outright the notion that the ball should not be held. Furthermore, many who had profited from the war—and thus, in most cases, who supported the Republican party—had money to spend on such frivolity. Perhaps to lessen the sense of guilt for holding the ball while the war raged, the inaugural committees announced that any profits from ticket sales would be "appropriated to the uses of our brave defenders in the field and in the hospitals."[46]

The ball had been in progress for more than an hour when President Lincoln, Mrs. Lincoln, and their party entered the Patent Office hall to the music of "Hail to the Chief" played by the military band. Speaker of the House Schuyler Colfax accompanied the president to the platform at the end of the hall, followed by Mary Lincoln and her escort, Senator Charles Sumner. Lincoln and Sumner had been at odds over a number of issues, and at the time of the inauguration a serious breach in their relationship appeared imminent because of their differences over reconstruction, a rupture that Lincoln sought to avoid.[47] The Radical Massachusetts senator chaired the Senate Foreign Relations Committee and after the war would be a key player on critical foreign policy issues. Thus, maintaining cordial relations with him was important for the president. Mary Lincoln's friendship with Sumner made the rapprochement between her husband and the sensitive senator much easier. Lincoln's gesture of goodwill toward Sumner on inauguration day, however, did not resolve their differences on reconstruction or on the proper role for the federal government in establishing and protecting black rights in the postwar South.

Lincoln, wearing a black suit, a black tie, and white gloves (perhaps to conceal his elongated, knotty hands), only sat for a moment on the presidential platform. He relinquished his chair to a senator's wife and joined the men by the wall at the back of the platform. He and Mrs. Lincoln did not venture onto the dance floor. (Lincoln had never learned to dance.) About midnight the presidential party finished their "supper" and prepared to leave. By this time good order had broken down in the hall, mainly because about half of the people had not been fed and little hope existed that they would be. The *New York Herald* described the scene: "The ladies were very angry—so were the men. Some bullied, some bribed the waiters, and some ate the remains of other people's suppers. The mass surged to and fro like a sea. Plates were broken by dozens. There was a general mess."[48]

The presidential party was forced to depart by a side door where few people would notice them. Leaving the hungry crowd behind, members of Lincoln's party "spoke in severe terms of the disorder" in the hall. When Mrs. Lincoln remarked that the scene was "a scramble," the president quipped, "well, it appears like a very systematic scramble." It was his only light remark of the night. Though Lincoln had retained his equanimity throughout the chaotic inaugural events, he was tired and dispirited. Within a week he would be sick and bedridden, mainly from fatigue. Mary Lincoln lamented to Elizabeth Keckly: "Poor Mr. Lincoln is looking so broken-hearted, so completely worn out, I fear he will not get through the next four years."[49] However, within a few days he had sufficiently recovered to conduct business and once again receive the swarm of visitors who gathered outside his office.

* * *

Except for Vice President Johnson's embarrassing behavior, the turmoil and disorganization that marred the inaugural festivities were soon forgotten. Lincoln's inaugural address, in contrast, received immediate and continuing attention. On leaving the Capitol after the speech, a prominent Protestant minister pronounced it "the finest state paper in all history." A "distinguished statesman from New York" (probably Seward) heard the minister and prophetically responded: "Yes, and as Washington's name grows brighter with time, so it will be with Lincoln's. A century from to-day that inaugural will be read as one of the most sublime utterances ever spoken by man. Washington is the great man of the era of the Revolution. So will Lincoln be of this [period], but Lincoln will reach the higher position in history." For Lincoln's supporters, the address reinforced their view that he had become a great president. Charles Francis Adams Jr., after reading the speech, wrote to his father, the American minister in London: "That rail-splitting lawyer is one of the wonders of the day. Once at Gettysburg and now again on a greater occasion he has shown a capacity for rising to the demands of the hour which we should not expect from orators or men of the schools. The inaugural strikes me in its grand simplicity and directness as being for all time the historical keynote of this war."[50]

Most conservative Unionists and Republicans praised the religious tone of the address. The *Washington National Intelligencer,* the bellwether of the old Whig party, applauded the president's reminder that the North, as well as the South, had succumbed to sin and needed to abandon the self-righteous attitude and pharisaical pride that it had developed during the war: "Our offences in the sight of Heaven, as a people, who, amid luxury and pride and political corruption, have forgotten the Almighty, are too manifold and rank to admit of such impious audacity." Lincoln in his inaugural speech, the paper's editor concluded, was attempting to awaken the nation to the need to be cleansed of its sinfulness.[51]

The *Boston Daily Advertiser,* a conservative Republican newspaper published in a state where Calvinistic theology was still taken straight, judged that it was altogether proper for Lincoln to stress the role of Providence in the war and in the destruction of slavery. It was also appropriate to remind Northerners that they should reflect on their own shortcomings and practice charity toward Southerners even while making war against them. Lincoln's religious sentiments "may be deemed 'Puritanical' by some," the *Advertiser* declared, "but we suspect that the majority of the loyal people will agree that the President was right." The neighboring *Boston Journal* agreed, contending that it was the religious "feature of the address which commends it to the approval of the sober, earnest and thoughtful portion of the people—not those alone who are professors of religion, but every one who recognizes the hand of God in dealing with nations as with individuals." The *Journal,* in answer to those who criticized the president for failing to provide a course of action for his second term, claimed that Lincoln's "recognition of Divine Providence in the war prevented [him] from making out a policy for the future," since he could not foresee what God's plans and purposes would be. The president's statement that the nation should pursue a policy "with malice toward none, with charity for all" could clearly "shadow forth" God's purpose for the future.[52]

The *Boston Journal* was responding to what it labeled "the Satanic press of New York" and Democrats who criticized Lincoln for mixing religion with politics in the inaugural address. The *New York World,* the leading Democratic newspaper in the Northeast, had charged that "Mr. Lincoln's substitution of religion for statesmanship is not less gratuitous than it is absurd. The President's theology smacks as strongly of the dark ages as does Pope Pius's [Pius IX] politics." Desperate to find fault with the popular president, the *Cincinnati Enquirer,* a leading midwestern Democratic paper, dismissed the address as Lincoln's "politico-theology" and charged that it was "a joint production . . . of the church, speaking through the Presidential conduit." Likewise, the Copperhead *Detroit Free Press* asserted that Lincoln's speech "is more worthy of a puritanical hypocrite than of an American Executive. It is chiefly made up of a short, flawed moral lecture on the impropriety of both sides appealing to the Almighty for the justice of their cause."[53]

At the other end of the political spectrum, the *New York Evening Post,* whose editor William Cullen Bryant had long criticized Lincoln for moving too slowly to free the slaves and on other issues, announced that the speech "will be a disappointment to perhaps a majority of readers [in] that nothing is said" regarding future policies. The Radical *Boston Commonwealth* declared that "Mr. Lincoln did not touch all of the chords of the American heart. He did not reach those" who would give "the black man the right of suffrage in all of the States . . . As it is, we must have four more years of warfare to gain this good of American liberty." The erstwhile Radical *New York Tribune* contended that the president's theological discourse about "the [harsh] judgments of the Lord" would do more harm than good in getting the rebels to lay down their arms and return to the Union. Despite the president's "charity for all" pronouncement, "last-ditch" Southern leaders, the *Tribune* argued, would construe the speech "as an official declaration from 'the despot Lincoln' that it is his purpose to prosecute the war to the total extirpation of slavery, though it may involve the extermination of the white race of the South and the destruction of their property, root and branch." The *Tribune* dismissed the address as "a little speech of 'glittering generalities,' put in to fill the programme, and as nothing more."[54]

Abroad, European journals expressed their approval of the address. The British press, which earlier had been contemptuous of Lincoln, charging him with hypocrisy on the slavery issue, especially praised his speech. The *Spectator* (London) asserted that his short address "for political weight, moral dignity, and unaffected solemnity has no equal in our time." This newspaper lauded Lincoln's recognition of God's purposes in the war and his expression of charity to Southerners: "No statesman ever uttered words stamped at once with the seal of so deep a wisdom and so true a simplicity. The 'village attorney' of whom many wise men wrote with so much scorn in 1861, seems destined to be one of those 'foolish things of the world' which are destined to confound the wise." The *Saturday Review* (London) also applauded Lincoln's willingness to be charitable to his enemies and his refusal to pass judgment on the rebels: "The President regards both combatants as the instruments and victims of a just retribution for a common crime." Even the *Times*, which had sympathized with the Confederacy for most of the war, saw the hand of a statesman in Lincoln's address. According to the *Times*, the speech revealed the central quality of the president's leadership: the steadfastness of his war and emancipation policies.[55]

* * *

Lincoln's second inaugural address, as some of his critics noted, did not set forth a policy for the future. Lincoln thought in broad terms;

he would leave the specifics to Congress, military commanders, and others. At the time of his inauguration in March 1865, he had already laid out his policies regarding the war and emancipation. These were now in the process of fulfillment to his satisfaction. He said in the address that he did not think it "fitting and proper" to provide, as he had done in his first inaugural speech, details "of a course to be pursued." Only his reconstruction policy might need refinement, but, with the war still raging and much of the South unsubdued, he did not know what changes in policy might be necessary after the rebel surrender. Perhaps God would provide guidance. He admonished the people to commit themselves in the months ahead to a policy of "malice toward none," "charity for all," and aid to the victims of the war in order that the nation might achieve "a just, and a lasting peace." After four years of bitter enmity it was problematic whether the majority of the Northern people would agree to such a forgiving and beneficent policy toward their fallen foes.

Lincoln thought that his inaugural address would "wear as well as—perhaps better than—any thing I have produced; but I believe it is not immediately popular." He took notice of the criticism directed at his injection of God's purpose in the war when he wrote to Thurlow Weed: "Men are not flattered by being shown that there has been a difference of purpose between the Almighty and them. To deny it, however, in this case, is to deny that there is a God governing the world. It is a truth which I thought needed to be told."[56] Although many antislavery stalwarts disagreed with the president's contention that the North was also to blame for the evils of slavery, Lincoln was correct in predicting that his speech would wear well in history. Indeed, no presidential inaugural address has received greater acclaim. But arguably Lincoln was wrong in asserting that history would attribute the Union triumph and the end of slavery to the divine will. Though Lincoln gave Providence its due in the inaugural address, posterity has recognized that it was his own statecraft in navigating the dangerous waters of the war for the Union and emancipation that produced these historic successes.

CHAPTER 6

BEYOND THE BATTLEFIELD

In the last months of the Civil War, when ending the fighting, Southern reconstruction, and the place of freed blacks absorbed most of Lincoln's attention, he also had to address serious problems not directly connected to the war in the South. Controversies flared up with Great Britain over Confederate raids from sanctuaries in Canada and with France over French intervention in Mexico. Conflict between Indians and settlers in the West and illicit trade through the military lines in the South also demanded the president's attention. These problems severely tested his leadership skill, his political dexterity, and even his mental and physical stamina.

★ ★ ★

Lincoln had only occasionally paid close attention to foreign affairs, but as the war wound down international issues assumed greater importance. Deteriorating relations with Great Britain proved especially troublesome. Despite British efforts to maintain a strict neutrality in the American conflict, Britain's toleration of small groups of Confederate raiders operating out of Canada made armed confrontation a real possibility. Many Northerners resented the aid, though technically neutral, that British citizens and merchants had given the Confederacy and believed the government in London had plotted against the Union. It was no secret that members of the British government and the upper class hoped that the South would win its independence and divide America into two less potent nations. Lincoln had pursued a policy of "one war at a time," but with the rebellion coming to an end, Northern pressure could be expected to increase on the president to make the British pay for their supposed unneutral acts and the incidents along the Canadian border.

At General Grant's headquarters in late March 1865, Lincoln seemed to favor retribution, though he stopped short of threatening war against the British. According to Horace Porter, Grant's aide-de-camp, the president, while sitting around the campfire and dodging the smoke, exclaimed: "England will live to regret her inimical attitude toward us. After the collapse of the rebellion John Bull will find that he has injured himself more seriously than us." Even after three years, the president still resented the British for an incident in late 1861: Captain Charles Wilkes of the U.S.S. *San Jacinto* had intercepted a British mail steamer, the *Trent,* and forcibly taken custody of two Confederate emissaries, John Slidell and James M. Mason. Slidell and Mason had been taken to Boston and incarcerated at Fort Warren. Lincoln, who at first opposed delivering up the prisoners, had been forced to surrender them to avoid war with Britain. Now he told Grant and his officers that "it was a pretty bitter pill to swallow, but I contented myself with believing that England's triumph in the matter would be short-lived, and that after ending our war successfully we would be so powerful that we could call her to account for all the embarrassments she had inflicted upon us."[1] The president's bellicosity on this occasion might have been triggered by a visit earlier in the day to the Petersburg battlefield, where he saw the bloody results of a failed Confederate attempt to breach the Federal lines. Like most Northerners, he partly blamed British aid to the Confederacy for the continuation of such carnage.

The main bone of contention between the United States and Great Britain late in the war was Confederate operations out of British-controlled Canada. These activities had increased by the fall of 1864. Confederate agents in Canada provided financial support to Copperhead candidates in midwestern elections and launched raids to free Confederate prisoners in the Great Lakes region. In September Confederate raiders operating from Windsor, Canada, attempted to seize the U.S.S. *Michigan* at Sandusky, Ohio, and to free Southern prisoners from nearby Johnson's Island. Though this mission failed, the rebel raiders, led by John Yates Beall, a former officer in the Confederate army who had been granted a naval commission to engage in privateering, captured two steamers on Lake Erie, took some of the property ashore in Canada, and scuttled one of the vessels at Windsor, reportedly while British Canadian authorities watched. Beall then crossed the border into New York to continue his raiding. Federal authorities captured him in December and a military commission in New York tried him for spying and conducting "irregular and unlawful warfare as a guerrilla." In February 1865 the commission sentenced him to be executed.[2]

Tremendous pressure was brought to bear on Lincoln to commute Beall's sentence to imprisonment. Orville H. Browning, John W. Forney, the Blairs, and other leading Republicans met with the president—some on more than one occasion—and appealed to him to stop the execution. In one visit, Forney, an influential Republican newspaperman and Lincoln supporter, was accompanied by Roger A. Pryor, a Confederate brigadier general who had been imprisoned with Beall but granted parole. The two men insisted that Beall was a commissioned Confederate officer and that his men had killed no one in the Lake Erie operation. Interceders from New York and Baltimore journeyed to Washington hoping to persuade the president to spare Beall's life. Even crusty Thaddeus Stevens, who had no love for rebels, told Lincoln that Beall "deserves clemency" and asked him to grant it "as a personal favor."[3]

At the same time, General John A. Dix, whose military commission had condemned Beall to death, importuned the president not to reverse the verdict. Despite Lincoln's well-deserved reputation for clemency, he agreed with Dix and refused to intervene to save Beall. On February 18 the raider went to the gallows at Fort Columbus on Governor's Island in New York harbor, still claiming that he had acted as a Confederate officer under the rules of war and did not deserve to be treated as a spy or a guerrilla.[4]

The Beall decision haunted Lincoln. A few weeks later he told a group of visitors: "There was this case of Beall on the lakes. That was a case where there must be an example." Beall's supporters "tried me every way. They wouldn't give up; but I had to stand firm on that, and I even had to turn away his poor sister when she came and begged for his life, and let him be executed. I can't get the stress out of my mind yet." Tears reportedly ran down Lincoln's cheeks as he spoke.[5]

Rumors of Confederate raids from British Canada had circulated throughout the upper North during the fall and early winter of 1864. The presidential campaign had only intensified the rumors. A spectacular attempt by eight Confederates operating out of Canada to burn hotels and other buildings in New York City added to Northern hostility toward the British. The rebel incendiaries entered the city in late October and mingled with the crowds, attended plays, listened to campaign speeches for Lincoln, and heard a sermon by Henry Ward Beecher while awaiting the moment to strike.[6] According to the confession of Captain Robert C. Kennedy, one of the arsonists, the plan was to set fire to thirty-two buildings on election night, but the phosphorus for igniting the fires was not ready and the attempt was postponed until November 25. The purpose, Kennedy said, was to retaliate for General Philip Sheridan's "atrocities in the Shenandoah Valley [and] let the people of the North understand . . . that they can't be rolling in wealth and comfort while we at the South are bearing all the hardships and privations." Ten hotels and Barnum's Museum, which, Kennedy admitted, he fired as "a huge joke," were only slightly damaged, mainly because the windows were closed and the oxygen supply was shut off. Fortunately, no one died or received serious injuries in the fires.

The incendiaries, or terrorists by today's reckoning, remained in the city for almost two days after their crime—and read about their exploits in the newspapers—then fled to Canada and safety. Kennedy, however, seeking to return to the South, crossed the border at Detroit and was captured by United States detectives. Tried before another of General Dix's military commissions—the kind of tribunal that the New York Times and New Yorkers demanded for him—Kennedy was convicted of "one of the greatest atrocities of the age" and sentenced to be hanged. Unlike the Beall case, no Northerners pleaded for his life. Kennedy appealed to Lincoln to commute the sentence, but the president turned a deaf ear. On March 25, 1865, one month after Beall's execution, Kennedy, defiant and "with curses on his lips," was hanged at Fort Lafayette in New York harbor. After the war federal authorities arrested the commander of the raid, Colonel Robert M. Martin, but he never came to trial. Held in close confinement for seven months, Martin received a pardon from President Andrew Johnson. He returned to New York in 1874 and became the manager of a tobacco warehouse in Brooklyn.[7]

Many in the United States believed, with some justification, that British North Americans were sympathetic to the Confederacy and were helping its agents and raiders. Northerners also assumed that British and Canadian authorities were doing nothing to break up Confederate plots. This view gained support after a bold rebel raid on St. Albans, Vermont, in late 1864, the raiders' escape across the border, and the Canadian officials' refusal to hand them over to American authorities.[8] Though the St. Albans raiders, about twenty strong, had instructions from Clement Clay, Jefferson Davis's representative in Canada, to "burn and destroy, but don't rob," they plundered the town, justifying their depredations as retaliation for the destructive behavior of Federal troops in the South. Their major objectives were to seize money from banks and ultimately to provoke an armed conflict between the United States and Canada. One Vermont citizen was killed and two wounded in a gunfight with the marauders. After failing to torch the town, the Confederates fled toward the border with $200,000 that they had stolen, mainly from local banks. A hastily organized posse pursued them into Canada and captured several, including Lieutenant Bennett Young, their twenty-one-year-old leader. Then a British major arrived on the scene and demanded that the prisoners be turned over to Canadian authorities, and after a tense moment the Vermont posse surrendered both the Confederates and the money.[9] Even worse, because of conflicting British and Canadian laws on extradition, Justice Charles Coursol, a Montreal police magistrate, rather than extradite the prisoners, released them. The incident aroused Northern anger to a fever pitch.

Some powerful Republicans in states bordering on Canada saw the St. Albans affair as part of a larger picture of British hostility toward the Union that needed to be redressed. Senator Zachariah Chandler of Michigan on December 26 wrote to John M. Forbes, a prominent Boston merchant who had cautioned against retaliation: "I hope that you do not represent the spirit of the New England commercial

States. If you do, the gulf between the commercial and North Western States" (he could have added Vermont and upstate New York) "is broader than I had hoped." The United States should punish "John Bull for his insolence, impertinence and criminality" during the war; if not, "we deserve the contempt of the world." Chandler declared that the Lincoln administration should act now when American forces were strong and battle-tested. And in fact even people in the "New England commercial States" thought that the "bloated aristocrats of England" needed a "thrashing," but that somehow it should be done peacefully and after the rebellion had been suppressed.[10]

Democrats, including Copperheads, and self-styled independents like James Gordon Bennett of the *New York Herald* joined the Republicans in demanding that the United States take Canada by the throat and throttle her "as a St. Bernard would throttle a poodle pup." The *New York Times,* reflecting upper Northern sentiment, agreed with the call for intervention. Such action, the *Times* admitted, might "lead to war with England. But if it must come, let it come . . . We were never in better condition for a war with England."[11]

* * *

One week before Justice Coursol's decision to release the St. Albans raiders, Lincoln in his annual message to Congress had taken a less bellicose but nonetheless important position. According to the Rush-Bagot agreement of 1817, neither Great Britain nor the United States could add to its naval force in the Great Lakes without six months' notice. Now Lincoln announced that because of "recent assaults and depredations committed by inimical and desperate persons, who are harbored [in Canada], it has been thought proper to give notice that after the expiration of six months . . . the United States must hold themselves at liberty to increase their naval armament upon the lakes." Lincoln threatened to require passports to enter the United States from Canada and also to end the reciprocal trade treaty of 1854 if Canadian officials did not take action to prevent rebel raids. To soften the threat, he added that "the Colonial authorities of Canada are not deemed to be intentionally unjust or unfriendly towards the United States; but, on the contrary, there is every reason to expect that, with the approval of the [British] imperial government, they will take the necessary measures to prevent new incursions across the border."[12]

Lincoln, like other Americans, must have been shocked by Coursol's subsequent release of the raiders. Secretary of the Navy Gideon Welles called it "an outrage that cannot be acquiesced in," and Secretary of State Seward wrote to Charles Francis Adams, America's minister in Britain, that "there is imminent danger of a war" over Coursol's action and the border incidents. General Dix, commanding in New York, did not wait for a reaction from Washington. He issued an order on December 14 for his troops to pursue rebel marauders across the border into Canada. Dix further directed that when apprehended "under no circumstances" were the raiders to be turned over to British Canadian authorities. The order, if implemented, could mean war with Britain.[13]

Lincoln recognized the danger of Dix's directive, as well as the bad precedent that would be created by army commanders acting on policy matters, a situation he had faced in 1861–1862 when Generals John C. Frémont and David Hunter had sought to free slaves in their military departments. The next day he revoked Dix's order. Speaking through Secretary of War Edwin M. Stanton, he told Dix that "the act of invading neutral territory by military commanders is . . . too grave and serious to be left to the discretion or will of subordinate commanders" and that "subordinate military authorities, when left to their own will or discretion, are too prone to act upon views of military necessity where none really exists, to be intrusted with the power of crossing neutral territory without specific authority." Still, Lincoln's message revoking Dix's order contained an implicit threat. If higher British-American authorities did not overturn Coursol's decision, round up the raiders, and extradite them to the United States, his administration would take action. "It remains to be seen," Stanton quoted Lincoln, "whether the Executive authorities in Canada will sanction the action of their judicial officer . . . If circumstances shall require military commanders to cross into Canada, or to pursue marauders, thieves, or murderers of any description into neutral territory, proper authority can be applied for, without any delay prejudicial to the public welfare." In that case, Lincoln promised to give the order to cross the border.[14]

Two days after revoking the pursuit order, the president, through Secretary of State Seward, directed that passports be required of all foreigners entering the United States, except bona fide immigrants. The Senate supported Lincoln and demonstrated its outrage over the release of the St. Albans raiders by unilaterally abrogating the reciprocal trade accord of 1854 with Canada. At the same time it gave the required six months' notice for the termination of the Rush-Bagot demilitarization agreement. The new organization of Irish nationalists in America, the Fenian Brotherhood, helped exacerbate tensions along the border. The Fenians saw the crisis as an opportunity to strike at the British in Canada. In addition to plotting raids into Canada, they offered their services to patrol the border for the United States. Lincoln wisely rejected the offer.[15]

★ ★ ★

Many Britons fully expected that the Lincoln administration, pressured by the Northern public, would use the border troubles as an excuse to invade and occupy Canada. "The most influential organs of public opinion in Great Britain," according to the *New York World*, reported "the existence of an equally irritable state of feeling in that country toward the Union" and talk of war was heard everywhere. Both the prime minister, Lord Palmerston, and Lord Lyons, the British minister in Washington, concluded that the United States was preparing for war with Britain. Rumors circulated in England that after the Civil War a combined Northern and Southern force would march into British North America. None other than the defeated presidential candidate George B. McClellan, who was visiting in Britain, assumed the task of convincing the Prince of Wales that the Lincoln administration had no such objective in mind. War between the United States and Great Britain, of course, might have allowed the tottering Confederacy to snatch victory from the jaws of defeat. As one Confederate official put it, "a [Union] war with England would be our peace."[16]

But there would be no war between the two Atlantic adversaries. Neither Palmerston, nor Lincoln, nor Canadians wanted war. Palmerston knew that if it occurred Canada would be lost and British commerce disrupted. Lincoln had no intention of abandoning his "one war at a time" policy or beginning an international conflict when his longing for peace at home might soon be realized. Canadian authorities were shaken by the prospect of thousands of American troops invading their province, and the livelihoods of many Canadians, dependent on trade with the North, would be ruined if the Union government closed the border. Already the passport requirement was placing a hardship on Canadians. News of Sherman's march through the South and the impending collapse of the Confederacy virtually wiped out remaining English belligerence toward the Union over Canada. Charles Francis Adams wrote to his son that "public sentiment" in Britain, "disappointed in its sanguine expectations of our ruin, is now taking a wholly new turn" in hopes of avoiding war.[17]

In Canada, Prime Minister John A. Macdonald and the British governor general, Stanley Monck, moved quickly to defuse the border controversy. Monck expressed appreciation to Lincoln for revoking Dix's "hot pursuit" order and promised to undo Coursol's release of the St. Albans raiders. Working with Canadian officials, Monck secured the re-arrest of nine of the fugitives. (However, the prisoners were not extradited to the United States but held for trials in Canada; they ultimately received no punishment.) Meanwhile, Macdonald called up the militia to patrol the border and took action to destroy the nests of Confederate plotters in his country. When the Canadian parliament in February agreed to pay $50,000 of the $200,000 stolen at St. Albans, Lincoln accepted this show of goodwill and rescinded the passport order. What happened to the remaining $150,000 is a mystery. Years later, Bennett Young, the leader of the raiders, claimed that he had sent the money to Confederate officials in Richmond. The historian Robin Winks, an authority on the incident, believes that the chief of police in Montreal seized the money and simply kept a large part of it.[18]

By March the border had settled down, and on both sides of the Atlantic talk of war had subsided, though Adams reported great uneasiness in London "in regard to what will be done by us" after the restoration of the Union. Palmerston, Benjamin Disraeli, and other prominent Britons began to speak "in the highest terms of the manner in which Mr. Lincoln's Administration had conducted its relations to foreign Powers."[19] Lincoln's measured response to the St. Albans raid, his revocation of General Dix's rash order for troops to pursue the raiders across the border, and his patience in dealing with Canadian authorities were crucial in defusing the crisis. The reduction in tension along the border freed Lincoln to focus on ending the Southern rebellion and restoring the states to the Union.

★ ★ ★

American relations with France in late 1864 and early 1865 fared little better than those with Great Britain. The problem was Mexico. Napoleon III had intervened in Mexico on the pretext that Mexicans had failed to pay their debts to Europeans, and in 1864 had installed Maximilian of Hapsburg as emperor. These actions clearly violated the Monroe Doctrine. The Lincoln administration, however, in its communications with France, did not mention the Doctrine lest it irritate the French and prompt Napoleon to recognize the Confederate States. Indeed, Lincoln seemed less concerned about the Monroe Doctrine than about the imposition of a nonrepublican, imperial government on the Mexican people. He saw America as "a model for the world" that would succeed not by force but by the strength of its ideas and the will and wisdom of its people to create and sustain republican institutions in the United States. The triumph of the Maximilian regime in Mexico would be a disturbing setback for the progress of republicanism and self-government in the Western Hemisphere.

Lincoln also feared that French forces might link up with Confederates in Texas, making the restoration of the Union in that state unlikely without an armed confrontation with France. He admitted in a confidential message to his commanders that the Red River military campaign of 1864, launched from New Orleans under the command of General Nathaniel P. Banks, was intended in part to counter the French threat to Texas.[20] (The campaign faltered in north Louisiana and never reached Texas.) Lincoln's fears of a French-Confederate military linkage were exaggerated: the French had enough of a fight on their hands with the Mexican resistance under Benito Juarez and were not likely to risk a war with the United States over Texas.

Despite his ideological opposition to an imperial regime in Mexico, Lincoln's main concern regarding the French was to prevent them from recognizing the Confederacy and expanding their material aid to the rebels across the porous border. With that in mind, even as Maximilian consolidated his position in 1864, the president and the secretary of state sought to reassure Napoleon III's government that the United States had no hostile intentions toward France or its puppet regime. In his annual message to Congress in December 1864, Lincoln referred to Mexico as "a theatre of civil war," avoiding any public suggestion of French imperialism. He also claimed: "While our political relations with that country have undergone no change, we have, at the same time, strictly maintained neutrality between the belligerents."[21]

Republicans in Congress, however, attacked Lincoln's appeasement of the French and Maximilian. Many Radical Republicans blamed Secretary of State Seward for the administration's failure to insist that the French abide by the Monroe Doctrine and withdraw from Mexico. The House of Representatives in April 1864 had unanimously adopted a resolution, introduced by Henry Winter Davis, chairman of the Committee on Foreign Affairs, asserting that members of Congress were "unwilling, by silence, to leave the nations of the world under the impression that they are indifferent spectators of the deplorable events now transpiring in the Republic of Mexico; and they therefore think fit to declare that it does not accord with the policy of the United States to acknowledge a monarchial government, existing on the ruins of any republican government in [North] America, under the auspices of any European power." Even before the House voted on the resolution, Seward wrote to William L. Dayton, the American minister in Paris, that the action of the House did not signal a change in U.S. policy. Lincoln, Seward told Dayton, wanted him to inform the French that he did not contemplate "any departure from the policy which this Government has hitherto pursued in regard to the war between France and Mexico." The matter of foreign affairs, Seward continued, "is a practical and purely Executive [power], and the decision of its constitutionality belongs not to the House of Representatives, nor even to Congress, but to the President of the United States." Still, he noted that the Davis resolution "truly interprets the unanimous sentiment of the people of the United States in regard to Mexico." Dayton showed Seward's letter to Edouard Drouyn de Lhuys, the French foreign minister, who expressed his "entire satisfaction" with it. The letter was subsequently printed and circulated in the European capitals.[22]

The Senate failed to approve the Davis resolution, but Davis and many other members of Congress were livid when they read the correspondence between Seward and Dayton, documents that were supplied to the House by Lincoln upon its request. Denouncing Seward's action as a sellout to France, Davis wanted his committee to make a blistering report to the House floor on the issue. But with the election campaign of 1864 beginning and the war at a critical juncture in Virginia and elsewhere, members of his own party blocked Davis's effort to embarrass the Lincoln administration.[23]

When Congress met in December, after Lincoln's re-election, a still defiant Davis introduced a resolution asserting the constitutional right of Congress to have "an authoritative voice in . . . prescribing the foreign policy of the United States as well as in the recognition of new powers [governments]; and . . . the constitutional duty of the President to respect that policy." In a direct slap at Seward, the resolution declared that a matter before Congress, "while pending and undetermined, is not a fit topic of diplomatic explanation with any foreign power." By a vote of 70 to 63 the House immediately tabled the new Davis resolution. While only 15 Republicans voted with Davis against tabling, Democrats, whose antebellum party had favored an aggressive policy toward Mexico, voted overwhelmingly against tabling the resolution. The *Boston Commonwealth* correspondent in Washington, a Republican, explained the votes of the majority of his party: "We are all in too good a humor with Mr. Lincoln" since his re-election "to criticise or complain." Though they were upset with "Mr. Seward for his apologies to France about the [earlier] House action on the Monroe doctrine," Republicans in Congress, the *Commonwealth* correspondent wrote, "have an idea that the polished Baltimore orator [Davis] is a very dangerous lion any way, needing to be kept under the most watchful restraint, lest he fall upon the administration party and rend it."[24]

When the vote went against him, Davis resigned as chairman of the House Committee on Foreign Affairs. In doing so, he made a passionate speech defending the resolution and attacking "the Secretary of

Henry Winter Davis, a harsh Republican critic of Lincoln in the House of Representatives and coauthor of the Wade-Davis Manifesto, who in 1864–1865 unsuccessfully sought greater authority for Congress in foreign policy.

State" (he never used Seward's name) for his lack of respect for Congress and his appeasement of the French in Mexico. Seeking to shame House members for not supporting his resolution, Davis exclaimed, "A free nation on our borders lay bleeding in the talons of the French eagle, and a vagrant adventurer, who had never seen the soil of Mexico, called himself an emperor." Compounding the humiliation, the "Secretary of State saw fit to enter into diplomatic communication with a foreign government, in order to rob the vote of this House" of "its legitimate and moral power." Davis denied that his resolution had attacked Lincoln, a claim that must have amused House members of both parties who knew otherwise. "There is no word in that resolution which assails the President, nor was it contemplated to assail him," Davis said.[25]

The Maryland congressman succeeded in shaming the House members, or at least a majority of them, into reconsidering his resolution.

In the debate on it, those Republicans (mostly Radicals) who favored the resolution clearly aimed their fire at Seward and not at Lincoln. They implied, however, that the president had neglected his constitutional duty by permitting, as Thaddeus Stevens charged, "an agent of this Government," Seward, to carry on foreign policy independently. Democrats remained gleefully quiet as their political foes, still flushed with victory in the fall elections, divided over Davis's resolution. Republicans both defended the authority of the president to conduct foreign policy, unhampered by Congress, and asserted the right of the legislative branch to participate in it.[26]

The vote on the resolution claiming congressional authority in foreign relations and criticizing Seward passed by a close margin of 68 to 59. The majority of Republicans, not wanting to antagonize Lincoln, voted against it. Strange bedfellows provided the victory: conservative Unionists and all but two Democrats, along with sixteen Radicals, sided with Davis. A few Republicans, who probably supported the resolution, deliberately absented themselves during the balloting.[27]

★ ★ ★

Davis's victory was short-lived. The Republican press overwhelmingly denounced the House's action, charging that the resolution had more to do with Davis's malevolence toward Lincoln and Seward, combined with bitter Democratic partisanship, than with the conduct of foreign affairs or the issue of the French in Mexico. The *New York Times* called the passage of the resolution "little more than a splenetic ebullition against the President, on the part of those who failed to prevent his re-election." The *Times* contended that "the House of Representatives has no right" to dictate to the president "upon any subject foreign or domestic; and any attempt to do so is simply an assumption of power with which it is not clothed." The *Times* further declared that no basis existed for charging that the president was weak in his support of the Monroe Doctrine; "he had repeatedly and earnestly warned the French Government that any attempt on their part to override the will of the Mexicans" and substitute a monarchy for the country's republican institutions would sooner or later "involve the two countries in war."[28] The *Times* was wrong on the last point: Lincoln had not threatened war if the French prevailed in Mexico, though conceivably friction between the two countries over the Maximilian regime after the Civil War might have led to American intervention.

Other Republican newspapers concluded that Davis's resolution was solely an attack on Seward. The resolution would have failed, the *Boston Daily Advertiser* claimed, if its supporters had not changed their tactic by making Seward the villain while downplaying the president's role.[29] Senators, led by Charles Sumner, chair of the Foreign Relations Committee, despite their distaste for Seward and the administration's appeasement policy toward the French, sensed public opposition and refused to challenge Lincoln on the issue. The Senate did not consider the House resolution, and the controversy over control of foreign affairs soon subsided—but the issue of Maximilian and the French in Mexico continued to trouble the Union.

James Gordon Bennett's *New York Herald,* reputedly the newspaper with the largest circulation in the North, did not permit Americans—or the Lincoln administration—to forget the egregious French violation of the Monroe Doctrine. In early 1865 the *Herald* repeatedly demanded the enforcement of the Doctrine in Latin America. It was "an imperative necessity," the *Herald* thundered on January 25, "that every European Power should be driven from this continent." Now was the time to act: "We are now more powerful than we ever were before, and in every way prepared to wage war on a vast and expensive scale." The *Herald* suggested that, as the Confederacy crumbled, defeated Southern soldiers could join Union veterans in a campaign to expel Maximilian and the French from Mexico; in the process, it said, several northern Mexican provinces could be annexed to the United States.[30]

Francis Preston Blair Sr., patriarch of the prominent Maryland political family, proposed, in the name of peace, to give practical effect to the *Herald*'s "grand Mexican idea" (see Chapter 4). His plan involved an armistice between the two sides in the Civil War, followed by combined Federal-Confederate operations against the French in Mexico. At the Hampton Roads peace conference on February 3, Lincoln, unmoved by the ebullitions in the *Herald,* firmly rejected any such unrealistic scheme. News of the proposal, however, and of Lincoln's willingness to engage in the peace talks that Blair had set afoot, made Napoleon III's ministers fear that the United States would abandon its policy of coexistence with Maximilian's regime.

This fear was compounded by bad intelligence provided by Louis de Geofroy, the French chargé d'affaires in Washington. Overreacting to Blair's mission to Richmond in January, Geofroy sent misleading information to Paris about Lincoln's intentions in the proposed peace talks. Just before the Hampton Roads conference, he reported that as part of the peace agreement the Confederate army "would be retained in its present organization and used beside that of the North in a great foreign war." Geofroy predicted that "within the next six months" we will "see the war transplanted to the borders of Mexico and Canada." He did note that Seward "continues to cast a skeptical eye on all of this," but he claimed that Lincoln "affects a great independence from members of this cabinet, and would be perfectly capable of making some great decision without consulting his advisors."[31]

Geofroy had wrongly informed his government that Lincoln differed sharply with Seward on the Union's Mexican policy. A French visitor who was often in the company of the president wrote to his wife that, though "Lincoln clearly saw that America was in a position which allowed her to speak firmly" to France, he wanted no war over Mexico. But Geofroy's dispatches convinced the French government that war with the United States was likely after the defeat of the Confederates.[32] Similar to British fears that an Anglo-American war would result in the loss of Canada, the French government expected to lose Mexico and perhaps other New World possessions if Lincoln decided to intervene against its puppet emperor. Napoleon's ministers toyed with the idea of a combined French-British force to put the American upstart in its place and preserve European possessions and interests in the Western Hemisphere. The French would supply the troops and the British the navy. But as long as the Lincoln administration refrained from armed intervention in Canada, Lord Palmerston would not agree to an alliance against the United States. Such an American intervention never occurred.[33]

Under these circumstances, the French government, while making plans to send eight elite regiments to Mexico, sought to placate Lincoln. According to the prominent New Yorker August Belmont, who was visiting Paris, French leaders began to speak "in glowing terms of the prospects of our Country." Though Napoleon was heard to comment that "the honor of France was engaged in the support of Maximilian," the French foreign minister indicated to John Bigelow, the American chargé d'affaires in Paris, that an agreement could be reached about Mexico. Bigelow wrote to Senator Edwin D. Morgan on March 2: "The French policy in Mexico is on the eve of an important change . . . Maximilian is likely to leave" the country, and with him, the French forces. Bigelow told Seward that he "hoped Congress & the Press of the U.S. will leave Maximilian and [the] Empire to the laws of gravitation," and cease their pressure on Lincoln to intervene. Seward assured Bigelow—and thus the French—that the administration's nonintervention policy "remains unchanged." If war occurred with France, Seward wrote, "it must be a war of her making, either against our ships or upon our territory . . . We shall attack nobody elsewhere." He told Bigelow, who would soon be promoted to the position of United States minister in France, that "all conjecture and collateral questions arising out of the war are left by us to the arbitrament of reason under the mutations of time." Seward confidently predicted that once the passions against Europe raised by the Civil War had passed, the American people would support the president in this policy.[34]

Lincoln, as he had suggested to Grant and his officers at City Point in March 1865, was more interested in securing redress from Great Britain for its aid to the Confederacy than in precipitating a conflict with France over its violation of the Monroe Doctrine in Mexico. Still, Lincoln's policy had been to avoid a foreign war while insisting that European nations not take advantage of America's preoccupation with its domestic war or permit the use of neighboring countries for infringements on its sovereignty. The Canadian border crisis during the winter of 1864–1865 had tested Lincoln's resolve to avoid an armed conflict with Great Britain and had led him to assume a greater role in foreign affairs than before.

* * *

In contrast to his late-war involvement in foreign affairs, Lincoln demonstrated little interest in mounting Indian troubles on the Great Plains. (In troublesome Utah, he pursued a "let alone" policy toward

Brigham Young and the Mormons.)[35] By 1864–1865 the continued penetration of Indian lands and serious abuses by white interlopers, military forces, and government agents had led to Indian uprisings in the West, especially in the central and southern Plains. Lincoln, with a civil war to fight and a need to keep European powers at bay, had delegated authority over Indian affairs to the War and Interior departments and, unfortunately, to local white citizens who wanted the "savages" either expelled from the area or exterminated. The president did not, in any sustained way, consider the plight of the Great Plains Indians or white encroachment on Indian lands in the West.[36]

Only once during his presidency did Lincoln take an active hand in Indian affairs. After a widespread Sioux uprising in Minnesota in 1862, as president, he was required by law to approve the death sentences of 303 Indians found guilty of "horrible outrages" by a military commission. Carefully considering each case, he pared down the list of condemned men to 39. He later ordered the release of some of the surviving prisoners after missionaries made an appeal on their behalf. In one case, in late 1864, the local military commander ignored a presidential order for the release of Big Eagle, one of the Sioux prisoners. Lincoln, informed that his directive had been disregarded, sent a sharp message to the general in command, demanding the prisoner's immediate release. This time the officer complied. The Big Eagle case was symptomatic of the difficulty the president and Washington officials had in managing affairs in the distant West, where anti-Indian prejudice among white settlers was endemic and resistance to eastern interference was strong. Most Indians, unlike Big Eagle, did not have missionary benefactors to call the president's attention to their plight.[37]

Lincoln's attitude toward the Great Plains Indians reflected many of the views of his contemporaries, especially in the Old Northwest (Midwest). He shared the prevailing view that the Indians were born into a savage state and were by nature nomadic hunters. Lincoln, however, was more sympathetic to their condition than most political leaders of his day. He believed that Native Americans could and should be civilized into Anglo-American ways. This attitude became clear in a White House meeting on March 27, 1863, with a group of western Indian chiefs. Talking down to them in an idiom used by many whites toward the Indians, Lincoln lectured the chiefs on "the great difference between [the] pale-faced people and their red brethren." Whites, he explained, "depend upon the products of the earth rather than wild game for a subsistence." "This is the chief reason of the difference," he went on; "but there is another." "Although we are now engaged in a great war between one another, we are not, as a race, so much disposed to fight and kill one another as our red brethren"—an assertion that later generations, and perhaps the Indian chiefs at the time, questioned. Reminding the chiefs that they had asked for his advice about the future, Lincoln declared: "I can see no way in which your race is to become as numerous and prosperous as the white race except by living as they do, by the cultivation of the earth." According to a press report, the chiefs applauded the president's remarks and went away in good spirits.[38]

Lincoln believed the Indians should be treated kindly and their trust not abused by whites, particularly by government agents, though he did not act forcibly to prevent mistreatment. He recognized the need to reform the federal management of Indian affairs, which had become an institutionalized structure of corruption and maladministration. In his annual message to Congress in December 1862, he referred to the Minnesota uprising and asked Congress to consider "whether our Indian system shall not be remodelled. Many wise and good men have impressed me with the belief that this can be profitably done."[39] The only action that Congress in the 1862–1863 session took on this issue was to authorize the negotiation of removal treaties with the Indians.

The president revealed in his next annual message, on December 8, 1863, that "stipulations for extinguishing the possessory rights of the Indians to large and valuable tracts of land" had been made. He "hoped that the effects of these treaties will result in the establishment of permanent friendly relations with such of these tribes as have been brought into frequent and bloody collision with our outlying settlements and emigrants." He also told Congress that "sound policy and our imperative duty to these wards of the government demand our anxious and constant attention to their material well-being, to their progress in the arts of civilization, and, above all, to that moral training which, under the blessing of Divine Providence, will confer upon them the elevated and satisfying influences, the hope and consolidation of the Christian faith." Prompted by a gloomy report on western affairs from Secretary of the Interior John P. Usher, Lincoln repeated his appeal for "remodelling our Indian system." He referred Congress to Usher's report and again expressed "the urgent need for immediate legislative action." Though Indian reform bills were introduced into the Senate and the House in 1864, they failed to pass. Congress, at Usher's suggestion, did provide for the reorganization of Indian lands in California, a plan that, Lincoln predicted in his last annual message on December 6, 1864, "will be attended with reasonable success."[40]

Lincoln could not avoid paying close attention to one aspect of western affairs—federal patronage in the territorial governments and in the Office of Indian Affairs. Squabbles over these federal positions became increasingly irksome as he approached his second term as president and many aspirants for office expected changes to be made.[41] The greatest pressure came from midwestern politicians in his party and old friends who wanted to replace William P. Dole as commissioner of Indian affairs. Though Dole had served competently and had attempted to protect the Indians, the position had long been considered a plum for office seekers who sought material gain for themselves and those whom they selected for Indian agencies in the West. Even Dr. Anson G. Henry, Lincoln's Springfield physician and friend, came to Washington in February to lobby for Dole's job. In the end, Lincoln wisely retained Dole as commissioner.[42]

As the troubles on the Plains multiplied late in the Civil War, Lincoln signaled, at least to one visitor, that he intended to take a more active role in Indian matters. Henry B. Whipple, the Protestant Episcopal bishop of Minnesota and a missionary among the Indians, spoke to him at this time about the mistreatment of the western Indians. Moved by Whipple's account, the president promised, according to the bishop, "if I live, this accursed system shall be reformed."[43]

* * *

A massacre of Indians in the Colorado territory in late 1864 led to a Senate investigation and a greater awareness among easterners about the deplorable situation in the West. After a series of violent white-Indian encounters, on November 29 a territorial force of volunteers under the command of the Indian-hater Colonel John M. Chivington attacked a large band of unsuspecting Cheyenne and Arapaho at Sand Creek in eastern Colorado. Though Black Kettle, the main chief, escaped, approximately 130 Indians, including women and children, died before the slaughter ended. Black Kettle had recently appeared at Fort Lyon and approved the U.S. army commander's terms for peace, an agreement that Coloradans refused to accept. After the massacre, Chivington and his men received a hero's welcome in Denver.[44]

Indian attacks on Colorado settlers followed the Sand Creek massacre and expanded the conflict into other areas of the Great Plains. Soon Federal troops—many fresh from fighting Confederates in the Missouri-Kansas district—moved against the Indians. News of the Sand Creek attack stunned members of Congress. One week after the incident and before its full meaning was known in Washington, Lincoln sent his annual message to Congress. In the message he did not mention the attack and only briefly commented on Indian affairs, reminding Congress of his earlier recommendation that "our Indian system [should] be remodelled . . . for the proper government of the Indians" in order to "render it secure for the advancing settler, and to provide for the welfare of the Indian."[45]

When confirmed reports reached the East of the brutal conduct of the Colorado troops, demands arose for a congressional investigation and for a review of the federal Indian policy. On January 9 Republican Senator James R. Doolittle, chair of the Committee on Indian Affairs and a Lincoln ally, announced that he had received reliable information from Colorado that should "make one's blood almost chill and freeze with horror." Senator Charles Sumner, whose public vision normally extended southward rather than westward, pronounced the Sand Creek attack "an exceptional crime; one of the most atrocious in the history of any country."[46] Senator James Harlan of Iowa also condemned the massacre and expressed grave concern that General James H. Carleton in New Mexico was planning an expedition against the Comanche. Harlan feared a general war in the area, and when it occurred, he declared, "we shall have to suffer the disgrace of the extermination of thousands of these comparatively inoffensive and unarmed people." On January 13 Doolittle introduced a resolution in the Senate to authorize a probe of the Sand Creek incident and of Indian affairs generally. The resolution passed after the two California senators, both Republicans, attempted to divert the debate from Chivington's action to the issue of "Indian barbarity" and the need to suppress the "savages." Friends of the resolution confidently predicted that the work of the Doolittle committee would "lead to a most thorough investigation of the Indians along the whole frontier" and "expose the plots of unprincipled adventurers in the Indian country for the promotion of their own selfish schemes."[47]

After a brief but fairly extensive investigation, the Doolittle committee made its report. It condemned Colonel Chivington for the Sand Creek massacre (but he never faced disciplinary action). Rather than recommending any radical changes in federal policy, the committee largely limited itself to explaining the causes of the problems on the Plains: "the aggressions of lawless white men" were to blame for most white and Indian conflict; the loss of tribal hunting grounds to miners, railroads, and settlers had contributed to the decline of the Indians. The committee did make two relatively important recommendations. It recommended that the Department of the Interior, despite the turmoil and violence in the West, should continue to control Indian affairs and without the military's interference. Interior officials, the committee opined, were more suited to educate the Indians and help them adjust to civilized life on the reservations. It also recommended that independent boards of inspection should be created to investigate abuses by Indian agency officials. Still, Senator Doolittle, who wrote the report, doubted that anything could be done to correct "the evils growing out of the nature of the case itself, which can never be remedied until the Indian race is civilized or shall entirely disappear." He predicted the "ultimate disappearance of nearly all [Indians] upon the continent." Only one of the committee's recommendations was realized: four years after its report the Board of Indian Commissioners, or inspectors, was created, and it functioned until 1934.[48]

On March 2, one day before the end of the congressional session, Republican Senator James Harlan, appalled by the injustices to Native Americans, introduced a plan for the formation of a large Indian territory in the Southwest. This plan, if approved, would break up small reservations, consolidate them into one, and grant the Indians control of their own affairs as long as their actions did not conflict with the United States Constitution. It was designed to protect tribal customs, regulations, and rights. Harlan, who a week later would be appointed by Lincoln as secretary of the interior to take effect in May, was influenced by the views of the commissioner of Indian affairs, William P. Dole. Since 1863, Dole had advocated a consolidation policy for the western Indians to protect them from white encroachments and conflict.[49] It is reasonable to assume that Dole and Harlan had the support of the president for such a significant reorganization of Indian lands and governance. Lincoln, however, made no public comment regarding the plan, and Congress, with Southern reconstruction issues diverting its attention, let Harlan's proposal die.

Lincoln had also stayed on the sidelines when Congress investigated the Sand Creek massacre and confronted the immediate abuses in the Indian system. In a paternalistic way, he sympathized with the Indians, as he had revealed earlier to Bishop Whipple, and he must have been outraged by the behavior of Chivington and his men. But he stopped short of intervening to correct the abuses under the federal administration of the western territories. Though a person of great sensitivity, Lincoln failed to perceive the full extent of the mistreatment and suffering of the Indians. The remoteness of the Great Plains from Washington and the brief, filtered anti-Indian reports he received contributed to his failure to act on the problem. Lincoln, though more enlightened regarding race and ethnic difference than most of his contemporaries, was a product of his time who believed that the Indians could not be elevated to the status of whites until they had been subdued and civilized in Anglo-American ways. While the Civil War raged, his focus and energy were on suppressing the Southern rebellion and destroying slavery. The management of Indians and public lands could be delegated to the Interior and War departments, unless the Constitution or federal law directly required presidential action as in the case of the Minnesota Sioux who were sentenced to be hanged for their uprising in 1862.

What Lincoln said privately to Doolittle, Harlan, and others regarding their efforts in early 1865 on behalf of changes in Indian policies is unknown. The only documented instance at this time of his involvement in the western problem was a proclamation, issued on March 17, directing that "persons dwelling in conterminous foreign territory" adjacent to the United States who were supplying arms to hostile Indians "to prosecute their savage warfare upon the exposed and sparse settlements of the frontier . . . shall be arrested and tried by Court Martial at the nearest post, and, if convicted, shall receive the punishment due to their deserts."[50] Had he lived, after the Civil War ended Lincoln might have devoted more time to Indian affairs, recognized the seriousness of the problem, and, in his compassionate way, acted to implement the Doolittle report and Harlan's reorganization plan. However, it is problematical whether Lincoln—or any nineteenth-century president—could have significantly reversed the white penetration of tribal lands, the corruption in western administration, and the abuses against unoffending Native Americans.

★ ★ ★

Closer to Washington, by the winter of 1864–1865 a storm was brewing over the increasingly lucrative trade being conducted with the rebels as the Union armies and gunboats penetrated farther into the South. This trade was helping to sustain Confederate armies, corrupting Federal officers, and bringing a wave of opportunistic Northern traffickers into the region.

Early in the war Lincoln, as authorized by an act of Congress, issued a proclamation prohibiting "all commercial intercourse" with rebel states. However, he exempted Southern states or any part of a state that "may maintain a loyal adhesion to the Union and the Constitution, or may from time to time [be] occupied and controlled by forces of the United States." An even more important concession was the provision authorizing the Treasury Department to issue special licenses to loyal citizens seeking to engage in the Southern trade.[51] The reasoning behind the concessions was to encourage Southern Unionism, bring out valuable cotton to aid Northern textile production for the war effort, and increase government revenues. By 1864 the trade concessions had become inviting loopholes for enterprising traders and speculators in Southern products, especially cotton. With the average price of cotton rising above sixty cents a pound (it had been eleven cents in 1860), many profit-minded Northerners, often with political influence, obtained licenses to buy Southern cotton in exchange for gold, greenbacks, salt, shoes, bacon, and other products. Supposedly the goods would not be used to supply the rebel armies.

In increasing numbers, military men in the South sought to profit from the trade. Some Federal army officers, having seen the "white gold" along the riverbanks while campaigning, resigned their commissions and became cotton entrepreneurs. A friend complained to Illinois Senator Lyman Trumbull in 1864 that he had traveled on the Arkansas River with a former brigadier general, two former colonels, and a former major, all of whom had "left the service in the full vigor of health to speculate in cotton." They "labor under the monomania known as 'Cotton on the Brain'—an infectious disease, supposed to be contagious and incurable north of Mason & Dixon's Line." General Nathaniel P. Banks reported from New Orleans that "the profits of an illicit commercial intercourse are so gigantic that it is almost impossible to prevent" military officers from engaging in it. The government's policy had been, as Secretary of the Treasury Salmon P. Chase expressed it, "to let commerce follow the flag." However, as the historian James M. McPherson has written, "the problem was that trade had a tendency to get ahead of the flag."[52]

Military commanders like Grant and Sherman vigorously opposed any commercial traffic with the rebels while the war lasted. Grant charged that "speculators who have trade permits" were "universally a worse class of people with an army than the worst rebels . . . I have always believed that entire non-intercourse with 'people in rebellion' would prove the most speedy way to bring about a permanent peace." Grant and other generals attempted to stop the trade within their commands, only to find themselves in a position not unlike that faced by King Canute in trying to sweep back the sea. They did have allies in Secretary of War Stanton and Secretary of the Navy Welles, but not Lincoln. In cabinet meetings Stanton and Welles protested, with little effect, the practice of "fighting and trading at the same time with the Rebels."[53]

Lincoln at first took a neutral stand on the Southern trade. However, as the war progressed, manufacturers in need of cotton to keep their spindles running and to meet lucrative military contracts repeatedly reminded him of the value of cotton to the Union cause. Edward Atkinson, a prominent Massachusetts textile entrepreneur, proved especially active in lobbying the president and others in Washington. Lincoln told his cabinet on July 5, 1864, that he had met with Atkinson and had been impressed by the New Englander's "striking facts" on the issue.[54]

Influential newspapers in the Northeast, without regard to political affiliation, joined Atkinson in pressuring Lincoln to encourage the trade. The *New York Commercial Advertiser* argued that Southerners "want money and the necessaries and comforts of life. Take their cotton and give them greenbacks, and they will speedily feel the force of the old tie, and be convinced that the Union, as of old, brought with it the richest blessings of individual and general prosperity." The *Washington Chronicle*, which Lincoln usually read, declared that, in addition to promoting loyalty in the South, a stream of cotton flowing north would bolster the gold standard, increase revenue to pay off the war debt without raising taxes, and improve American credit abroad. The *Boston Advertiser* made a similar argument, indicating that "we are glad that the plan for opening a free trade in cotton with the insurgent States attracts increasing attention, and commends itself to the minds of men of the most diverse views." The *New York Herald* exclaimed: "Our mills need the cotton. Every bale of it which arrives here reduces the price of gold, and so sustains the credit of the government and mitigates the distress caused by a depreciated currency." Still, both the Democratic *New York World* and the Republican *New York Times,* which supported the trade, warned against Northern cotton traders plundering the Southern people and thereby creating a "lasting and bitter animosity toward their oppressors."[55]

At the same time, Lincoln came under strong pressure, especially from his military commanders, to end trade with the South. Reports of the permit system's pernicious effects on the war began to reach him by mid-1864. General Daniel E. Sickles, still recovering from the loss of a leg at Gettysburg, in the late spring had visited the Mississippi Valley at Lincoln's request to investigate general conditions in the occupied region. Sickles wrote to Lincoln that he found illicit trade with the rebels everywhere. At Memphis, "goods to the amount of half a million a week went through our lines, sold for currency or exchanged for cotton. Boats loaded with supplies have had almost unrestricted opportunities for trade on the Mississippi, and some of its navigable tributaries, stopping every where along the river, and dealing with anybody."[56]

General Cadwallader C. Washburn, commanding in West Tennessee, bombarded his brother Elihu Washburne, an Illinois congressman, with letters in 1864 about the situation in Memphis. (The brothers spelled their last name differently.) "The amount of contraband trade that has been carried on through this point is enormous," the general wrote to his brother, who soon would chair the congressional committee investigating the illicit traffic. "I suppose that there is hardly any article that the rebels need that they could not get here." In May 1864 Washburn predicted that trade behind rebel lines would soon reach $36 million a year. He concluded that "for every dollar's benefit that the treasury will derive from allowing the trade, we shall have to pay thousands of dollars additional expense in crushing the rebellion." He expected his brother to talk to the secretary of the treasury and probably the president about the pernicious impact the commerce along the Mississippi was having on the Union cause.[57]

General Banks, commanding in the lower Mississippi Valley, reported to Secretary of War Stanton in early 1864 that the rebel army was obtaining not only clothing but also equipment and arms through the illicit trade. General Edward R. S. Canby, Banks's successor, in December 1864 told his superiors in Washington, probably with some exaggeration, that "the rebel armies east and west of the Mississippi river have been supported during the last twelve months by the unlawful trade carried on upon that river." Canby mentioned a contract by an English firm for the purchase of 200,000 bales of cotton in Confederate Mobile in exchange for supplies and gold and its shipment through New Orleans, which, according to the contractors, promised a profit of $10 million.[58] He predicted that if the trade with the enemy continued it would have the effect of adding 50,000 men to the rebel army in his district. If Washburn, Banks, and Canby were correct, the fall in July 1863 of Vicksburg and Port Hudson, the last important rebel outposts on the Mississippi, did not do the irreparable damage to the Confederate cause that historians have assumed.[59] The trade in cotton, by bringing needed products into the region, partly compensated the Confederates for the Federal seizure of the river and its tributaries.

Reports reached Lincoln in 1864 from the Virginia theater that Norfolk had become a convenient base for Northern speculators and unpatriotic entrepreneurs engaged in the "nefarious traffic" through the lines. Benjamin F. Butler, commanding the Department of (eastern) Virginia and North Carolina, permitted his favorites and others to bring out cotton, tobacco, naval stores, and other Southern products in exchange for food and supplies, much of which by late 1864 had found its way to Lee's army. Butler, who preferred to believe that Northern provisions went only to needy nonbelligerents, revealed his connivance in the North Carolina trade when he chastised a friend for taking out more than his share of cotton and tobacco. Butler wrote to C. B. Dibble, a "merchant prince" of New York, that the $400,000 he had made "would satisfy a reasonable man's avarice; and as the trade is a special and limited one in North Carolina, you at least had had your share in that trade, and might give way to a less fortunate man."[60]

General George H. Gordon, who replaced Butler in January 1865, was appalled by the extent of the trade and its importance in sustaining the rebel forces in Virginia and North Carolina. He concluded that it did little to aid the local inhabitants for whose benefit it had ostensibly been begun. Gordon reported that upon assuming command he had immediately ordered a halt to the trade, but not before "Lee's army had been largely supplied with food and munitions of war." Despite his efforts, Gordon added, some of the "rascals" continued to bring out cotton, bragging that "they had the President's ear" and did not have to obey military commanders.[61]

* * *

Though Northern cotton traffickers never had Lincoln's permission to ignore military orders or trade regulations, by the late stages of the war the president had become an important convert to the policy of providing commercial privileges in the South. At a cabinet meeting on September 9, 1864, he rejected Secretary of the Treasury William P. Fessenden's plan to authorize the trade for only a select group of individuals. Supported by other members of the cabinet—but not Welles and Stanton, who wanted the trade prohibited—Lincoln directed that Treasury Department licenses should be available for all loyal applicants. He explained that if permits were restricted to a few enterprising persons, others would violate the policy. Wholesale plunder by Federal soldiers, Lincoln told his cabinet, would occur in the large no-man's-land between the armies where an abundance of cotton was offered for sale by nonbelligerent owners.[62] His decision, however, encouraged more enterprising Northerners and reputed Southern Unionists to apply for trade permits. Once they had these documents, the military could not normally interfere with their cotton operations.

The *New York Herald* reported on January 14, 1865, that "the President and the Financial Department of the government have been doing all that they can to encourage and stimulate the bringing out of cotton, believing that its result will not only be beneficial in increasing the revenue of the government, but also in reducing the price of gold." Lincoln, true to his traditional Whig view that economic well-being was a powerful political motivation, thought that turning the cotton into U.S. currency would encourage Southern planters to withdraw their support from the rebellion. The *Herald* indicated that instructions had been sent to Treasury Department agents "to see that all cotton that is possible got out." At the same time, this newspaper revealed that "the president is getting his back up" against the military commanders who oppose his liberal trade policy.[63]

Lincoln expected the U.S. Treasury to receive one-fourth of the cotton proceeds. However, by the winter of 1864–1865 Treasury regulations were more often honored in the breach than in practice, including the collection of the government's share. Treasury agents themselves were implicated in the profiteering. When General Canby in December 1864 protested against the illicit commerce in cotton, the president wrote him that the trade had become "immensely important to us to get the cotton away from [the rebels]." Otherwise, he said, the Confederates, with the price six times as high as before the war, would sell cotton abroad, despite the blockade, in exchange for supplies. "Better give him guns for it, than let him, as now, get both guns and ammunition for it." This specious reasoning aside, the president was on sounder ground when he told the general, "our finances are greatly involved in the matter": "The way cotton goes now carries so much gold out of the country as to leave us paper currency only, and that so far depreciated, as that for every hard dollar's worth of supplies we obtain, we contract to pay two and a half hard dollars hereafter. This is much to be regretted." He concluded: "And if pecuniary greed can be made to aid us in such effort, let us be thankful that so much good can be got out of pecuniary greed." He reassured Canby, however, that where the cotton trade affected military operations the army commander "must be judge and master."[64]

In addition to his general encouragement of the trade, Lincoln proved generous in giving permits to individuals to go south and contract for cotton and other products. His Illinois friends, including the Copperhead James W. Singleton, who combined his peace mission to Richmond in early 1865 with commercial transactions, especially found the president willing to provide trading permits. Orville H. Browning, a former senator and Lincoln's longtime friend, served as the intermediary with the president and Treasury officials for Singleton and a number of other aspiring traffickers. Leonard Swett, another old Lincoln political associate, received three permits to bring out a total of 150,000 bales of cotton from the South. The value was more than $20 million, which, even after he paid his agents and the Treasury Department took its 25 percent—if indeed it received the money—promised to provide the Illinois politician-entrepreneur an enormous profit.[65]

Robert Lamon, brother of Lincoln's friend Ward Hill Lamon, was granted three permits, totaling 50,000 bales. James H. Patterson of Chicago wrote to Ward Hill Lamon, who was also U.S. marshal for the District of Columbia, that a business associate, after receiving a permit from Lincoln, had told him "that such permits are obtained by proper influences." Patterson, a partner of Robert Lamon, wanted the marshal to secure a permit in Robert's name. He declared: "I can make more money than a Jackass can pack, but it must be through your instrumentality." Ward Hill Lamon became part of the scheme and interceded with the president for his brother and Patterson—as well as for others. Indeed, he soon sought his own permit as he explained to Lincoln, "to effect . . . an exchange of commodities, provisions and dry goods for cotton" in the South. In his request, the marshal, with his own interest in mind, reminded the president of his administration's "unceasing attention . . . to the cotton question." It "proves that your Government is determined to deprive the Confederacy of its greatest element of material strength, and at the same time, to make, if possible, cotton the basis of this government's currency: for cotton is gold."[66]

The outgoing vice president, Hannibal Hamlin, also sought to engage in the trade. He asked Lincoln, "as a favor," for a permit for one Fergus Peniston to transport through the lines 23,640 bales of cotton and 17,200 barrels of naval stores in southern Mississippi and Louisiana. Hamlin obviously expected to share in the proceeds of the enterprise. The president obliged and admonished "all officers of the army or navy of the United States & civil officers" to extend to Peniston "all facilities that may be required to carry out the design of this permit which is the introduction of cotton and naval stores within the Military lines of the United States."[67]

Prominent Southern Unionists requested cotton permits for themselves or their friends. They usually argued from the standpoint of restoring loyalty in the South and, like Lamon, the financial boost that the trade would give to the nation. Michael Hahn, soon to be elected Union governor of Louisiana, wrote to Lincoln in January 1864 that "the recent arrival of a few thousand bales of cotton" in New Orleans "from Natchez produced such a sensation as to cause a large number of persons to take the oath of allegiance in order to resume their business." In April 1864 the Unionist Cuthbert Bullitt, U.S. marshal of eastern Louisiana, wrote to the president: "Commerce is still King. You have it in your power to reduce the price of gold, pacify the clamor for cotton from abroad, make friends for yourself & our country, & put into the exchequer from this department some 30 to 40 millions [of] dollars." Impressed by such arguments, Lincoln in August issued a cotton permit to the military governor of Texas, Andrew Jackson Hamilton, or "any person authorized in writing by him." The president specifically granted Hamilton and associates the authority to ship cotton through the blockade from Galveston or Sabine Pass and deliver it to the Treasury official at New Orleans, where the government's share would be deducted before it was sold. Lincoln told General Canby and Admiral David G. Farragut, Federal commanders in the area, that "the passage of such person, vessels and cargoes shall not be molested or hindered."[68]

Several weeks later Farragut sent Secretary of the Navy Welles a copy of the Hamilton permit and complained that it constituted a serious violation of the blockade. Welles, furious, confronted Lincoln with the order. "The President," Welles wrote in his diary, "seemed embarrassed but said he believed it was all right." Welles asked, "How right?" Lincoln answered by uncharacteristically casting blame elsewhere: "It was one of Seward's arrangements, that he guessed would come out all right." He made no further explanation. Since Welles had long viewed Seward as a schemer, he accepted this ex-

planation. "It is another specimen of the maladministration and improper interference of the Secretary of State," he concluded. "There
are times when I can hardly persuade myself that the President's natural sagacity has been so duped."[69] Though Seward supported the policy of bringing out Southern cotton, Lincoln had not been forthright
in blaming him for the Hamilton permit.

Welles, still seething, discussed Hamilton's permit with Seward,
who explained that it "was one by which certain important persons in
the Rebel cause were to be converted." Seward told the navy secretary
that the order to Canby and Farragut had not been his idea. Only "by
special request of the President" had he drawn it up, and he himself
did not have much faith that it would amount to anything. "The President," Seward indicated, "believed there would be results." Pressure
from Welles and to a lesser extent Farragut finally caused Lincoln to
revoke the permit.[70]

Lincoln, however, did not abandon his policy of using cotton to
encourage loyalty in the rebel states. In late 1864, after talking to
the former Confederate congressman and peace advocate Augustus
R. Wright, he issued a pass for Wright to return to North Georgia
and arrange for the shipment of five hundred bales of cotton. On his
part, Wright promised to work for the restoration of Georgia to the
Union.[71]

Two days before his assassination, Lincoln met with William C.
Bibb, an Alabama planter and a member of a prominent Southern
political family. The omnipresent Orville H. Browning accompanied
Bibb to the White House. Bibb had a letter of introduction from Navy
Lieutenant John L. Worden, whom the planter had befriended after
his capture by Confederates in 1861. Bibb's mission in the North was
both commercial and political. He wanted to ask Lincoln about his
views on reconstruction, perhaps with the hope that the president
would appoint him to a postwar office in the South. He also needed a
pass to return south after transacting cotton and plantation business
in Baltimore and New York. In a postwar account Bibb strongly suggested that he had sought a federal contract to collect Confederate
cotton in Alabama and, for a fee, turn it over to the Treasury official
in his district. He ultimately secured a contract, but later claimed, "I
did not collect a single bale."[72]

Bibb's talk with Lincoln focused on the president's reconstruction speech delivered at the White House the night before. According to Bibb, the president indicated that he would continue his liberal reconstruction policy and would soon issue a general amnesty proclamation. At the end of the conversation, Lincoln wrote a pass allowing Bibb to return to the South. At this point the Alabamian admitted that he had not taken the oath of allegiance and would not do so until the surrender of all Confederate armies. As Bibb remembered, Lincoln momentarily cast his eyes downward and a shadow passed over his face. Then he looked at his visitor and said: "I respect your scruples. Probably under the same surroundings I should have entertained them myself."[73]

Another remarkable meeting of a Southerner with Lincoln occurred on March 18. Thomas C. Teasdale, a Baptist minister and agent of the Mississippi State Orphans Home, traveled to Washington to seek presidential approval for the purchase of cotton in Mississippi (with Confederate money) and its shipment through the lines to New York. Teasdale planned to sell the cotton and use the proceeds to buy supplies for the orphanage. He carried with him a petition from the orphanage board describing its poverty and appealing for assistance. Teasdale, a native of New Jersey who had held pastorates in several Northern cities, including Lincoln's home town, had secured Jefferson Davis's endorsement of the mission before making a hazardous trip through the lines to reach Washington.

Lincoln recognized the minister and greeted him warmly. Teasdale explained the purpose of his visit and handed the president the board's petition. According to Teasdale's account, apparently written soon after the meeting, Lincoln read the entire document, and "then, turning it over, he read on the back of it the cordial endorsement placed upon it by President Davis." Perhaps piqued at seeing Davis's endorsement, Lincoln said, "You ask me to give you relief in a case of distress, just as we have been striving to produce it." Then he smiled and added, "We want to bring you rebels into such straits, that you will be willing to give up this wicked rebellion." Teasdale, who thought Lincoln was not serious, responded, "It is the hapless little ones that are involved in this suffering, who, of course, had nothing to do in bringing about the present unhappy conflict between the sections." They deserved the "sympathy and commiseration" of all government leaders. The president immediately softened his tone and declared, "That is true; and I must do something for you."[74]

Lincoln wrote a note to General Canby authorizing, but not ordering, him "to give Rev. Mr. Teasdale such facilities in the within matters as he, in his discretion, may see fit." Then he added his endorsement to the back of the orphanage board's petition, directly under that of Jefferson Davis. The endorsement read: "Refd to the Sec'y. of Treasury, and the Sec'y of War for conference with Rev. Dr. Teasdale, in connection with the praiseworthy effort in which he is engaged." Lincoln also gave Teasdale a pass through the lines "with convenient baggage." When he returned to Mississippi, Teasdale completed the arrangement for shipping the cotton to New York. But the end of the war rendered the Confederate currency worthless and the scheme collapsed, leaving the state orphanage in a desperate condition.[75]

* * *

Meanwhile, by early 1865, the disturbing revelations of General Canby and other military commanders regarding the "nefarious traffic" with the enemy caused the Northern press to demand an investigation. The *Boston Commonwealth,* a Radical Republican newspaper that had earlier given tepid support to the policy of bringing out the cotton, declared that the reports from the South, "taken in connection with the favoritism of this system of permits, reveal a very shameful state of things." This newspaper, which was ever vigilant to find fault with the Lincoln administration, charged that the evil in the system was immense; in addition to favoritism, it included "corruption, bribery, aid and comfort to the enemy, and enhanced prices to honest and loyal citizens." The *Commonwealth* demanded: "In the name of patriotism, of justice, of common decency, we call upon Congress to stop it."[76]

In January the House of Representatives directed its Committee on Commerce to "inquire into all the facts and circumstances connected with the trade with the rebellious States since the breaking out of the rebellion." The Senate soon agreed to a House request for the formation of a joint committee on the matter, chaired by Representative Elihu B. Washburne of Illinois. On March 1, after gathering extensive documents and testimony, the committee made its report. It found that the trade with the rebel states, "apparently under the sanction of law, has been of no real benefit to our government; but, on the other hand, has inflicted very great injury upon the public service" and corrupted and demoralized the army and the navy. The trade "has induced a spirit of speculation and plunder among the people . . . and has fed that greed of gain which must wound the public morals." It had also "led to the prolongation of the war, and cost the country thousands of lives and millions upon millions of treasure." A great deal of the trade "has been carried on within the rebel lines with rebel agents, and for the use of rebel armies. The amount of supplies necessary for the support of rebel armies which, under the cover of this trade, has been sent through the rebel lines at New Orleans, Memphis, Norfolk, and other places, almost surpasses belief."[77]

The Washburne committee proposed that Congress repeal an earlier law authorizing the secretary of the treasury, with the approval of the president, to appoint government agents to purchase products in the insurrectionary states. The intent of the repeal bill was to shut down the Southern trade until after the end of the war and the restoration of the states to the Union. On March 3, the last full day of the congressional session, the measure, which was full of important loopholes, passed both houses of Congress, with only three voting against it in the Senate and none in the House. Lincoln, however, stunned Washburne and others when, without an official explanation, he pocket vetoed the bill. He believed that the measure, if enacted, would unconstitutionally invalidate commercial contracts that had been made and would undermine the Treasury Department's efforts to secure the government's share of Southern cotton and other products. John M. Forbes, a New England merchant and lobbyist for textile interests who claimed that he wanted to end the favoritism in the permit system, wrote to a friend: "You can hardly imagine my disgust . . . that old Abe had pocketed our Grand bill—I could have wrung his long neck. I suppose the cotton speculators around him were too many for him."[78] Though Lincoln (and his Treasury agents) was willing to grant trade permits in a relatively indiscriminate fashion, Forbes exaggerated the influence of cotton entrepreneurs on his policy. Lincoln believed that the public interest would be better served if the Southern trade remained open to all who legitimately obtained permits.

On March 8 General Grant, reinforced in his opposition to the traffic by the Washburne committee's report of the extent of the trade through Norfolk, asked Secretary of War Stanton for permission to prohibit all trade and to annul all permits in the Southern interior. Stanton referred the request to Lincoln, who immediately authorized the general to suspend Treasury permits southeast of the Alleghenies. Grant then drafted an order for the suspension of "Treasury Trade permits" in that area and submitted it to Stanton for approval. The secretary of war, without consulting Lincoln, told Grant that the order was too limited. "So as to meet the whole mischief," Stanton said, it should "include all 'Trade permits' by whomsoever granted, so as to cover every species of trade license including unauthorized licenses by Military commanders as well as the Treasury permits and also to prevent abuses under the President's permit." The order that went out on March 11 or 12 incorporated Stanton's change, suspending all trade permits, "by whomsoever granted," in Virginia (excluding two small counties on the Eastern Shore), North Carolina, South Carolina, and coastal Georgia. Grant directed the military to seize all products under contract and hold them for the benefit of the government. The only exception to the trade prohibition would be to meet "the wants of those living within the lines of actual military occupation"—and only in cases of absolute necessity. Stanton and Grant had managed to circumvent Lincoln's earlier veto of the Washburne bill and order the closure of the trade in the South Atlantic region.[79]

One month earlier Grant had given "wide discretion" to General Canby to restrict trade in the lower Mississippi Valley. He had informed his subordinate that both Lincoln and Stanton supported him in this action.[80] Canby attempted to stop the traffic in the remaining weeks of the war, but the illicit trade in his department was too widespread and too lucrative for his effort to succeed.

Grant's prohibition of the trade in the South Atlantic created consternation among cotton traffickers. "Cotton speculators" descended upon the War Department and the White House seeking the administration's intervention. Stanton brusquely sent them away from his office. Lincoln told them that he had long favored the effort to get out the cotton, but that General Grant was responsible for the conduct of the war, and "I shall not, therefore, interfere with the order under any circumstances." Frustrated by the problems inherent in the trade and no longer concerned about its impact as the war ended, Lincoln in the cabinet meeting on the last day of his life asked the secretaries of the treasury, war, and the navy to develop a trade policy, and he promised to approve it.[81]

The issue of the Southern trade soon became moot. With the ending of the war and the opening of commerce throughout the former Confederate states, controversy over reconstruction and the place of blacks in the South took center stage in Washington. The Washburne committee, which in March had announced that it would continue its work, never revived the investigation into the illicit trade. After the war, the report of a collateral investigation by General George H. Gordon at Norfolk documenting the extent of the traffic through the lines was filed away lest it reflect unfavorably on the martyred president. Even die-hard Radical adversaries of Lincoln like Senator Benjamin F. Wade and Representative George W. Julian, who believed that the president had violated the law in granting trade permits and refusing to provide Congress with the relevant documents, muted their criticism after his death.[82]

Cotton continued in great demand after the war. Many Northerners, assisted by Southerners who knew where the valuable bales were hidden, moved into the interior, seizing the cotton on the grounds that it had belonged to the Confederate government and thus could now be taken. Confederates had claimed at the beginning of the war that "cotton was king" and would secure European support for their cause. They had discovered that it was a false monarch. However, by the end of the war cotton had achieved regal importance for Northerners and for others seeking financial gain in the defeated South; it would reign for at least a year after the conflict.

Lincoln's trade policy may have contributed to Northern financial stability and influenced some Southerners like Augustus R. Wright and William C. Bibb, who possessed cotton, to renew their allegiance to the Union. But the abuses and corruption associated with the trade, including his granting of permits to Illinois associates, contributed to the decline of values that he held dear—honesty, respect for the law, patriotism, and fairness. When it became clear in 1864 that the commerce had become a lucrative operation for dishonest and unpatriotic entrepreneurs and was helping to keep the rebellion alive, Lincoln, at the behest of his commanders, should have acted vigorously to end the trade. He did not. The erosion of moral standards and ideals in government and business as reflected in the loose and illicit wartime trade would become increasingly apparent during the postwar period. Some blame for this condition of affairs should attach to Lincoln for his poor judgment in encouraging the trade through the lines.

* * *

On issues relating to Southern trade and Western affairs, Lincoln did not demonstrate the kind of close attention and able leadership that he gave to winning the war, ending slavery, and restoring the South to the Union. His involvement in issues beyond the battlefield, including the Canadian border crisis, was more reactive than deliberate and thoughtful. Although perhaps understandable, Lincoln's fixation on the war in the South and emancipation caused him to neglect his other important responsibilities as president. On these matters, he could have done better.

CHAPTER 7

AT THE FRONT

On March 20, 1865, the bone-tired president received a message from General Grant inviting him to visit his headquarters at City Point, Virginia. Grant, a protégé of the influential Republican congressman Elihu Washburne, recognized the need to cultivate the favor of prominent political leaders, and none was more prominent than Lincoln. Lincoln had first visited Grant's headquarters in June 1864, at a difficult time when the Federal forces had suffered tremendous casualties and the offensive against Lee's army had stalled. The relationship between the two men had blossomed since then, yet Grant brushed off his wife's suggestion that he invite the president to City Point with the comment, "If President Lincoln wishes to come down, he will not wait to be asked." But when Robert Todd Lincoln, a captain on Grant's staff, mentioned that his parents might come "if they were sure they would not be intruding," Grant put aside some uneasiness about presidential interference in his impending military operations and invited Lincoln to visit "for a day or two." When the invitation arrived, Lincoln wrote to Grant that he had been thinking of going to Virginia "after the next rain." As it turned out, instead of staying for only a day or two, he remained with the army for more than two weeks.[1]

On March 23 President Lincoln and a small party, including Mary and Tad, left Washington on the *River Queen,* a sidewheeler operated by a civilian crew. The navy had originally assigned the gunboat *Bat,* commanded by Captain John S. Barnes, to transport only the president to City Point. When Lincoln met with Barnes to plan the trip, he told the captain that the Spartan accommodations aboard the *Bat* were sufficient for him. But Mary announced that she and Tad wanted to go, necessitating the switch from the *Bat* to the more spacious and comfortable *River Queen.* The navy, however, fearing a Confederate attack on the *River Queen* similar to the one that had destroyed her sister boat, the *Greyhound,* assigned the *Bat* to escort the president's vessel to City Point. The two-day trip, which was uneventful, carried the party down the Potomac, into the Chesapeake, to Fort Monroe, and finally up the James River to Grant's headquarters.[2]

Lincoln's departure from Washington produced a wave of speculation in the North. The *Chicago Tribune* told its readers that the president "has been driven from the capital, . . . to escape the pertinacious crowds of irrepressible office-seekers and pelt-hunters who, fierce as hungry wolves, have hung upon his steps, dogged him in his private apartments, and given him no peace, until he has finally fled to save his life." The *New York Herald* reported that Lincoln had gone to City Point not only to escape office seekers but to renew peace negotiations with rebel leaders. The *New York Tribune* agreed and declared that the president's purpose was to bring peace on the basis of reunion and emancipation. The *Tribune* surmised that if no understanding with "the Rebel Chief" could be reached on these points, Lincoln would appeal "to the good sense and right feeling of the Southern people" to end the bloodshed.[3]

Secretary of the Navy Gideon Welles provided a more accurate assessment of Lincoln's reasons for visiting Grant. He wrote in his diary: "The President has gone to the front, partly to get rid of the throng that is pressing upon him, though there are speculations of a different character . . . No doubt he is much worn down; besides he wishes the War terminated, and, to this end, that severe terms not be exacted of the Rebels" by the military commanders.[4] Lincoln wanted to impress upon Grant, in person, his desire to end the war with as little additional fighting as possible and with liberal surrender terms for the rebels. These terms were simple: rebel soldiers must lay down their arms, promise not to fight again, go home, and renew their peaceful pursuits. Already Lincoln had told Grant that he should not negotiate a political or reconstruction settlement with General Lee or any Confederate authorities. The president remained the master on such issues. In visiting the army at this critical time, Lincoln, whose popularity with the troops had grown during the war, also hoped that his presence would lift the morale of the men and inspire them as they launched the final offensive against Lee's army.

* * *

The president and his party arrived at City Point during the evening of March 24. Grant, his wife, Julia, and Robert Lincoln greeted them at the docks and went aboard the *River Queen* for a brief social visit. Lincoln and Grant retired for a few minutes to a cabin, where the general reported on the latest military developments around Petersburg. The evening ended with the Lincolns accepting an invitation to review the troops the next day.[5]

Daylight on March 25 gave Lincoln his first opportunity to view

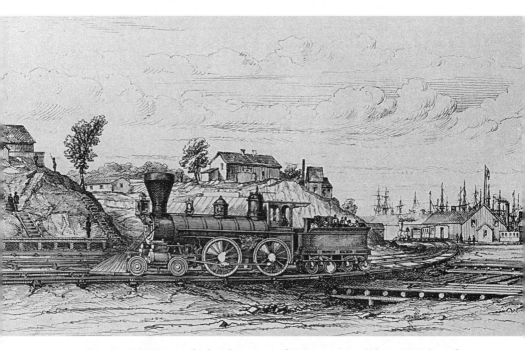

City Point, Virginia, the headquarters of U. S. Grant and the staging base for operations against Robert E. Lee's forces during the last months of the war. Lincoln visited the army at City Point from March 24 to April 8, 1865.

the massive military buildup at City Point, where the Appomattox River flowed into the James. Vessels of every description—steamers, gunboats, ironclads, transports, and hospital ships—greeted his gaze. Many were tied up at the wharves preparing to load or unload their cargoes. On the bluffs he could see Grant's rustic headquarters, surrounded by hundreds of tents and barracks with defensive works and lookout towers. By midmorning the area was a beehive of activity.

The president could also hear the booming of artillery fire a few miles to the southwest on the Petersburg battle line. Lee had chosen this day to launch a desperate counterattack to disrupt Grant's plan to encircle his forces. If the assault succeeded, Lee would dispatch part of his army to North Carolina to assist General Joseph E. Johnston in his attempt to stop General Sherman, after which both Confederate armies would return to Petersburg to face Grant. The weak link in the Federal line was Fort Stedman, eight miles southwest of City Point, and it was there that Lee focused his main attack. The assault, under the command of General John B. Gordon, a future Georgia governor and U.S. senator, began before dawn, and the rebels temporarily took the small earthen fort. By midmorning, though, the Federal forces commanded by General John G. Parke had retaken Fort Stedman, restored the Union line, and captured about sixteen hundred prisoners.[6]

Clearly, Grant's plan for the Lincolns to review the army had to be abandoned. Lincoln, however, despite the risk, asked if he could go to the vicinity of the fighting. At first Grant refused to expose the president to the danger of enemy fire, but when reports reached him later in the morning that the rebel attack had been repulsed and the battlefield secured, he arranged for an army train to take the Lincoln party and himself close to the front. On the trip Lincoln carried a map of the area, which he often took out of his pocket and examined. At Patrick's Station Lincoln and Grant mounted horses and rode on to General George G. Meade's headquarters, while Mrs. Lincoln, Mrs. Grant, and a military aide followed in an open horse-drawn ambulance. The horse Lincoln rode had been seized from Jefferson Davis's plantation by Grant and named "Jeff Davis." The horse was almost too small for the tall president, who quipped: "Well, he may be Jeff Davis and a little too small for me, but he is a good horse."[7]

At Meade's headquarters Lincoln saw from a distance the Confederate prisoners captured in the morning's action and commented on their sad condition. Colonel Theodore Lyman, a Harvard-educated member of Meade's staff, wrote to his wife a close-up description of Lincoln: "The President is, I think, the ugliest man I ever put my eyes on." Citing Lincoln's habit of telling "coarse stories," Lyman continued:

> There is also an expression of plebeian vulgarity in his face that is offensive . . . On the other hand, he has the look of sense and wonderful shrewdness, while the heavy eyelids give him a mark almost of genius. He strikes me, too, as a very honest and kindly man; and, with all his vulgarity, I see no trace of low passions in his face. On the whole, he is such a mixture of all sorts, as only America brings forth. He is as much like a highly intellectual and benevolent Satyr as anything I can think of.

The colonel's concluding comment was peculiar, revealing the respect for Lincoln's leadership that many of the New England elite had grudgingly given while still displeased with his "vulgar" habits. "I never wish to see him again," Lyman wrote, "but, as humanity runs, I am well content to have him at the head of affairs."[8]

In the afternoon Lincoln reviewed a division of troops that had marched up to support the Union line. As he "rode down the ranks, plucking off his hat gracefully by the hinder part of the brim," Lyman reported, "the troops cheered quite loudly." Hardly had he finished the review when nearby Federal artillery opened up on Confederate pickets, an action that the president observed. Lincoln, escorted by Grant and Meade, then visited other Federal positions along the line, including Fort Stedman, where the dead and wounded still lay on the ground. Everywhere he went, he was heartily cheered by the troops, who found it remarkable—and inspiring—that the president would risk visiting the battlefield.[9]

Later in the afternoon Lincoln returned to City Point on a train filled with wounded men. Deeply affected by what he had seen, he said he had witnessed enough of war and hoped that the fighting near Petersburg was the beginning of the end of the bloodshed.[10] At City Point, he sat around the campfire talking for a time, but, exhausted from his venture, he declined an invitation to eat with Grant and went to his cabin on the *River Queen*.

The next day Lincoln climbed the bluffs to Grant's headquarters, where he found the general-in-chief conferring with his officers and with Admiral David D. Porter, who commanded the naval forces on the James. While discussing plans for the day, Lincoln found three orphan kittens meowing at his feet; they seemed instinctively to recognize a friend. The president put the kittens in his lap and whispered: "Poor little creatures, don't cry; you'll be taken care of." He turned to Grant's adjutant and directed him to "see that these poor little motherless waifs are given plenty of milk and treated kindly." On several occasions during his visit to City Point, Lincoln picked up the kittens, wiped the matter from their eyes with his handkerchief, and gently stroked their fur. Horace Porter, Grant's aide-de-camp, found it "a curious sight at an army headquarters, upon the eve of a great military crisis" to see the nation's leader "tenderly caressing three stray kittens. It well illustrated the kindness of the man's disposition, and showed the childlike simplicity which was mingled with the grandeur of his nature."[11]

Since the president had seen a "fight instead of a review" the previous day, it was agreed that the party should go up the James, witness General Philip H. Sheridan's forces crossing the river, and review a part of General Edward O. C. Ord's Army of the James. During the trip the president fretted that while the generals were gone Lee might renew his assault and take City Point. Grant and the other officers assured him that it could not happen. Lincoln's mood brightened when he heard Sheridan's troops cheering him as they crossed the James on pontoons. Not to be outdone, sailors in Porter's fleet let loose with wild cheers for "Father Abraham" as he passed them on the river.[12]

Arriving at Varina Landing at midday, Lincoln and the officers mounted horses and rode the three miles to the review grounds on Malvern Hill, the site of the last battle in the Seven Days campaign of 1862. Mrs. Lincoln and Mrs. Grant followed in an army ambulance. The first units the president reviewed were black troops in General William Birney's brigade. Their shouts for Lincoln resounded across the old battlefield, greatly pleasing the president. He received a similar reception as he passed in front of the other brigades.[13]

An embarrassing scene with Mary Lincoln, however, marred the day. A rough ride on the corduroyed road had given Mrs. Lincoln a headache (probably triggering a migraine). When she and Julia Grant arrived on the field, the review had already begun and Mary Ord, the general's attractive wife, was riding down the line with the president. When Mrs. Ord approached to pay her respects, a furious Mary Lincoln called her names and demanded to know "what she meant by following up the President." (Generals Ord and Grant had also ridden with Lincoln, a fact that Mrs. Lincoln ignored.) That night at dinner on the *River Queen,* with guests present, Mary chastised her husband for flirting with Mrs. Ord. Later, after everyone had retired, the president knocked on the door of Captain Barnes of the escort gunboat *Bat,* who was staying on the *River Queen,* and asked him to come to his cabin. There Barnes found a still angry Mrs. Lincoln. The president, according to the young captain, "very gently suggested"—probably not for the first time—that he had barely noticed Mrs. Ord's presence during the review of the troops; "but Mrs. Lincoln," Barnes recalled, "was hardly to be pacified and appealed to me to support her view" of the incident. He refused to do so, and the next day Mrs. Lincoln successfully pressured him to leave the *River Queen.*[14] This incident reveals the verbal abuse that Lincoln was sometimes subjected to by Mary. It also demonstrates his patience, learned from experience, in dealing with outbursts from a wife whose anxieties often got the better of her.

* * *

The morning after the visit to General Ord's army, March 27, Lincoln again climbed the bluffs to Grant's log cabin to be briefed on the war and to await developments. His good humor had been revived, and he enlivened the conversations with colorful anecdotes. Horace Porter, who was usually present during these visits, recalled Lincoln's knack for storytelling: the president "did not tell a story merely for the sake of the anecdote, but to point a moral or to clench a fact . . . He seemed to recollect every incident in his experience and to weave it into material for his stories." According to Porter, Lincoln seldom smiled "until he reached the climax of a humorous narration; then he joined heartily with the listeners in the laugh which followed." While visiting the army, he "usually sat on a low camp-chair, and wound his legs around each other, as if in an effort to get them out of the way, and with his long arms he accomplished what he said with all sorts of odd gestures."[15]

Later in the day the president and a small party, including Mary and the Lincolns' two sons, took an excursion up the Appomattox to the Point of Rocks. They saw the oak tree that reputedly marked the spot where Pocahontas had saved Captain John Smith's life. They walked through the woods to a Federal army signal tower, which Lincoln climbed and which gave him a good view of the area. Apparently it was also during this walk that Lincoln, seeing an old country cemetery, turned to Mary and remarked, "When I am gone, lay my remains in some quiet place like this." While at the Point of Rocks, the president visited a hospital for wounded officers.[16]

The president returned to City Point in midafternoon and met on the *River Queen* with Generals Grant, Mortimer D. Leggett, and Marsena R. Patrick, provost marshal of the Army of the Potomac. They visited for more than half an hour. Patrick recorded in his diary that Lincoln "was very happy and talked very freely about many persons in high position; as freely as I would talk to them in my own family."[17] With victory in sight and unrestrained by obvious political considerations, Lincoln at City Point abandoned his usual reticence on sensitive matters and opened up to the officers around him. Despite the fact that the war raged nearby, he felt more relaxed with the troops in the field than in Washington, where demands on him came from all sides.

That evening, General William Tecumseh Sherman arrived from North Carolina to confer with Grant regarding military operations to end the war. When the generals boarded the *River Queen,* the president recognized Sherman, having met him early in the war; he greeted the conqueror of Georgia and South Carolina with an expression that Sherman found gratifying. This first meeting, though largely social, gave Lincoln an opportunity to question Sherman about his recent march through South Carolina and into North Carolina.[18]

The next day, March 28, Lincoln, Grant, and Sherman again conferred on the *River Queen;* Admiral Porter also was present for some of the discussion. As it turned out, this meeting was the only high-level conference for mapping strategy for the ending of the war. Lincoln began the talks by expressing his concern that Johnston's army in North Carolina, though beaten at Bentonville a few days earlier, might take advantage of Sherman's absence to strike at Union forces in the state and then attempt to link up with Lee's army at Petersburg. Sherman reassured the president that Johnston's army had been shattered and, in retreat toward Raleigh, no longer posed a threat to Federal forces in North Carolina. Grant informed Lincoln that at that very moment Sheridan's cavalry, near Petersburg, was moving to flank Lee's army, gain control of the strategic Southside Railroad, and prevent Lee from joining Johnston. Sherman confidently said that he could take care of Johnston's retreating army.[19]

Lincoln then turned to the matter that had increasingly occupied his thoughts since his re-election—ending the bloodshed as soon as possible. His tour of the battlefront a few hours after the bloody clash at Fort Stedman had reinforced his desire for peace. At the beginning of 1865 Lincoln had expected the war to continue into the summer or even later and to require extended hard war tactics. But the fall of Fort Fisher, Sherman's march into the Carolinas, and other military successes early in the year had convinced him that victory was near. By the time of his visit to City Point, he fervently wanted his generals to avoid the kind of fierce fighting that had produced so much death and suffering on both sides. In the conference on the *River Queen*, the president repeatedly urged Grant and Sherman to end the fighting quickly and humanely. When Sherman predicted that one more battle would be necessary, Lincoln exclaimed, "Must more blood be shed! Can not this last battle be avoided?" Sherman said that he believed "both Jeff. Davis and General Lee would be forced to fight one more desperate and bloody battle." Grant agreed, indicating that he expected Lee to make another effort to prevent the encirclement of his army.[20]

Sherman, who did more talking in the conference than Grant, asked if Lincoln had plans for the disbandment of the rebel armies and the treatment of the leaders. The president replied that all he wanted was the end of the rebellion and for the men to go home, "whereupon they would be guaranteed all their rights [in] a common country." In an account based on notes made that evening after the meeting, Admiral Porter reported Lincoln as saying: "Let them once surrender and reach their homes, they won't take up arms again. Let them all go, officers and all . . . Let them have their horses to plow with, and, if you like, their guns to shoot crows with. I want no one punished; treat them liberally." The president insisted that his only desire was for "those people to return to their allegiance to the Union and submit to the laws." Though Porter's recollected words may not have been exactly what Lincoln said, the president's statement conveyed clear instructions to Grant on the treatment of the defeated rebels. Two weeks later, at Appomattox Court House, Grant gave Lee the surrender terms that Lincoln wanted.[21]

Lincoln also told Grant and Sherman that "in his mind he was ready for the civil reorganization of affairs at the South as soon as the war was over." The president, Sherman later wrote, "distinctly authorized me to assure Governor [Zebulon B.] Vance and the people of North Carolina" that, once they had laid down their arms, "to avoid anarchy the State Government, with their civil functionaries, would be recognized by him." Sherman had misunderstood Lincoln's policy, a mistake that became important when, after the president's death, he offered political as well as military terms to the Confederate army in North Carolina. Lincoln, as he had made clear to Grant earlier, did not want his generals arranging a reconstruction settlement with the rebels. Sherman's political terms included the recognition of the rebel state governments after their officers and legislators took the loyalty oath. They also included restoration of the rights and property of the people, which conceivably could have extended the life of slavery until the ratification of the Thirteenth Amendment. These terms created a firestorm in Washington. They suggested a Confederate-style reconstruction for the defeated South, and Stanton and Radical Republicans made wild charges that Sherman was in league with the rebels. President Johnson quickly reversed Sherman's extraordinary action, and the Confederate troops in North Carolina were given only the military terms that Lee had received at Appomattox.[22]

* * *

The conference on the *River Queen* ended at noon on March 28, and that afternoon Sherman boarded a steamer for his return to North

U. S. Grant, General-in-Chief of the Union armies,
whose warm relationship with Lincoln blossomed
during the president's visit to his headquarters.

Carolina. The next morning Grant, with his plans completed and his army in readiness, launched the long-awaited offensive against Lee. His great fear—and Lincoln's also—was that Lee's army would escape in strength before he could flank and shatter its lines. When Grant boarded the army train for the short trip to the front, Lincoln came ashore to bid him and his staff godspeed. Horace Porter remembered that the president "looked more serious than at any time since he had visited headquarters. The lines in his face seemed deeper, and the rings under his eyes were of a darker hue. It was plain that the weight of responsibility was oppressing him."[23]

Perhaps to relieve this weight and the tension among the men, Lincoln insisted on telling one more story before Grant and his staff left for the front. A Grant comment about a crackpot's proposal to win the war by supplying Union troops with bayonets longer than those of the Confederates prompted the president to relate an encounter he had had with cold steel. "I had a chance to test it once myself," he began.

> When I was a young man, I was walking along a back street in Louisville one night about twelve o'clock, when a very tough-looking citizen sprang out of an alleyway, . . . pulled out a bowie-knife that seemed to my stimulated imagination about three feet long, and planted himself square across my path. For two or three minutes he flourished his weapon in front of my face, appearing to try to see just how near he could come to cutting my nose off without quite doing it. He could see in the moonlight that I was taking a good deal of interest in the proceeding, and finally he yelled out, as he steadied the knife close to my throat: "Stranger, kin you lend me five dollars on that?" I never reached in my pocket and got money out so fast in all my life. I handed him a bank-note, and said: "There's ten, neighbor; now put up your scythe."[24]

As the train departed City Point, Grant and members of his staff raised their hats in respect to the president. Lincoln returned the salute, and "in a voice broken by emotion," he exclaimed, "God bless you all! Remember, your success is my success." At Grant's suggestion, the president remained at City Point to await reports on the campaign.[25]

Lincoln's relationship with Grant had become warmer during the president's stay with the army. He enjoyed the informality of Grant's headquarters and the skill with which the general and his staff went about planning the offensive against Lee's army. Lincoln reveled in the camaraderie with the officers and with the troops and sailors, who, unlike the "throng" in Washington, made no demands upon him. Elizabeth Keckly, who visited City Point with Mrs. Lincoln, remembered that "Mr. Lincoln, when not off on an excursion of any kind, lounged about the [*River Queen*], talking familiarly with every one that approached him."[26]

Grant appreciated the fact that the president did not seek to interfere with his military plans. As he told his staff on the train ride from City Point to the front on March 29, "the President is one of the few visitors I have had who have not attempted to extract from me a knowledge of my movements, although he is the only one who has a right to know them."[27]

★ ★ ★

For the next few days Lincoln anxiously waited at City Point for dispatches from the front. Hearing the guns in the distance only added to his anxiety. He reported to Stanton that on the first night of the battle he heard "a furious cannonade, soon joined in by a heavy musketry-fire" that lasted about two hours. "The sound was very distinct here, as also were the flashes of the guns upon the clouds." He repeatedly wired Grant for news of the fighting—and the general immediately replied. Meanwhile, the president joined Admiral Porter in visits to military and naval facilities along the James. He also welcomed Secretary of State Seward to City Point for a two-day visit, renewing speculation that peace negotiations were imminent.[28]

On the morning of April 2 Lincoln received the good news that the Federal forces, as he wired Stanton, "have all broken through the enemy's intrenched lines" and reached the Southside Railroad. Before the day was over, Grant reported that his troops had enveloped Petersburg itself. He suggested that the president "might come out and pay us a visit to-morrow." That evening Lincoln sent the general "the nations grateful thanks" for the "magnificent success" of his army, and he accepted the invitation to visit the front. By the next morning

Petersburg had fallen, and Grant dispatched a squad of troops to escort Lincoln into the town. At eight A.M. the president telegraphed Stanton that he planned to start for Petersburg "in a few minutes." The war secretary immediately wired Lincoln that he was thunderstruck by the president's decision. He admonished Lincoln not "to expose the nation to the consequences of any disaster" to himself "in the pursuit of a treacherous and dangerous enemy." Lincoln did not receive Stanton's message until after he returned from Petersburg. He probably would have ignored it anyway.[29]

By nine A.M. Lincoln and a small party that included Admiral Porter and Tad and Robert had left City Point for Petersburg. They took the train to Hancock Station, where they mounted horses for the ride into the town. Near Petersburg Lincoln saw the bodies of Union and Confederate soldiers, a sight that brought tears to his eyes. Grant had established a temporary headquarters in Petersburg at a residence on Market Street. Horace Porter, Grant's aide-de-camp, recorded the meeting of the two Union leaders. The president "dismounted in the street, came in through the front gate with long and rapid strides, his face beaming with delight. He seized General Grant's hand as the general stepped forward to greet him, and stood shaking it for some time, [while] pouring out his thanks and congratulations . . . I doubt whether Mr. Lincoln ever experienced a happier moment in his life." In a conversation that lasted almost half an hour, Lincoln talked about the civil complications that would follow the destruction of the Confederate armies. According to Porter, the president "intimated very plainly . . . that thoughts of leniency to the conquered were uppermost in his heart." Grant soon took his leave and went west to join his army in pursuit of Lee.[30]

The president remained in the war-scarred town until the afternoon. He called at the house where paroled Confederate General Roger A. Pryor, whom he had met earlier in Washington, was staying. Mrs. Pryor met Lincoln at the door and politely told him that her husband could not meet with the head of the enemy government as long as General Lee was still in the field.[31] (Ironically, after the war Pryor moved to New York, became a prominent attorney, and ended his career as a justice on that state's supreme court.)

Lincoln found a more cordial welcome in the streets of Petersburg.

Learning that the Great Emancipator was in town, liberated blacks turned out to cheer him. He also received friendly greetings from a few white citizens, including a Mr. Wallace, an old Whig acquaintance of Lincoln who lived in the house Grant was using as his temporary headquarters. Before leaving Petersburg, once the major tobacco marketing center in the South, the president and Admiral Porter grabbed a few bundles of tobacco leaves as souvenirs.[32]

★ ★ ★

Returning to City Point in late afternoon, Lincoln learned that Richmond had fallen to the Union forces. He immediately told Admiral Porter, "I want to see Richmond." During the night Porter's sailors worked to remove the "torpedoes" (underwater mines) and other obstructions in the James River near Richmond. The next morning, April 4, Lincoln boarded the *River Queen* for the trip upriver to rendezvous with Porter on the *Malvern*. After Lincoln joined the admiral on the *Malvern*, the vessel ran aground as it entered the dangerous waters below Richmond. The presidential party transferred to a navy barge, pulled by a tugboat and escorted by the *Bat* with thirty marines and armed sailors on board. Above Drewry's Bluff they came upon a startling sight. Run aground on pilings thrown up by the Confederates was the steamer *Allison,* commanded by Admiral David F. Farragut but inadvertently still flying the Confederate flag. On an impulse, Farragut and General George H. Gordon, commanding at Norfolk, had made an overland dash into Richmond soon after its fall and were now returning downriver. After exchanging pleasantries and while waiting for the tug to pull the *Allison* off the obstructions, Lincoln shouted out to Farragut, "How is Libby [prison]?" "Very full of Rebel prisoners," came Farragut's reply. That seemed to satisfy the president, who would soon see the prison himself.[33]

By midmorning the president and his party, including Tad, had arrived at the Richmond landing. The docks were virtually deserted, but a group of black workers recognized the tall president, touching off a celebration among the newly freed slaves as he climbed the hill. The news of his bold visit spread "as if upon the wings of lightning," wrote Thomas Morris Chester, a black reporter for the *Philadelphia Press.* Above the landing Lincoln saw a familiar face, Charles Carlton

Coffin of the *Boston Journal,* and he asked Coffin for directions to General Godfrey Weitzel's headquarters in the suddenly evacuated residence of President Davis. As he walked through the still smoldering city, guarded only by twelve marines and sailors, crowds of former slaves rushed forward to shake and kiss his hand and shout their praise. Coffin later wrote, "Abraham Lincoln was their Savior, their Moses." They surged around the president "in a wild delirium of joy; . . . they leaped into the air, hugged and kissed one another." Chester reported that one black woman exclaimed, "I know that I am free, for I have seen Father Abraham and felt him."[34]

Lincoln, exhausted by the walk and the adoration in the streets, wearily ascended the steps of the Davis mansion and took a seat in the reception room that also had served as the office of the Confederate president. One observer noted that as he sat down "there was no triumph in his gesture or attitude." His first words were "I wonder if I could get a glass of water," a request that was quickly granted. General Weitzel and other officers soon arrived and hurriedly organized a lunch reception for the president. Lincoln also met with some "gentlemen" of the city, whom he received kindly. One of the "gentlemen" was a Confederate assistant secretary of war, John A. Campbell, a former U.S. Supreme Court associate justice who had participated in the Hampton Roads peace conference in February. The president hoped that Campbell had an official offer of surrender, but Campbell informed Lincoln that, though he wanted peace, he had no authority to act. He encouraged the president to reach out to prominent Confederates, including Virginia legislators and General Lee, who, he suggested, would be eager to end the war even on Union terms. Lincoln saw an opportunity to stop the bloodshed and gain the support of influential Southerners for the pacification of their communities. He asked Campbell to meet with him the next day.[35]

After lunch at the Davis mansion, General Weitzel provided carriages and a cavalry escort for the president and his party to tour Richmond. Many whites opened their windows to view the man who, they believed, had been the cause of their troubles. During the day some Richmond citizens indicated to Admiral Porter that they were beginning to have second thoughts about the tall Union leader they had earlier vilified.[36]

That night Lincoln slept on the *Malvern* near Richmond. The next morning he met with Campbell on the warship. Campbell brought with him Gustavus A. Myers, a Richmond attorney, who a few days later wrote an account of the meeting. Weitzel also attended the conference. The president repeated his liberal peace terms—the end of armed hostilities against the government, the restoration of the Union, and the abolition of slavery. To facilitate an early termination of the war, Lincoln, according to Myers, said that "he was thinking over a plan by which the Virginia legislature might be brought to hold [a] meeting" in Richmond "for the purpose of seeing whether they desired to take any action on behalf of the State in view of the existing state of affairs." Asked whether he required the oath of allegiance to reestablish loyalty, Lincoln replied that "he had never attached much importance" to the oath, but that he would leave it with General Weitzel to decide for Richmond citizens. The general agreed that no test should be required. Finally, Myers recorded, Lincoln "declared his disposition to be lenient towards all persons, however prominent, who had taken part in the struggle" and that he was "disposed" to return confiscated property.[37] During the final weeks of the war, the president repeatedly declared his wish to forgo the arrest and prosecution of rebel leaders. What to do with Jefferson Davis, however, greatly perplexed him. He hoped that Davis, "unbeknownst to myself," would flee the country and never be seen again, thereby obviating the need for him to act.[38]

After returning to City Point on April 5, Lincoln put in writing for Campbell the "three things" indispensable to peace that he had mentioned in Richmond. In a separate dispatch, he authorized Weitzel to allow the "gentlemen who have acted as the Legislature of Virginia" to meet for the sole purpose of recalling state troops from the rebel army. Weitzel's call for the Virginia legislators to return to Richmond prompted a barrage of protests from Radicals and other Republicans who believed that his action would have the effect of recognizing a rebel state government before political reconstruction had been achieved. George W. Julian, a member of the Joint Committee on the Conduct of War, declared that "this false magnanimity" on Lincoln's part "is to be our ruin after all." After his return to Washington, the president reassured members of his cabinet and Governor

Francis H. Pierpont of the Restored (Union) Government of Virginia (then at Alexandria) that he had not intended to recognize the rebel legislators for any purpose other than withdrawing the state's troops from the war. On April 12, three days after Lee's surrender at Appomattox, Lincoln revoked his recall order, explaining to Weitzel that Grant "has since captured the Virginia troops," thus removing the reason for the legislature to meet.[39]

* * *

At noon on the day of the president's return to City Point from Richmond, Mary Lincoln and a party that included Speaker of the House Schuyler Colfax, Senator Charles Sumner, and other influential congressmen arrived at the dock. After a visit with the president on the *River Queen,* Mrs. Lincoln's entourage went on to Richmond to see the city that had symbolized the rebellion in Northern minds. Lincoln, who remained at City Point to await news from Grant as he pursued Lee westward, received a message from Seward encouraging him to return to Washington. "We need your personal sanction to several matters here which are important and urgent in conducting the Government." One matter was the issuance of a presidential proclamation closing all rebel ports preparatory to reopening them and restoring Southern commerce at the end of the war. Seward admitted, however, that "the public interest will not suffer by you remaining where you are." Secretary of the Navy Welles disagreed. He lamented in his diary that the routine affairs of the government were suffering because of the president's absence. At least one member of the cabinet, Secretary of War Stanton, hoped that the president would remain at City Point, because, as he confessed to his colleagues, he "was much less annoyed" when the president was out of town. The *New York Herald* correspondent in Washington reported that office seekers were "getting out of pocket and out of patience in consequence of the President's prolonged stay down at City Point." This reporter impishly suggested that those wanting a favor from the president should join Grant's army; that "will carry them to 'Old Abe' when everything else fails."[40]

Lincoln, having settled into a relatively relaxed routine at City Point, had no desire to reenter the Washington cauldron. Still, on

April 5 he telegraphed Seward that he would soon return. Seward, deciding that his business could not wait, prepared to visit Lincoln again. But before he could depart he suffered severe injury in a carriage accident, causing the president grave concern. When Stanton reported on April 6 that Seward was not in danger, Lincoln extended his stay in Virginia for an additional two days.[41]

Meanwhile, he kept busy reviewing troops and visiting the bulging military hospitals in the area. The fighting to the west and elsewhere had filled the hospitals with men from both armies. The day he left City Point, Lincoln insisted on visiting all the hospitals and shaking hands with the patients. The army's chief surgeon tried to dissuade him from the visit, pointing out that it would tax his strength and damage his hand and arm. The president responded with a smile and said that he "guessed he was equalled to the task. At any rate he would try, and go as far as he could; he should never, probably, see the boys again, and he wanted them to know that he appreciated what they had done for their country."[42] Lincoln later told Seward that he "worked as hard at [shaking hands] as sawing wood." Indeed, to prove to the surgeons that his arm had not suffered and to demonstrate to the troops that he was still strong, the president, after completing the handshaking, chopped wood for a few moments, then held the heavy ax straight out from his body. Strong men in the crowd reportedly admitted that they could not replicate this feat.[43] As this incident revealed, the bond between Lincoln and his troops had grown stronger during his visit to City Point and with the imminence of Union victory in the war.

In his visits to the hospitals, the president made no distinction between Union and Confederate soldiers. At one bed a wounded rebel soldier, with tears running down his cheeks, extended his hand and exclaimed, "Mr. Lincoln, I have long wanted to see you, to ask your forgiveness for ever raising my hand against the old flag." The president was also moved to tears while heartily clasping the hand of the repentant rebel.[44] A Union soldier later reported watching as the president approached another wounded Confederate, about seventeen years of age, whose leg had been amputated. The young rebel's face "was cold and harsh and half-averted." The president sensed the boy's defiance, and "without an instant's further hesitation, stepped close up to the boy, took his hand cordially in his own, and with a warm pressure and a look of respectful sympathy, said simply: 'My boy, I hope we shall agree better some day,' and passed on." The young soldier "lay thoughtfully a few moments, and at last turned his face to his pillow and sobbed like a child."[45]

The president, from a distance, also saw the thousands of ragged and poorly nourished Confederate prisoners who were marched into City Point for processing and shipment to camps. On one transport boat that passed the *River Queen*, a group of prisoners, having been generously fed, shouted three cheers for "old Abe." One of the men called out, "Halloo, Abe, your bread and meat's better than [the] popcorn" that he had subsisted on in Lee's army.[46]

★ ★ ★

On April 5, the day Lincoln returned to City Point from Richmond, he had a remarkable meeting with a Confederate general who had been captured west of Petersburg. General Rufus Barringer, a member of a prominent North Carolina family, was an old Whig who had opposed secession until after the war had begun. Then he had joined the Confederate army and become one of Jeb Stuart's ablest brigadiers. Learning of Lincoln's presence at City Point, he asked General Charles H. T. Collis, his captor and the post commander, to point out the president to him. Collis mentioned Barringer's request to Lincoln, who indicated a desire to meet him. When they met, Lincoln at first mistook the general for his brother Daniel Moreau Barringer, who had served with him in Congress, even sitting at the same desk and eating at the same boardinghouse. "He was my chum, and I was very fond of him," Lincoln told the prisoner. The president and Barringer, along with Collis, went into a nearby tent, where, according to Collis, the "discussion drifted from Mr. Lincoln's anecdotes of the pleasant hours he and [Daniel] Barringer had spent together, to the war, thence to the merits of the military and civil leaders, North and South, illustrated here and there by some appropriate story, entirely new, full of humor and sometimes of pathos." Finally, the president asked Barringer, "Do you think I can be of service to you?" Though Lincoln at first failed to "realize the innocent simplicity of the inquiry," everyone else in the tent laughed at this question, coming from the commander in chief of the Union armies and directed to a rebel prisoner of war.[47]

Barringer responded, "If anybody can be of service to a poor devil in my situation, I presume you are the man." Lincoln drew from his pocket a card with his name engraved on it, adjusted his glasses, turned up the wick of the lamp, and wrote a note to Secretary of War Stanton. While writing, he kept up a steady conversation with Barringer. The note read: "This is General Barringer, of the southern army. He is the brother of a very dear friend of mine. Can you do any thing to make his detention in Washington as comfortable as possible under the circumstance?" Overcome with emotion, Barringer left the tent and broke down in tears outside. He later wrote in his diary these terse words regarding Lincoln: "Pleased with him. His leadership & manners have been misrepresented South." Barringer never forgot Lincoln's kindness, and after the war he assisted in the organization of the martyred president's political party in North Carolina, the Union Republican party.[48]

On April 7, two days after meeting Barringer, Lincoln received an encouraging message from the Federal army pursuing Lee. General Sheridan, commanding Grant's vanguard, telegraphed the president that "if the thing is pressed I think that Lee will surrender." Lincoln, citing Sheridan's message, immediately wired Grant: "Let the *thing* be pressed."[49] Even without Lincoln's admonition, the tenacious Grant had no intention of permitting Lee's army to escape.

While waiting for additional news from the front, Lincoln made a second trip to Petersburg, this time with Mrs. Lincoln and her party, including Tad and Senator Sumner. Also in the entourage was Elizabeth Keckly, Mrs. Lincoln's seamstress, who sought out friends from her days as a slave in Petersburg. On this visit the president insisted on showing the group a large, peculiarly shaped oak tree on the outskirts of the town that he had noticed earlier. Lincoln took pride in his knowledge of trees; he had an almost mystical feeling about them, probably derived from his youth as a rail-splitter. On the way back to City Point, Lincoln again, as with the kittens, demonstrated his tender concern for "poor little creatures" when he stopped the train to rescue a terrapin on the side of the track. The president had the brakeman bring the terrapin to him, and he and Tad played with it until they reached City Point.[50]

* * *

With the fighting in Virginia near its end, Lincoln could no longer justify his stay at City Point. On April 8 he decided to return to Washington. After visiting the hospitals for the last time, he boarded the *River Queen* for the voyage home. He asked the headquarters band, which had come to the landing to send off the presidential party, to play the "Marseillaise" in honor of the Marquis de Chambrun, a member of Mrs. Lincoln's entourage. The French imperial government had banned the anthem in France, prompting Lincoln to remark to the marquis that he had to come to America to hear it. The president also asked the band to play "Dixie," which surprised the musicians and those on the *River Queen*. Lincoln explained his choice, apparently in all seriousness: "That tune is now Federal property, and it is good to show the rebels that, with us in power, they will be free to hear it again."[51]

On the first part of the trip to Washington, Lincoln remained absorbed in thought and somewhat distant from the other passengers. When the *River Queen* entered the Potomac on Sunday, April 9, his demeanor changed. The Marquis de Chambrun recorded in his diary that Lincoln spent the day discussing literary subjects with Sumner and others. "Lincoln read aloud to us for several hours," Chambrun wrote. "Most of the passages he selected were from Shakespeare, especially *Macbeth*." Macbeth's moral torment after he murdered Duncan especially impressed the president; he read the scene twice. When the *River Queen* passed Mount Vernon, the marquis predicted that Lincoln's home at Springfield someday "will be equally honored in America" as that of Washington. Ignoring the compliment, the president responded, "Springfield, how happy I shall be four years hence to return there in peace and tranquility!"[52]

Arriving at Washington in the early evening, Lincoln immediately visited the badly injured Seward. The president sat on his friend's bed, told him that "we are near the end, at last," and for about half an hour described his experiences at the front. After Seward fell asleep,

Lincoln quietly left for the White House. They never saw each other again. Before he went to bed that night, Lincoln learned that Lee had surrendered to Grant at Appomattox Court House near Lynchburg.[53]

* * *

April 10 dawned in Washington with the booming of cannons and people rushing into the streets to celebrate the news from Virginia. Offices closed for the day. At the White House, the cannonade rattled the windows. Lincoln, however, was at his desk early in the morning, scanning his mail and handling urgent business. Throughout the day a horde of visitors descended upon the waiting room; many would go away disappointed, having been unable to see the president.[54]

By early afternoon an immense crowd had gathered outside the White House, filling the yard, the carriageway, and passages. The *Washington National Intelligencer* described the scene: "The bands played, the howitzers belched forth their thunder, and the people cheered. Call after call was made for the President, and his failure to appear only made the people cry out the louder." Finally, about five o'clock, Lincoln came out, and after the crowd gave him "three loud and hearty cheers," he spoke briefly. "I am very greatly rejoiced," he began, "to find that an occasion has occurred so pleasurable that the people cannot restrain themselves." He declined to make a speech but said that he would be prepared "to respond" the next night if "some sort of a formal demonstration" occurred. For the moment, he asked the band to play "Dixie one of the best tunes I have ever heard. Our adversaries over the way attempted to appropriate it, but I insisted yesterday that we fairly captured it." Lincoln claimed that he had "presented the question to the Attorney General, and he gave it as his legal opinion that it is our lawful prize." The celebrants laughed and roared their approval. The president ended by asking the crowd to give three cheers for the troops and the sailors.[55]

The next night, when another crowd gathered, Lincoln, as promised, had a written speech to deliver. It would be his last public address. "We meet this evening, not in sorrow, but in gladness of heart," he began. "The evacuation of Petersburg and Richmond, and the surrender of the principal insurgent army, give hope of a righteous and speedy peace whose joyous expression can not be restrained."

Then Lincoln, reflecting his deepening religious faith, reminded the crowd—and by extension all Americans—"In the midst of this, however, He, from Whom all blessings flow, must not be forgotten." The president announced that he would soon issue "a call for a national thanksgiving." He praised the officers and men of the army and the navy for producing the victory. "I myself was near the front," he said, "and had the high pleasure of transmitting much of the good news to you; but no part of the honor, for plan or execution, is mine."[56] This was a remarkable denial of credit by a political leader; nevertheless, Lincoln knew that the American public gave him considerable credit for the Union's success in the war.

The president then turned to the reconstruction issue, which he declared was "fraught with great difficulty" because "there is no authorized organ for us to treat with" in the rebel states: "No one man has authority to give up the rebellion for any other man." He said that differences among "the loyal people" regarding "the mode, manner, and means of reconstruction" had caused "additional embarrassment." The president blamed these disagreements on the Radicals and others who criticized his reconstruction plan, announced in December 1863, and specifically his action in setting up and sustaining the conservative Union government in Louisiana. By that time Radicals had wanted a reconstruction policy that would disfranchise rebel leaders and provide federal protection for black freedom, including political rights.

Lincoln launched into a long defense of Louisiana reconstruction. He admitted that he preferred that "the elective franchise" "were now conferred on the very intelligent" blacks in Louisiana "and on those who serve our cause as soldiers." But he would not impose it upon the leaders of the new state government who, he contended, were "fully committed to the Union, and to perpetual freedom." These Unionists, the president insisted, were "committed to the very things, and nearly all the things the nation wants." He put pressure on Congress, scheduled to meet in December, to seat the senators and representatives from Louisiana and his other loyal Southern governments, warning that "if we reject, and spurn them, we do our utmost to disorganize and disperse them." Such a course would hurt both whites and blacks, he asserted. "We in effect say to the white men 'You are worthless, or worse—we will neither help you, nor be helped by you.' To the blacks we say 'This cup of liberty which these, your old masters, hold to your lips, we will dash from you, and leave you to the chances of gathering the spilled and scattered contents in some vague and undefined when, where, and how.'" Furthermore, Lincoln argued, restored Louisiana would add one more vote toward the ratification of the Thirteenth Amendment, a vote that might be necessary in securing the three-fourths of the states "to validly ratify" it.[57]

★ ★ ★

The president, despite his strong opposition to slavery and his sympathy for blacks, had not changed his fundamental policy of permitting white Unionists to control their states' relationship with the freed slaves. Once the rebellion had been suppressed, order restored, and emancipation completed, he did not conceive of an extension of federal authority in the Southern states. As the historian Don E. Fehrenbacher has written, "in the closing days of the war, his outlook on race relations continued to be guided and restricted by his traditional view of federal relations," which left such matters in the hands of the states. Lincoln's concept of governmental authority reflected "the orthodox [American] conception of the United States as a relatively decentralized federation in which the state governments played the most active and versatile part."[58]

Nonetheless, Lincoln, who believed in human progress and in opportunity for all, including blacks, to rise in life, assumed that the former slaves would gradually be elevated to first-class citizenship. As suggested in his reconstruction plan of 1863, education and free labor would be important agencies in this rise. White prejudice against blacks would fade, a point Lincoln had seemed to make in his annual message of December 1, 1862, when he had argued that by 1900 "those whose habitual course of thought" was opposed to black freedom would "have passed away" and the new generation of Southern whites would accept it.[59]

Had Lincoln survived to observe conditions in the South after the war, he would not have been so hopeful about progress toward black equality. Faced with the suppression of black freedom, perhaps he would have grasped the reality of the situation for the former slaves.

Rather than intervene with federal power, he might have used his formidable political influence to sustain Unionists in the South and to insist that they protect black freedom in their states, policies that his successor, Andrew Johnson, did not pursue. In this way, Lincoln might have prevented the early return of former Confederates to power and their enactment of anti-black laws, known as Black Codes, that, until an outraged Congress intervened in 1866–1867, restored a form of slavery.

But such speculation is counterfactual history. A judgment regarding Lincoln and black Americans must be based on his actions and policies, particularly during the last part of his presidency. This much seems clear: Lincoln's leadership was indispensable in bringing about emancipation, and this major success made possible the elevation of the former slaves, despite the tortured road that followed emancipation. Though paternalistic toward blacks, Lincoln did not envision a permanently inferior status for them in American society. Like the abolitionist William Lloyd Garrison at this time, he expected emancipation to bring its own rewards, and with only a minimum of federal intervention after the war. His support for the Freedmen's Bureau, a temporary agency authorized by Congress in March 1865 to aid blacks in their adjustment to freedom, was a notable exception to his nonintervention policy.

* * *

Lincoln in his April 11 address continued to insist that "the sole object of the government" in regard to the rebel states was "to again get them into their proper practical relation with the Union." The policy for each state, he said, must be flexible while the "important principles"—emancipation and loyalty—"may, and must, be inflexible." In conclusion, he indicated that "it may be my duty to make some new announcement to the people of the South." He probably had in mind a declaration extending temporary military control to states where no local Union governments existed, a purpose that became clearer when he met with his cabinet three days later.[60]

The reconstruction speech received what in the early twenty-first century would be called a strong public approval rating. Writing from Washington the next day, John W. Forney ("Occasional") reported in the *Philadelphia Press* that everyone he had talked to endorsed "the remedies suggested in the speech." He admitted, however, that some die-hard Radicals would criticize it for failing to call for the punishment of rebel leaders. But not even the Radicals, Forney indicated, were united on the issue of reconstruction; some, like Senator James Harlan, recently selected as secretary of the interior, had spoken in favor of the president's policy. Forney himself declared: "We have no time to give to vengeance, now that we have vindicated our Government, defeated the rebellion, and consolidated a great party around our faithful Chief Magistrate. Let us take his counsel, and confide in him as we have heretofore done, and the end of the war will [bring] endless peace and prosperity."[61]

Likewise, the independent *New York Herald* reported that the president's April 11 address "meets with approbation from a large majority of the people." The *Herald* also acknowledged that "a very active minority of the more radical of the republicans" opposed Lincoln's reconstruction policy. "Although comparatively few in number," the *Herald* claimed, the Radicals "are very active, and include many prominent and influential members of the dominant party." As before, this newspaper professed confidence that the president would prevail if challenged, since he "relies on the good sense of the people, and their desire to secure lasting peace and quiet as speedily and with as little difficulty as possible." The *New York Times*, the *Chicago Tribune,* and other Republican newspapers provided similar support for Lincoln's policy. Even the Copperhead (Democratic) *Detroit Free Press* expressed surprise that the president had not caved in to the Radicals in his party and indicated approval of Lincoln's conclusion in the speech "that the people of the States must reorganize and administer the State governments themselves" without federal interference.[62]

* * *

Meanwhile, the victory celebrations continued in the capital and elsewhere. At night in Washington, public buildings, hotels, shop fronts, and homes were brilliantly illuminated with gas and candles. National flags, colored lanterns, and transparencies covered the city. The streets were crowded with celebrants. Bands at several government buildings played patriotic music, with a backdrop of bonfires and rockets.[63] Many people concluded that God had willed the salvation of the Union and the end of the cruel war. Easter Sunday, April 16, promised to exceed all other religious observances in the history of the republic. Great preparations were under way for a marvelous day of religious ceremonies and thanksgiving. Indeed, had not Lincoln on April 11 suggested such a day of remembrance and "national thanksgiving"?

CHAPTER 8

MARTYRDOM

April 14, 1865, Good Friday for Christians, dawned in Washington full of promise that soon the last Confederate army would surrender and peace would be restored to the country. The day would end in tragedy.

On that Friday, in faraway Charleston Harbor, General Robert J. Anderson, who had been the commandant of Fort Sumter when the war began, raised the United States flag over the fort, marking the fourth anniversary of the surrender of the Federal garrison and symbolically proclaiming the Union victory in the war. The prominent antislavery minister Henry Ward Beecher spoke at the ceremony. That evening fireworks from the Federal fleet in the harbor lit up the sky.

In North Carolina, meanwhile, the main body of General Sherman's army encamped around Raleigh, while the vanguard pursued General Joseph E. Johnston's defeated army westward. Sherman, from his headquarters in Raleigh, prepared to meet with Johnston and offer surrender terms. President Davis and other Confederate officials conferred with Johnston at Greensboro to determine their next move. The general made it clear that he would surrender on the terms Grant had offered Lee at Appomattox Court House a few days earlier. Davis, still hoping for a miracle, refused to cooperate and continued to flee southward; he would be captured by Federal troops in May. Johnston would meet with Sherman near Durham Station, North Carolina, and on April 26 would surrender more troops than Lee had done at Appomattox. Except for minor skirmishing in Tennessee, Texas, and elsewhere, the war would be over—but only after claiming its most eminent casualty, Abraham Lincoln.

That Lincoln's assassination occurred on the traditional anniversary of Jesus' crucifixion was viewed by Americans in the Union states as more than a coincidence. It carried a profound spiritual meaning for an anguished people who had increasingly turned to religion to explain the terrible price exacted by the war. As Jesus had suffered on the cross for humankind, so Lincoln had suffered and died for God's objectives in the Civil War. He had become a martyr to the Providence-ordained purposes of republicanism—liberty, freedom, self-government, and Union. Lincoln's apotheosis as an American hero had begun well before the assassination, but his exaltation as a divine instrument of the Union effort in the war came with his death and the outpouring of grief that followed.

* * *

Lincoln's day began with the usual morning routine in the White House. He ate breakfast at eight o'clock with his family, including Robert, who was fresh from Grant's army in Virginia. Robert gave the family tantalizing details of Lee's surrender, which brightened his father's mood.[1] The president's first visitors were Speaker of the House Schuyler Colfax and Representative Cornelius Cole, who were preparing to leave for California, Cole's home state. When Colfax expressed strong views against permitting secessionist leaders to return to power in the South, Lincoln changed the subject and asked him about his trip to California. "How I would rejoice to make that trip," Colfax reported the president as saying; "but public duties chain me down here, and I can only envy you its pleasure." However, Lincoln asked Colfax to take a message for him to the western miners. He had some "very large ideas of the mineral wealth" of the West: the silver and gold from the mountains would make "so much easier" the payment of the large war debt. Furthermore, he said, "We shall have hundreds of thousands of disabled [discharged?] soldiers, and many have feared that their return home in such great numbers might paralyze industry by furnishing a greater supply of labor than there will be demand for. I am going to try to attract them to the hidden wealth of our mountain ranges." Lincoln also planned to direct immigrants to the opportunities in the West. "Tell the miners for me that I shall promote their interests to the utmost of my ability, because their prosperity is the prosperity of the nation, and we shall prove in a very few years, that we are indeed the treasury of the world."[2]

With the war coming to an end, Lincoln's interest in national economic growth and western development—a product of his Whig background—had clearly revived. In his April 14 conversation with Colfax, he ignored the effect that the exploitation of western mineral wealth would have on the Indians and rather focused on its economic potential for the nation. In closing, he asked Colfax to join him at Ford's Theatre that night. The Speaker, however, told Lincoln that he had "engagements" to attend to before leaving town the next day.[3]

At some time during the day—probably that morning—Lincoln replied to a letter in which a former general, James H. Van Alen of New York, praised his conservative course on reconstruction. Van Alen also cautioned him "to guard his life and not expose it to assassination as he had by going to Richmond." It was a warning to be taken to heart, but the president had had similar warnings and had taken them lightly. He thanked Van Alen for his concern and added, "I intend to adopt the advice of my friends and use due precaution." He also thanked the New Yorker "for the assurance that you give me that I shall be supported by conservative men like yourself, in the efforts I may make to restore the Union, so as to make it, to use your language, a Union of hearts and hands as well as of States."[4]

Before meeting with his cabinet at eleven o'clock, Lincoln visited the War Department to learn whether Johnston's army had surrendered. Secretary of War Stanton had no news from North Carolina. When Stanton expressed concern about Lincoln's plan to attend the theater that evening, the president turned and asked Major Thomas T. Eckert, chief of the military telegraph office and a man noted for his strength, to accompany him and Mrs. Lincoln to the play. Eckert declined, citing the pressure of work.[5]

Returning to the White House, Lincoln met for three hours with his cabinet. Not all members were present. Seward, still suffering from his carriage injury, sent his son Frederick to represent him. General Grant attended the meeting at Lincoln's invitation and received a warm welcome and congratulations for the military's success. Asked if he had news from Sherman in North Carolina, Grant replied that he hourly expected word. In a cheerful mood, Lincoln said he had no doubt that a report would come soon and that it would be favorable. The previous night, he explained, he had dreamed he was in an indescribable vessel, moving rapidly toward the shore. He had had similar dreams before, and they had always been followed by great events of the war. Therefore, he told the cabinet and Grant, "we shall, judging from the past, have great news very soon. I think it must be from Sherman."[6]

The main topics for the April 14 cabinet meeting were the reopening of trade and the restoration of civil society in the South. When the cabinet could not agree on the question of restoring trade and communications in the collapsing Confederate states, Lincoln asked the secretaries of treasury, war, and navy to develop a policy to be implemented by their departments. The discussion then turned to a "rough plan" drawn up by Stanton for the appointment of a military governor for Virginia and North Carolina. The governor would be responsible for establishing order and initiating the return of civil authority. The president said that Stanton's draft needed "some modifications." Welles pointed out and Lincoln agreed that Governor Francis H. Pierpont's administration had been recognized as the legitimate government of Virginia and should be detached from any plan involving North Carolina. Lincoln asked Stanton to have a revised draft ready for the regular cabinet meeting on April 18.[7]

According to Frederick Seward, the president declared, as if to emphasize his commitment to a liberal reconstruction policy: "We can't undertake to run state governments in all these southern states. Their people must do that, though I reckon at first, they may do it badly." When asked about the possible escape of rebel leaders, he replied: "I should not be sorry to have them out of the country; but I should be for following them up pretty close to make sure of their going." He spoke highly of Lee and other Confederates. In a pointed aside, he said he was glad that Congress was not in session to complicate the work of restoration.[8]

At two o'clock the cabinet meeting ended and Lincoln ate lunch with Mary in a private room. At three he met for twenty minutes with

Andrew Johnson, apparently his first meeting with the vice president since the embarrassing incident at the inauguration. They probably talked about reconstruction in Tennessee, where the recently formed Union government had abolished slavery in the state, to the delight of both men. After Johnson left, the president talked briefly with Congressman Samuel Shellabarger of Ohio about local patronage matters.

About the same time, the War Department received a telegram from the provost marshal in Maine reporting "positive information" that Jacob Thompson, the chief Confederate agent in Canada, would "pass through Portland to-night" and take a steamer to England. Assistant Secretary of War Charles A. Dana asked Stanton what instructions he should send to Maine authorities regarding Thompson. Stanton said, "Arrest him." But as Dana was leaving the room, Stanton called, "No, wait; better go over and see the President."[9]

At the White House, Dana found Lincoln in a side room washing his hands. "Hallo, Dana, what is it? What's up?" the president greeted him. On hearing the telegram, Lincoln asked, "What does Stanton say?" Dana replied, "Arrest him, but that I should refer the question to you." The president, while slowly drying his hands, said, "No I rather think not," and explained, "When you have got an elephant by the hind leg, and he's trying to run away, it's best to let him run." Back at the War Department, Dana relayed the president's answer to Stanton, who snapped, "Oh, stuff!" (Actually, his language was probably stronger than what Dana recorded.) The next morning, a few minutes after Lincoln breathed his last, an officer arrived at Dana's door with a message from his boss: "Mr. Stanton directs you to arrest Jacob Thompson." Dana sent the order to Portland, but Thompson had taken a Canadian route to Nova Scotia and later to England.[10]

In late afternoon Lincoln and Mary rode out to the Navy Yard, where they viewed three damaged ironclads and talked to some of the men. During the ride Mary laughingly remarked, "Dear Husband, you almost startle me by your great cheerfulness." He replied: "And well I may feel so, Mary. I consider *this day*, the war has come to a close."[11] He said he looked forward to returning to Springfield, a desire that he had also expressed to his old law partner John Todd Stuart and to the Marquis de Chambrun.[12]

By six o'clock the Lincolns had returned to the White House, where the president found Governor Richard J. Oglesby, Senator Richard Yates, and other Illinois political leaders hoping to see him. He greeted them warmly and invited them to his room. Lincoln apparently avoided any serious discussion of politics or the war; instead, he read aloud four chapters of the humorous *Nasby Papers,* and was still reading when called to dinner.[13] He ate hurriedly with Mary, Robert, and Tad, then took his usual after-dinner walk to the War Department to read the latest telegrams from the South. On his return he found callers waiting for him. About eight o'clock Mary broke into the conversation and asked, "Well, Mr. Lincoln, are you going to the theater with me or not?" Lincoln grabbed his hat and coat and prepared to leave. George Ashmun, a prominent Republican congressman from Massachusetts, was waiting downstairs to talk with him about a client's cotton claim and also about an undisclosed matter relating to Judge Charles P. Daly of New York. Saying that he did not have time to talk because he had to leave for the theater, Lincoln asked Ashmun to return with Daly the next day. He wrote on a card for the congressman, "Allow Mr. Ashmun & friend to come in at 9 A.M. tomorrow." These were Lincoln's last written words.[14]

In their carriage, the Lincolns went to pick up their theater guests, Major Henry R. Rathbone and his fiancée, Clara Harris. When they took their seats in the presidential box at about eight-thirty, the play *Our American Cousin,* featuring Laura Keene, was in progress. The president's plan to attend had been announced in advance, and many people in the audience had come mainly to see him. (They also expected General Grant to be there.) The orchestra interrupted the actors and played "Hail to the Chief." The audience rose and cheered wildly. Lincoln, according to a witness, "stepped to the box rail and acknowledged the applause with dignified bows and never-to-be-forgotten smiles."[15] He then settled back into the rocking chair the theater had provided him and watched the play.

★ ★ ★

The assassination of Abraham Lincoln is a familiar but often distorted story. Many writers and assassination buffs, especially during the early and mid twentieth century, advanced broad conspiracy theories to explain the murder. Their accusations reached into the Confederate government and even the federal administration in Washington (for example, claiming that Vice President Johnson and Secretary of War Stanton were involved). The circumstances surrounding Lincoln's death continue to be misrepresented in popular literature as well as historical texts.

A murder conspiracy indeed existed, but only a narrow one—and it was not hatched until the last week of Lincoln's life. It grew out of an earlier plot by Confederate sympathizers in Washington and Maryland to kidnap the president and exchange him for Southern prisoners. That plan, led by the popular Maryland actor John Wilkes Booth, was to seize Lincoln on March 17 as he rode in his carriage to attend a play at a hospital near the Soldiers' Home. This scheme collapsed when Lincoln decided to remain in Washington rather than ride out to the hospital. After this failure, most of the conspirators, with the war ending, went their own way. But not Booth, who blamed the country's troubles on Lincoln and saw himself as God's instrument for the punishment of the Northern tyrant. The president's statement in favor of black suffrage in his April 11 address had reinforced the actor's determination to kill him. Booth, listening to the speech on the White House lawn, allegedly turned to his co-conspirator Lewis Powell and declared: "That means nigger citizenship. Now, by God, I'll put him through."[16]

Three days later the announcement that Lincoln would be at Ford's Theatre that evening gave Booth the opportunity to act. He gathered together three other conspirators, including Powell, and made final preparations to kill not only Lincoln but also Vice President Johnson and Secretary of State Seward. Booth hoped that murdering these leaders would ignite a revolution in the North, bring down the Republican or war party, and save the Confederacy. Of the three would-be assassins, only Booth succeeded. George A. Atzerodt, assigned to kill Johnson, lost his courage and did not attack the vice president. Powell forced his way into Seward's home and stabbed him in his bed, but not fatally.

Soon after ten o'clock Booth slipped into the presidential box, where Lincoln, Mrs. Lincoln, and their young guests were watching the play. He placed his derringer pistol close to the back of the president's head and fired a bullet into his brain. Booth momentarily struggled with Major Rathbone, wounding him with a knife, then leaped to the stage. When he jumped, he caught his spur in the flag draped over the presidential box and broke the fibula in his left leg. Nevertheless, he escaped out the back door of the theater.[17]

Pandemonium broke out. Two doctors in the audience rushed to Lincoln's side and quickly determined that he could not survive. Breathing heavily, the president was taken across the street to the Petersen House, where the deathwatch began.

News of the assassination and the stabbing of Seward spread rapidly through Washington, producing fears and wild rumors of more attacks in the city. Cabinet members, awakened during the night, hurried to the Petersen House, not knowing what to expect. Stanton took charge and acted decisively to secure the city and track down the assassins. Before dawn he knew the identities of the attackers and had launched a massive search for them. Booth was killed at a farm in Virginia; the other conspirators survived to be tried for their crime. At 7:22 A.M. on April 15, Lincoln's labored breathing stopped. Stanton, choking back tears, quietly announced, "Now he belongs to the ages."[18]

* * *

The outrage and anguish following Lincoln's death reached heights never before seen in America. He was the first American leader to be assassinated. Such crimes, many believed, occurred where despots ruled, not in republican America where constitutional liberty and self-government, with the blessings of God, prevailed. Lincoln's popularity had soared in the North since the stalemated war of the summer of 1864 and the bitter fall election. He had risen to heroic stature in the Union states; but now a dastardly assassin had struck him down at the moment of his triumph in the war. Northerners concluded that the assassination plot must have involved more than a handful of embittered men led by an actor. How could so few bring down such a mighty leader? Rumors of a widespread conspiracy had already been circulating, promulgated by Southern rebels and Northern traitors with the aim of destabilizing the Union. Many Unionists assumed that Jefferson Davis and his subordinates had planned the murder in a desperate act against Lincoln and the government. Now they were bereft and sought revenge.

"Vengeance on the rebel leaders is the universal cry heard from one end of the country to the other," the Marquis de Chambrun reported a few days after the assassination; "Lincoln's recommendations" of leniency toward the South "are forgotten." The *Washington Chronicle,* normally the voice of moderation in the capital, exclaimed ten days after the act: "The thugs of the Confederacy are among us, and nothing can surely protect us from the assassin's knife but the wholesale terror inspired by a stern and strict execution of the law . . . The satisfaction of seeing [the assassins] dangling at the end of a rope would be a sorry compensation for the great grief they have caused the nation." With biblical cadence, the *Chronicle* thundered, "Vengeance is Mine, I Will Repay, Saith the Lord." In New York, a prominent Republican ruefully commented: "One consolatory fact connected with Lincoln's death is that he cannot pardon his murderer."[19]

No segment of the Union population was more deeply affected than the troops in the field. The death of "Father Abraham" hit hardest with the men in Virginia whom he had recently visited. Tears flowed freely when they heard the news. "The fountains of feeling have been so deeply stirred by this horrid event, that other events scarcely matter at all," a young soldier wrote home from City Point, Virginia. "Mr. Lincoln was different from everybody; so sagacious, so straight-forward in all that he did, so apt in all that he said, and withal so kind-hearted and honest, he was winning the admiration of the whole world." But he "has been murdered—murdered by the same fiendish spirit, begotten in hell, and fed by slavery, that has brought forth this rebellion." Black soldiers profoundly felt the loss of the man many of them viewed as a father figure. Throughout the army, commanders and chaplains held mass meetings of both white and black troops to mourn their fallen leader. Only a few Union soldiers dared express contempt for Lincoln and proclaim good riddance in his death. Some barely escaped lynching at the hands of their comrades.[20]

Only military discipline and threats from their commanders stopped the men in the ranks from taking revenge upon Southerners, including prisoners of war. In Raleigh, where thousands of Sherman's troops were encamped, General John A. "Black Jack" Logan prevented the sacking and burning of the North Carolina capital. Logan placed an artillery battery in the main street and warned an infuriated mob of soldiers that if they did not disperse he would issue the order to fire. Still seething, the troops returned to camp.[21]

Southern Unionists sharply felt the death of their patron. Hurriedly organized public meetings in Raleigh and other occupied Southern towns adopted resolutions expressing "abhorrence of the atrocious deed." Former Confederates attended these rallies in hopes of reducing the threat of revenge on their communities. In Richmond, a number of houses were draped in mourning, and, according to a Northern correspondent, "all citizens who expressed any opinion, denounced" the assassination "without qualification." In Petersburg, Roger A. Pryor, whose wife two weeks earlier had refused to admit Lincoln to their house, declared that "the South, in this crisis, had lost its best friend." Pryor joined other prominent citizens of the town in a call for a public meeting to express their strong disapproval of the murder.[22]

Many Southerners, however, privately applauded or excused the assassination of the Northern "tyrant." Catherine Ann Edmondston, a die-hard Confederate of North Carolina, wondered why Booth had delayed so long to kill "Lincoln the oppressor." Still, Confederates seemed to realize that reconstruction would be harsher and more difficult as a result of Booth's action. Even Edmondston acknowledged that while "Lincoln the rail splitter was bad enough, Johnson, the renegade tailor, is worse."[23]

Radical Republicans may have felt a certain glee at Lincoln's death. The morning after the shooting, Senator Benjamin F. Wade reportedly clasped the hand of the new president, Andrew Johnson, and exclaimed: "I thank God you are here. Mr. Lincoln had too much of human kindness in him to deal with these infamous traitors, and I am glad that it has fallen into your hands to deal out justice to them." Johnson seemed to agree. He told Wade and the other Radicals: "Treason is a crime, and crime must be punished . . . Treason must be made infamous and traitors punished." Congressman George W. Julian attended a meeting of Radicals on the same day and recorded in his journal that "hostility toward Lincoln's policy of conciliation and contempt for his weakness were undisguised, and the Universal feeling among radical men here is that his death is a godsend." Radical Republicans like other Northerners denounced the assassination as a dastardly deed committed by desperate rebels, but they saw the hand of Providence in the event and in Lincoln's replacement by Johnson. Henry Winter Davis, who had several axes to grind with the Lincoln administration, told a friend that the "assassination was a great crime, but the change is no calamity. I suppose God has punished us enough for his weak rule—& ended it." Senator Zachariah Chandler wrote to his wife, "The almighty continued Mr. Lincoln in office as long as he was useful, and then substituted a better man to finish the work."[24]

Several Radicals dutifully delivered eulogies for the fallen president. Even Wendell Phillips, who had refused to support Lincoln in the 1864 election despite the serious consequences for the antislavery cause had the Democrats won, provided tepid praise for Lincoln in an address on April 23. As the years passed and the Radicals turned to recalling their relationship with Lincoln, they ignored or played down their disagreements with him. Senator James W. Grimes of Iowa, who had once proclaimed the president "a disgrace," recognized as early as the day after the assassination that the force of history would be on Lincoln's side in the accounts of the political battles of the Civil War. He predicted: "Mr. Lincoln is to be hereafter regarded as a saint. All his foibles, and faults, and shortcomings, will be forgotten, and he will be looked upon as the Moses who led the nation through a four years' bloody war, and died in sight of peace."[25]

Frederick Douglass, a Radical Republican who had often castigated Lincoln for his slowness in ending slavery and his failure to support racial equality, after the president's death revealed a truer appreciation of the man whom many members of his race idolized. On April 15 Douglass told an audience in Rochester, New York, that the assassination was "a severe stab at Republican institutions. I feel it as a personal as well as a national calamity; on account of the race to which I belong and the deep interest which that good man ever took in its elevation." This African-American leader predicted that "some good may be born of the tremendous evil." The nation had been "in danger of losing a just appreciation of the awful crimes of the rebellion, but that should be ended with the assassination." "In the inscrutable wisdom of Him who controls the destinies of Nations," Douglass said, "this drawing of the Nation's most precious blood was necessary to bring us back to that equilibrium which we must maintain if the Republic was to be permanently redeemed." Today, the "North is a unit" and would be resolved to "exact ample security for the future" of the Union and for both races. "Let us not forget that justice to the negro is safety to the Nation," he declared.[26]

At the other end of the political spectrum from the Radicals, Northern Democratic leaders and newspapers also denounced "that most horrible crime" against the nation. Even the *Detroit Free Press,* which had repeatedly referred to Lincoln as a tyrant, said after his death: "There is one universal feeling of detestation at the crime; one universal cry of vengeance on the perpetrators, and all those who have aided, abetted, or counselled this most atrocious deed."[27] The *Dayton Empire* proclaimed the president's death "a great national calamity," and told its readers that at the time of the assassination Lincoln had been "maturing plans for the pacification of the country, which would have met the approval of the masses." This Copperhead newspaper admitted its longtime opposition to Lincoln, but now "believed that he was sincerely desirous of arranging our affairs upon a proper basis, notwithstanding the threats of radical men." The *Cincinnati Enquirer,* another Democratic newspaper that had vigorously fought against Lincoln's re-election, agreed that his death was "a great public calamity" and indicated that Southerners had lost their best friend in Washington. "The best traits of the man," the *Enquirer's* editor wrote, "were his general sensitiveness and humanity."[28]

The *Enquirer's* Republican counterpart, the *Cincinnati Gazette,* asserted that the "calamity binds the patriot closer to his country, and in proportion strengthens its foundations. The flag appears more precious to-day than previously . . . The blood of our murdered President has brought the people closer together, healed divisions, and thus the very act that was intended to weaken and destroy the Government has given it a new strength." America, according to the *Gazette,* was special. "Our reliance as a Nation is, under God, on the people. Herein we differ from other nations, and herein lies our strength."[29]

Despite Democratic expressions of outrage and the belief of some Republicans that the assassination had united the people, Copperheads, those peace Democrats who had bitterly opposed Lincoln, were targets of mob violence. In Westminster, Maryland, a mob destroyed a Democratic press and a "vigilance committee" killed the editor, who had been an "abusive" critic of the president. In San Francisco, a crowd "wrecked" several newspapers thought to be disloyal; only the timely intervention of General Irvin McDowell prevented violence against the editors and proprietors. Nevertheless, McDowell ordered the suppression of any newspaper and the arrest of any person in the Military Department of the Pacific expressing satisfaction over the assassination. In Philadelphia, a mob assaulted Edward Ingersoll, a member of a distinguished family who reputedly had made a pro-Southern speech a few days earlier. The mob also threatened to destroy the city's Democratic newspaper. The *Philadelphia Press,* a Republican newspaper, condemned the violence and threats against Democrats and cited an incident in which a staunch Union man was set upon by a mob simply because someone pointed to him and cried, "Copperhead!" In Indianapolis, when Democratic Senator Thomas A. Hendricks attempted to speak at a meeting called to deplore the assassination, men rushed the platform brandishing weapons and shouting, "Kill him! Hang him! Don't let the traitor speak!" Fortunately, Governor Oliver P. Morton, a popular war supporter, was present and quelled the unruly crowd.[30]

★ ★ ★

Many Protestant editors and clergymen contributed to the vengeful spirit engulfing the North. Methodist and Congregational divines, in the name of just punishment for rebel evildoers, were the most active in calling for retribution. In Boston, the Congregational minister Daniel C. Eddy exclaimed to his communicants on April 16: "Over the grave of Abraham Lincoln let this nation demand a reign of retribution."[31]

The *Christian Advocate and Journal* (New York), the leading Methodist journal in the Union states, proclaimed after the assassination: "A fouler deed never darkened the records of human crime, or stood forth as a development and indication of the dark and damning turpitude of the spirit of rebellion . . . This foul murder is only one of tens of thousands attempted or achieved by the rebel chiefs and their minions, and the miscreant who murdered the President is the fit companion in guilt of those who fired our cities, or threw railroad trains from their tracks, or starved to death our captured soldiers, and robbed our ships and murdered our sailors upon the high seas." In another editorial, the paper indicated that until Lincoln's assassination "we have been in danger of too lightly estimating the greatness of the sins of treason and rebellion, and attendant crimes." The editor suggested that Lincoln himself had been partly to blame for cultivating "the prevailing sentiment of dealing easily with the conquered leaders of the rebellion, and there was a prospect that after the ruin, and desolations, and deaths they had caused, they would escape all the punitive visitations of law." The editor asserted that Lincoln's murder had ironically changed all that, and the "sickly, soulless sentimentalism" in the North "against the laws of God and man" had been eradicated. Punishment of the rebel leaders would now be sure and severe.[32]

Hundreds of ministers took to their pulpits to preach a similar doctrine of retribution against the "wicked and traitorous rebels." "Preachers' meetings" passed resolutions expressing outrage and, as a Philadelphia Methodist assembly put it, "detestation of the rebellion which has culminated in a crime so deep and dark there is no name for it." The resolutions also expressed the clergy's "deep affliction in the loss of a President so universally beloved." A Cleveland Congregational Church conference sent a resolution to President Johnson denouncing the "demonical assassination" as "one of the legitimate fruits of American Slavery" and demanding "the condign punishment of all active, persistent traitors."[33] R. S. Cushman of the Congregational Church of Manchester, Vermont, contended that before the assassination "mistaken views of Christian mercy [had] poisoned and demoralized so many minds and hearts among us," but that this error had now been corrected. Another Congregational minister, William I. Budington of Brooklyn, exclaimed that Lincoln's murder "checks that unreasonable [and] unchristian charity, which ignores the guilt of sin, and denies the necessity of punishment." J. E. Rockwell, a New York Lutheran minister, told his congregation that "God has permitted this great crime . . . to awaken us to a sense of justice and to a full exaction of the penalty of God's law upon those who have planned and accomplished the horrible scenes of the past four years." Those people in the North, declared Alfred S. Patton, a Baptist minister in Utica, New York, who "are still begging mercy for these heartless traitors" were either "blind adherents of perverted systems of morals and politics, or else, being in sympathy with treason, they have themselves a wholesome fear of justice."[34] Such pulpit calls for a harsh judgment, in a society that had increasingly turned to the church to explain the internecine war, fueled the demand among Northerners for retribution against Southerners for Lincoln's death and the sin of rebellion.

Only a few clergymen whose sermons are extant called for a continuation of Lincoln's policy of charity toward the defeated rebels. The prominent Rabbi Sabato Morais of Philadelphia, perhaps concerned that Northern outrage would be turned against Jews, who already faced a strong undercurrent of anti-Jewish prejudice in America, warned against the "intemperate zeal" of those who had "laid against our General-in-Chief the charge of excessive leniency" toward Southerners. Morais urged moderation in response to the assassination. "Our great Abraham," he told his congregation, "would prefer magnanimity to severity, forgiveness to vengeance."[35]

Many ministers, however, like the Radical Republicans, expressed the conviction that the martyred president had had too much of the milk of human kindness to deal properly with the traitors and evildoers after the war. Lincoln in winning the war had accomplished God's purpose for him, and now he had been replaced by a sterner leader who would punish the rebels, especially their leaders. Daniel C. Eddy told his Boston congregation, "We have had the administration of mercy and forbearance; and I trust we are now to have an administration of justice and retribution." Isaac E. Carey, a Presbyterian minister of Freeport, Illinois, emphasized that Lincoln "had fulfilled the purpose for which God had raised him up, and he passed off the stage because some different instrument was needed for the full accomplishment of the Divine purpose in the affairs of our nation."[36]

In their immediate reaction to the assassination, Protestant clergymen and editors generally shied away from advocating black political equality or a reordering of Southern society after the war. They sought revenge on the leaders and those guilty of war crimes, not on the South generally. A notable exception was an article by a "Western Correspondent" that appeared in the *Christian Advocate and Journal*. This Methodist writer demanded that, in addition to the gallows for the leaders who had incited Southerners to rebellion, "all who have participated in the crime of treason [should] be disfranchised, and forever rendered incapable of holding any office of trust or profit in the gift of freemen." He insisted "that every vestige of the sin and curse of slavery should be removed from the land, and that the semi-civilization in which this VIPER of all our woes lived and moved . . . be destroyed and superseded by the freedom, of education, of Christianity." "Last but not least, . . . all the political rights of freemen and citizens" should be extended to the former slaves, since "their agency has been wielded with great courage in the salvation of the nation; let it also be made available in the country's preservation" in the future.[37]

The call by Northern Protestant leaders for a political revolution in the South would become louder after President Johnson disappointed them by adopting a reconstruction policy that failed to exact guarantees for the Union and secure bona fide black freedom. Northern Protestant divines would be in the forefront of those supporting congressional or military reconstruction in 1867–1868.[38] Nevertheless, despite the passions stirred by Lincoln's assassination and the heavy casualties suffered by the Union in suppressing the rebellion, congressional reconstruction proved remarkably mild. Military rule was relatively brief (no more than sixteen months in most former Confederate states), and black enfranchisement, required by Congress, did not produce a political or social revolution in the South. The rights of the great majority of Southern whites were not seriously affected. The nineteenth-century American commitment to the Founding Fathers' system of federalism, painstakingly sustained by Lincoln during the Civil War, stood firm against the demand of Northern clergymen and Radical Republican congressmen like Thaddeus Stevens for a thoroughgoing reconstruction of Southern politics and society.

★ ★ ★

Public mourning and reflections on the life and character of Lincoln soon paralleled the shock, outrage, and calls for revenge. The funeral ritual, including the profoundly emotional journey of Lincoln's body back to Springfield for burial, created a compelling occasion for an outpouring of eulogies and commentaries on the murdered president. Lincoln, whose elevation to hero status had begun a few months earlier, now assumed godlike qualities in the minds of the Northern public. He had become a martyr for God and the Union, a civil-religious juxtaposition that had been forged during the last part of the war. God's mission for America, achieved in blood and sacrifice, had been fulfilled, many believed; and Lincoln had been the Almighty's agent on Earth for this achievement. He had ensured that the United States would continue to be a model of Christian republicanism and liberty for the world. Northerners concluded that Lincoln, like Jesus, had died for the future of humankind. This historical judgment endured in the consciousness of the Civil War generation and of many Americans into the twentieth century.

Three days after his death, the embalmed body of "the good and great man," as Gideon Welles characterized him, was placed in a richly ornamented coffin on a catafalque in the East Room of the White House. There at noon on April 19 the first of many funeral rites for Lincoln occurred. Offices and shops in Washington—and in many other towns and cities—closed for the day, and flags flew at half mast. Only invited officials, their wives, diplomats, high-ranking army and navy officers, and delegations representing various city and state authorities were admitted to the ceremony. Robert Lincoln was the only member of the family present. General Grant, as if guarding his deceased commander in chief, sat at the head of the open coffin. Dr. Phineas D. Gurley of the New York Avenue Presbyterian Church, which Lincoln had occasionally attended, preached the sermon. George Templeton Strong, an erudite New Yorker and diarist, counted "it a great privilege" to be present at "the most memorable ceremonial this continent has ever seen." "There will be thousands of people ten years hence," he recorded in his diary, "who would pay any money to have been in my place."[39] Strong could have easily written "one hundred years hence."

After the White House funeral, a procession formed and a hearse, with a military escort, took the body on a winding route to the Capitol. Along the streets, tens of thousands of mourners gathered under a cloudless sky to pay their respects. Welles wrote, "There were no truer mourners . . . than the poor colored people who crowded the streets, joined the procession, and exhibited their woe, bewailing the loss of him whom they regarded as a benefactor and father."[40]

Lincoln's body lay in state in the Capitol's rotunda. The casket was opened for almost two days while thousands of people filed past and looked upon their dead president's pale face. Early on the morning of April 21 the coffin, along with Willie Lincoln's disinterred remains, was taken to the Washington depot and placed on a train consisting of a specially outfitted mourning car, eight passenger cars, and an engine. From Washington the train took a long circuitous route to

Springfield, a trip that took thirteen days and covered more than sixteen hundred miles. The War Department designated the tracks over which the train traveled military roads and cleared them of traffic for the cortege.[41] Everywhere along the route farmers, laborers, clerks, mechanics, professionals, women, children, and elderly people stood reverently as the slow-moving train passed. Towns and cities prepared funeral displays and, when the train stopped, held commemoration services.

At Baltimore, the first extended stop (five hours), a large procession, headed by state and city dignitaries and consisting of thousands of people, escorted the coffin to the Merchants' Exchange building, where it was opened. As in Washington, on every Baltimore street crowds of African Americans, "the saddest of the sad," according to an observer, watched as the hearse passed. During the two hours allocated for public display in Baltimore, only about one-fifth of those who had waited, many since dawn, were able to view the body. Four years earlier the president had had to slip through the city to avoid assassination, and in the same year Union troops had been attacked in the streets by a mob cursing the name of Abraham Lincoln. Now, as George Lansing Taylor reported in the inimitable style of the times, those who filed by Lincoln's coffin looked upon a "face, calm as an infant's in unutterable sweet peace, . . . bathed in a blessed, unfathomable, supreme sereneness shed from heaven."[42]

That afternoon the train continued its mournful trip, stopping first at Harrisburg, where the casket was taken to the Pennsylvania state capitol and opened. A long line of people waited, many in vain, to pay their respects. In Philadelphia on April 23 the body lay in state in Independence Hall all day and for four hours that night. The line of people waiting to see the martyred president extended as far as three miles through the city's streets. Army Major Henry S. Wilson, watching from an upstairs window in the historic hall, saw several women and children almost "mashed to death" by the "dense crowd striving to get in to see the remains." In addition, Wilson wrote, "over one hundred women had fainted in the midst of the jam."[43] An estimated one million people crowded into Philadelphia to take part in the demonstrations of respect.

Early the next morning the cortege left for New York. When the train entered New Jersey, the governor and other dignitaries met it at the state border. It stopped briefly in several New Jersey towns, including Trenton, but the casket remained in the car. At Jersey City the coffin was placed on a mourning-draped ferry for the crossing to New York, a city that had twice voted against Lincoln. Thousands of people in Manhattan watched from buildings as the coffin was transferred to a hearse for the procession to City Hall. The events in New York had an ecumenical tone. Protestant and Catholic leaders marched side by side in the procession, and a Jewish rabbi participated in a memorial service at Union Square at which the historian George Bancroft delivered a stirring address. Bancroft, who like many northeastern intellectuals had found Lincoln wanting during most of the war, told an emotional crowd: "The grave that receives the remains of Lincoln receives the martyr to the Union. His enduring memory will assist during countless ages to bind the States together, incite the love of our one undivided country, [and] plead forever for the freedom of man."[44]

Half a million people viewed the body in the New York City Hall rotunda on April 24 and 25. By this time Lincoln's features had deteriorated, partly because of the dust and spring pollen that had accumulated in the casket. His facial color was now leaden, almost brown, his eyes sunken, and his cheeks hollowed and deeply pitted. Charles B. Brown, a master embalmer who had accompanied the cortege from Washington, could do nothing to preserve the body but clear the dust and pollen from it.[45]

Leaving the city in the late afternoon of April 25, the train moved northward toward Albany. The reception was everywhere the same, with crowds of mourners gathered along the route. Thousands came from New England, a region that for practical reasons had been left off the cortege's itinerary. At Syracuse thirty thousand people braved a storm at midnight to greet the train with wreaths, arches, bells, and cannon fire. "A pillar of fire by night" guided the locomotive as it chugged along the countryside and through the towns. At Batavia the aging Millard Fillmore, who had publicly opposed Lincoln's re-election, joined the cortege for the trip to Buffalo. Then on to the Midwest, where the crowds seemed to grow even larger. In Richmond, Indiana, a number far greater than the town's population turned out at three-fifteen in the morning to see the train pass. In Cleveland one hundred fifty thousand mourners from northern Ohio, Michigan, and Pennsylvania viewed the coffin in the public square, where a special pavilion had been constructed. In the state houses in Columbus and Indianapolis these scenes were repeated. In Chicago, where the train arrived on May 1, thirty-six young women, dressed in white and each representing a state, including the Southern states, escorted the coffin to the courthouse. The open casket remained in Chicago for almost two days while Lincoln's fellow Illinoisans paid him their final tribute.[46]

* * *

Finally, on May 3, the funeral train arrived at its last station—Springfield. For twenty-four hours a steady stream of friends and people from the area filed past Lincoln's coffin in the state capitol and viewed the "noble face of our martyred President," as one mourner wrote to her brother. A controversy arose over the burial site when Mary Lincoln vetoed the local committee's plan to bury Lincoln in a grove of trees in the city. It was settled by an agreement to inter his remains outside the town in the Oak Ridge Cemetery.[47] There, on May 4, a simple ceremony ended the funeral rites that had begun in Washington on April 19.

A Methodist bishop, Matthew Simpson, delivered the burial sermon. His oration was a celebration of Lincoln's life and his importance in American history. It was also a paean to the Union's and God's purposes in the war, purposes that had become merged in the minds of most Northerners: "The conviction has been growing on the nation's mind, . . . especially in the last years of his administration, that, by the hand of God, [Lincoln] was especially singled out to guide our government in these troublesome times." Beginning early in life, Simpson announced, God had prepared Abraham Lincoln physically and mentally "for enduring [the] herculean labors" that he would face as president. Akin to this preparation was Lincoln's "identification with the heart of the great people, understanding their feelings because he was one of them, and connected with them in their movements and life." Simpson described the "mental characteristics" on which Lincoln's "greatness rested": a "quick and ready perception of

Matthew Simpson, a prominent Methodist Episcopal bishop and a brilliant orator, who delivered the graveside eulogy for Lincoln in Springfield on May 4, 1865.

the facts" of a case; "a memory unusually tenacious and retentive; and a logical turn of mind, which followed sternly and unwaveringly every link in the chain of thought on every subject which he was called to investigate." Nonetheless, it was his "moral power [that] gave him pre-eminence" and "gained him such control over mankind." Lincoln's honesty, Simpson explained, led men "to yield to his guidance." They "saw in him a man whom they believed would do what is right . . . It was this moral feeling which gave him the greatest hold on the people, and made his utterances almost oracular."[48]

Simpson went on to relate Lincoln's achievements during the war, none surpassing his "giving freedom to a race." All his policies, the bishop contended, were directed toward fulfilling the principles of liberty, Union, and self-government. The American "contest was for human freedom, not for the republic merely; not for the Union simply, but to decide whether the people, as a people, in their entire majesty, were destined to be the government, or whether they were to be subject to tyrants or aristocrats, or to class-rule of any kind." "The result of the contest," Simpson predicted, "will affect the ages to come; republics will spread in spite of monarchs, all over this earth." This, he averred, was the supreme meaning of the war and would be Lincoln's legacy.[49]

The oration concluded with a rhetorical flourish: "Chieftain! farewell! The nation mourns thee. Mothers shall teach thy name to their lisping children. The youth of our land shall emulate thy virtues. Statesmen shall study thy record and learn lessons of wisdom . . . Hushed is thy voice, but its echoes of liberty are ringing through the world, and the sons of bondage listen with joy . . . Thou didst fall not for thyself . . . We crown thee as our martyr—and humanity enthrones thee as her triumphant son."[50]

Abraham Lincoln's life and character, Simpson and other eulogists proclaimed, would forever be a shining example for Americans and others to follow. On the day of Lincoln's burial, the journalist John W. Forney, with great historical vision, enunciated this heroic image of the fallen president:

All men see him and know him, and through all the ages his life and example will never be absent. Long after this generation is dead and forgotten—long after the events of this marvellous time are wrapped in mystery—the life and doings of this man will be read with far more interest than that now given to Julius Caesar. Children will look deep into the line of his face, in bust and picture, to see what manner of man it was that wrote Emancipation. His body we give to the grave, but his manhood we consecrate to everlasting emulation and fame. He has done his work for America, and now America gives him to mankind.[51]

* * *

In Europe, the news of the assassination struck "with a thrill of horror." In London the *Times* reported that within twenty-four hours after hearing the news England was filled "with grief and indignation." Everywhere in Britain "the terrible event was the theme of conversation." The *Liverpool Shipping Gazette* could find "no face in which grief was not depicted," and noted that, despite "strong feelings for the Southerners" during the war, "there is nothing but detestation at the foul murder with which this fratricidal war has been crowned." The British reformer John Bright wrote to Senator Charles Sumner that for fifty years no event "has created such a sensation in this country as the great crime which has robbed you of your President. The whole people positively mourn, and it would seem as if again we were one nation with you, so universal is the grief and the horror at the deed."[52]

Memorials for Lincoln were held throughout Britain, and the House of Lords took the unprecedented action of expressing its outrage and sympathy to the American people. The *Times,* though insisting that "the preponderating sentiment is sincere and genuine," admitted that some of the declarations of sympathy were partly motivated by a concern that Lincoln's death had removed "one valuable guaranty for the amity of the two nations" after the Civil War. The *London Examiner,* however, asserted that the assassination had brought "the people of America nearer to us than we have sometimes remembered of late; nearer [in] their fundamental laws and ideas of order and authority; nearer in their religious sentiments and observances; nearer in their intellectual culture and the great sanctions of domestic life, than any other great people of the world."[53]

An American visitor in Paris reported finding "all over this part of the Globe the most intense horror for the crime and the sincerest sympathy for our loss." The American minister to France, John Bigelow, wrote to Secretary of State Seward: "I had no idea that Mr. Lincoln had such a hold upon the hearts of the [people] of France, or that his loss would be so properly appreciated." French democratic republicans, especially, reacted to the assassination with outrage and a feeling of kinship with America and the cause of liberty and equality that, they believed, Lincoln had nobly represented. The imperial government of Napoleon III sent its condolences to the American people. The French foreign minister, Drouyn de Lhuys, praised Lincoln's "exalted wisdom" and his "examples of good sense, of courage, and of patriotism which he has given" to his country. The prestigious French Academy created an award for the best poem about the death of Lincoln.[54]

Elsewhere in Europe, too, people were shocked by the assassination. Norman Judd, the American minister to Prussia, reported from Berlin: "Mr. Lincoln is being canonized in Europe. A like unanimity of eulogy by Sovereigns, Parliaments, corporate bodies, by the people and by all public journals was never before witnessed on the continent." In autocratic Russia, Czar Alexander II, who had been friendly to the Union during the Civil War, informed Americans that Lincoln's tragic death was "a cause of nation[al] mourning" in his country.[55]

The press of Western Europe, which had rarely said a kind word about Lincoln in his lifetime, tried to make amends. The *Constitution*, a French journal, announced that "the death of Mr. Lincoln is a cause of mourning for all civilization." *Le Pays* confessed that it had been a critic of the Lincoln administration, but added, "We lament from the bottom of our hearts this cruel death." In London, even the editor of *Punch*, a magazine that had gleefully ridiculed the prairie politician throughout the war, admitted that Lincoln "had lived to shame me for my sneer." The *Times*, whose columns had abounded in pro-Confederate and anti-Lincoln commentaries, now acknowledged that Lincoln "had slowly won for himself the respect and confidence of all." It was due to Lincoln that "in the whole of this sanguinary strife, notwithstanding the exasperation of popular feeling, there has been no political blood-thirstiness" in the North.[56]

The *London Review*, which also had criticized Lincoln during the war, now found "something great in that humble, uncouth, gigantic, half-educated rail-splitter from Illinois. He sometimes astonished, sometimes annoyed the refined statesmanship of Europe; but in the end he wrung from it respect, which in the last few weeks was rising into admiration, and which his bloody death will heighten and consecrate." Like other eulogists, the *Review*'s editorial writer saw Lincoln as a peculiar product of nature and specifically the American frontier: "Nature had fashioned him gaunt, and huge, and craggy, the better to encounter the grim work to which he had set his hand." This writer concluded: "Abraham Lincoln has won for himself, by consistency, by firmness, and by a certain progressive and expanding power, the most conspicuous place next to Washington in the list of American Presidents." The *Liverpool Daily Post* summarized the sentiments of many Europeans: "There stands before the world a man whose like we shall not look upon again."[57]

In Canada, where tension with the United States had grown during the winter, "the feeling of horror" was said to be "intense, amounting nearly to stupefaction." In Latin America governments proclaimed days of mourning and men wept in the streets. From around the world, dispatches and letters of condolence from governments, churches, societies, and individuals flooded Washington. Later the federal government compiled and published these materials as an appendix to the diplomatic correspondence of 1865.[58] Lincoln had become an inspiration for many world leaders and a democratic symbol for millions of their subjects.

* * *

Americans, who had long coveted the approval of Europeans while disdaining their autocratic governments and presumed decadence, delighted in the outpouring of sympathy for Lincoln. This favorable world response contributed to the canonization of the late president and, paradoxically, to the affirmation in Northern minds of American exceptionalism.

The virtual deification of Lincoln in the United States had been achieved by early summer. Numerous public meetings were held to commemorate his life and character. These meetings, whose proceedings were often published, gave orators, intellectuals, politicians, and others opportunities to reflect on the late president's place in history; they also contributed to his veneration as an American icon. Memorialists repeatedly linked Lincoln with George Washington, a connection that some staunch Lincoln supporters like John W. Forney had made before his death. While Washington had created a nation, Lincoln had saved the republic and redeemed it for freedom. He had made possible the greatness that Washington and other Founding Fathers had envisioned for America.

Legislative bodies authorized official Lincoln memorials to be read and printed. Congressman Henry C. Deming of Connecticut, speak-

ing to his state's general assembly, delivered perhaps the most elo-
quent and penetrating of these eulogies. Deming declared that Lincoln's magnificent success had derived from his hard and practical
frontier experience, a theme that Bishop Simpson and others had also
emphasized. Lincoln, though "born from a rude stock" in a wild forest, "was nurtured and molded by constant warfare with wilderness
life, and [by] iron fortune and frontier hardships." He was "ennobled
by no patent but that of nature, with no diploma but his record." He
brought to the presidency an "uncompromising common sense [and]
a keen insight into human nature." He also had "an intimate acquaintance with the spasmodic movements of the American mind . . . and in
detecting the occult relations of political cause to political effect." He
formed his policies with "great caution, honesty, and sincerity of purpose." Deming cited, as an example of these qualities, the careful evo-
lution of Lincoln's emancipation policy. Deming closed his address
with the prediction that the "forest born liberator's . . . fame will grow
brighter and grander as it descends the ages, and posterity will regard
him as the incarnation of democracy in its pure childhood and the em-
bodiment of those ideas of universal emancipation, which were the
glory of its youthful epoch."[59]

When Congress convened in December 1865 for its first session
since the end of the war, it provided for the preparation of an official
Lincoln memorial address. President Johnson, after Edwin M. Stanton had declined, chose George Bancroft, America's most prominent
historian, for the task. Bancroft had addressed mourners at Union
Square in New York when Lincoln's body lay in state at City Hall. A
longtime Democrat, Bancroft, when he met Lincoln during the war,
had dismissed him as "a president without brains." Still, he had supported the war and Lincoln's antislavery policy. As the lesser of evils,
he had voted for Lincoln in 1864 (but not in 1860).[60]

On February 12, 1866, Bancroft delivered his Lincoln memorial
address before a joint session of Congress and packed galleries. He
devoted the first third of the oration to the nation's history and its triumph over slavery. Not until page twenty-six did he mention Lincoln,
and then he described the late president as "in every way a child of nature, a child of the West, a child of America." After a brief and rather

bland account of Lincoln's rise to prominence and his firmness in the secession crisis of 1861, Bancroft easily—and eloquently—slipped into a glorification of American exceptionalism and progress and a denunciation of the autocratic governments, hierarchical social organizations, and reactionary religious institutions of the Old World. He singled out Great Britain and France for criticism and unfavorably compared the late Prime Minister Palmerston with Lincoln, asserting that Palmerston represented the "narrowness" of the British aristocracy, while Lincoln "thought always of mankind as well as his own country": "Lincoln took to heart the eternal truths of liberty, obeyed them as the commands of Providence, and accepted the human race as the judge of his fidelity. Palmerston did nothing that will endure." The oration was not what Congress had bargained for in a memorial address. It received mixed reviews in the United States and rekindled anti-American sentiment in Britain and France. John Hay, a member of the United States legation in Paris, pronounced Bancroft's speech "a disgraceful exhibition of ignorance and prejudice."[61]

It was left to the poets to provide the most moving tributes to the fallen president. Newspapers, journals, and literary periodicals published odes and elegies combining tributes to Lincoln with paeans to the Union and those who had died for it during the war. Most of these attempts at memorializing Lincoln and the war heroes have been forgotten. But some endure. Few memorial poems compare with Walt Whitman's "When Lilacs Last in the Dooryard Bloom'd." Without mentioning Lincoln's name, this poem combines Whitman's sense of loss at Lincoln's death with great hope for the future made possible by Lincoln's exemplary life and the sacrifices of Union soldiers. Literary critics have proclaimed "Lilacs" America's most beautiful elegy, though Whitman's sentimental "O Captain! My Captain!" is the best known of his four poetic tributes to Lincoln.[62]

James Russell Lowell, a strong wartime defender of Lincoln in northeastern intellectual circles, owed much of his success as a poet to his "Ode Recited at the Harvard Commemoration" of Harvard men who had died in the war. Though the poem is long and somewhat rambling, at times it achieves remarkable heights. Like Whitman's "Lilacs," Lowell's "Ode" expresses great sorrow at Lincoln's death and at the sacrifices of soldiers for the Union cause and America's future glory. The final verses in the "Ode" stand out as perhaps the greatest epitaph for Lincoln:

Our children shall behold his fame.
The kindly-earnest, brave, foreseeing man,
Sagacious, patient, dreading praise, not blame
New birth of our new soil, the first American.[63]

Few tributes, however, surpassed the four verses that William Cullen Bryant hurriedly composed while Lincoln's body lay in state in New York in April. Bryant, the editor of the *New York Evening Post* and a distinguished man of letters, had often criticized Lincoln for his slowness in moving against slavery and also for his support of the conservative Seward-Weed wing of the New York Republican party. After the Democratic party's adoption of a peace platform in the 1864 campaign, Bryant rallied behind Lincoln but not before he had written a friend: "I am so utterly disgusted with Lincoln's behavior" in making federal appointments in New York "that I cannot muster respectful terms in which to write him." Bryant rejoiced in his party's victory in the election and later wrote that Lincoln "had earned the love of his countrymen to a greater degree, perhaps, than any other person who filled the President's chair, scarcely excepting the 'Father of his Country.'"[64]

The last two verses of Bryant's poetic tribute to Lincoln, which was read by a friend at Union Square on April 24, expressed the poet's deep feeling for the martyred president:

Thy task is done; the bond are free
We bear thee to an honored grave,
Whose noblest monument shall be
The broken fetters of the slave.
Pure was thy life; its bloody close
Hath placed thee with the sons of light,
Among the noble host of those
Who perished in the cause of right.[65]

More than one hundred thirty years after these verses were written, they testify to the importance of this extraordinary man in his own era, to his character, and to the persistence of his spirit in our nation's history. In the last months of his life, Lincoln overcame great adversity and public disparagement to emerge as a leader equaled only by Washington in the pantheon of American heroes. In death, he became a martyr to humanity, to the Union that he had saved, and to the democratic ideals that he had expressed and lived.

Brooks, *Lincoln Observed*
Lincoln Observed: Civil War Dispatches of Noah Brooks, ed. Michael
Burlingame. Baltimore: Johns Hopkins University Press, 1998.

Brooks, *Lincoln's Washington*
*Mr. Lincoln's Washington: Selections from the Writings of Noah
Brooks, Civil War Correspondent,* ed. Philip J. Staudenraus. South
Brunswick, N.J.: Thomas Yoseloff, 1967.

Browning Diary
The Diary of Orville Hickman Browning, ed. Theodore Calvin Pease
and James G. Randall. 2 vols. Springfield: Illinois State Library, 1925–
1933.

Chambrun, *Impressions*
Adolphe de Chambrun, *Impressions of Lincoln and the Civil War: A
Foreigner's Account,* trans. Aldebert de Chambrun. New York: Random House, 1952.

Chase Papers
The Salmon P. Chase Papers, ed. John Nevin, 5 vols. Kent, Ohio: Kent
State University Press, 1993–1998.

Collected Works
The Collected Works of Abraham Lincoln, ed. Roy P. Basler et al. 9
vols. and 2 supplements. New Brunswick, N.J.: Rutgers University
Press, 1953–1955, 1974, 1990.

Grant Papers
The Papers of Ulysses S. Grant, ed. John Y. Simon. Vol. 14: *February
21–April 30, 1865.* Carbondale: Southern Illinois University Press, 1985.

Hay Diary
*Inside Lincoln's White House: The Complete Civil War Diary of John
Hay,* ed. Michael Burlingame and John R. Turner Ettlinger. Carbondale: Southern Illinois University Press, 1997.

Herndon's Informants
Douglas L. Wilson and Rodney O. Davis, eds., *Herndon's Informants:
Letters, Interviews, and Statements about Abraham Lincoln.* Urbana:
University of Illinois Press, 1998.

LC
Manuscript Division, Library of Congress.

Lincoln Papers
Abraham Lincoln Papers, Manuscript Division, Library of Congress.

McPherson, *Political History*
Edward McPherson, ed., *The Political History of the United States of America, During the Great Rebellion.* Washington: Philp and Solomons, 1865.

Nicolay and Hay
John G. Nicolay and John Hay, *Abraham Lincoln: A History.* 10 vols. New York: Century, 1890.

NYT
New York Times.

OR
The War of the Rebellion: A Compilation of the Official Records of the Union and Confederate Armies, 128 vols. Washington: Government Printing Office, 1880–1901.

Pierce, *Memoir of Sumner*
Edward L. Pierce, ed., *Memoir and Letters of Charles Sumner.* 4 vols. Boston: Roberts Brothers, 1878–1894.

Recollected Words
Don E. Fehrenbacher and Virginia Fehrenbacher, eds., *Recollected Words of Abraham Lincoln.* Stanford: Stanford University Press, 1996.

Rice, *Reminiscences*
Allen Thorndike Rice, ed., *Reminiscences of Abraham Lincoln by Distinguished Men of His Time.* New York: North American Review, 1889.

Segal, *Conversations*
Charles M. Segal, ed., *Conversations with Lincoln.* New York: Putnam, 1961.

Strong Diary
The Diary of George Templeton Strong, ed. Allan Nevins and Milton Halsey Thomas. 4 vols. New York: Macmillan, 1952.

Welles Diary
Diary of Gideon Welles: Secretary of the Navy under Lincoln and Johnson, intro. by John T. Morse Jr. 3 vols. Boston: Houghton Mifflin, 1911.

INTRODUCTION

1. Louis A. Warren, comp., *A Man for the Ages: Tributes to Abraham Lincoln,* with a biographical sketch of the author and a bibliography of his writings by John David Smith (Fort Wayne, Ind.: Louis A. Warren Library and Museum, 1978), 57.
2. Message to Congress in Special Session, July 4, 1861, *Collected Works,* 4:426.
3. Annual Message to Congress, Dec. 6, 1864, *Collected Works,* 8:154; Gideon Welles, *Selected Essays by Gideon Welles: Civil War and Reconstruction,* comp. Albert Mordell (New York: Twayne, 1959), 182.
4. Fourth Debate with Stephen A. Douglas, Sept. 18, 1858, *Collected Works,* 3:146; Frederick Douglass in Rice, *Reminiscences,* 193. On Douglass's relationship with Lincoln, see David W. Blight, *Race and Reunion: The Civil War in American Memory* (Cambridge, Mass.: Harvard University Press, 2001), 15–18. Blight maintains that Lincoln after the Emancipation Proclamation was not fundamentally at odds with Douglass on the place of blacks in American society.
5. Speech at Pittsburgh, Pa., Feb. 15, 1861, *Collected Works,* 4:214.
6. Response to a Serenade, Feb. 1, 1865, *Collected Works,* 8:254–255.
7. Entry for Feb. 12, 1865, "George W. Julian's Journal—Assassination of Lincoln," *Indiana Magazine of History* 11 (Dec. 1915): 328. *Radical,* when referring to a specific dissident or stalwart faction in the Republican party, will be capitalized. Unlike the Radicals, the conservatives did not represent a faction in the minds of Northerners; therefore, I will use the lower case when referring to them. At the other end of the political spectrum from the Radicals were Democrats and some border-state Unionists who opposed Lincoln and the Republicans. I have also chosen to capitalize the Federal army but not the federal government.

1. RE-ELECTION

1. Brooks, *Lincoln Observed*, 142–143. Some of the material in this chapter also appears in my essay "Lincoln's Role in the Presidential Election of 1864," in Charles M. Hubbard, ed., *Lincoln Reshapes the Presidency* (Macon, Ga.: Mercer University Press, 2003), 173–198.

2. The delegates believed that Johnson, a hero in the North because of his aggressive Unionism in Tennessee, would bring greater strength to the ticket than Hamlin, who had little support in New England and New York where he should have been strong. The belief that Lincoln dictated the choice of Johnson as vice president is effectively refuted by Don E. Fehrenbacher in "The Making of a Myth: Lincoln and the Vice-Presidential Nomination of 1864," *Civil War History* 41 (Dec. 1995): 273–290.

3. Kirk H. Porter and Donald B. Johnson, eds., *National Party Platforms, 1840–1968* (Urbana: University of Illinois Press, 1973), 34.

4. Entry for Nov. 8, 1864, *Hay Diary*, 243.

5. Ibid.; *Chicago Tribune*, Nov. 9, 1864; *Washington National Intelligencer*, Nov. 9, 1864. On the election in New York, see *New York Tribune*, Nov. 9, 1864. While agreeing with Butler that the election was "quiet and orderly," the *Tribune* charged that fraud in Democratic precincts had reduced the vote for Lincoln. The reported plan to set fire to buildings in New York was real, but it had to be postponed until late November and then failed to do significant damage (see Chapter 6).

6. Entry for Nov. 8, 1864, *Hay Diary*, 245.

7. Ibid.

8. Ibid., 244.

9. Charles A. Dana in Rice, *Reminiscences*, 372–373. About midnight, an oyster supper was provided by Major Eckert. John Hay reported that the president "went awkwardly and hospitably to work shoveling out the fried oysters." Entry for Nov. 8, 1864, *Hay Diary*, 246.

10. Brooks, *Lincoln Observed*, 144; Response to a Serenade, Nov. 8, 1864, *Collected Works*, 8:96. John Hay later transcribed the impromptu speech for the press; entry for Nov. 11, 1864, *Hay Diary*, 248.

11. Response to a Serenade, Nov. 10, 1864, *Collected Works*, 8:100–101.

12. Ibid.

13. Lincoln to Thomas Swann and Others, July 10, 1864, *Collected Works*, 7:437–438.

14. Interview with Alexander W. Randall and Joseph T. Mills, Aug. 19, 1864, *Collected Works*, 7:506–507.

15. Lincoln to Henry W. Hoffman, Oct. 10, 1864, *Collected Works*, 8:41.

16. Memorandum Concerning His Probable Failure of Re-election, Aug. 23, 1864, *Collected Works*, 7:514.

17. Entry for Nov. 11, 1864, *Hay Diary,* 248.
18. John G. Nicolay to John Hay, Aug. 25, 1864, in Helen Nicolay, *Lincoln's Secretary: A Biography of John G. Nicolay* (Westport, Conn.: Greenwood, 1971), 212; Lincoln to Henry J. Raymond, Aug. 24, 1864, *Collected Works,* 7:517, 7:518n.
19. Chase to Kate C. Sprague, Sept. 17, 1864, *Chase Papers,* 4:432.
20. J. K. Herbert to Benjamin F. Butler, Aug. 6, 1864, in *Private and Official Correspondence of Gen. Benjamin F. Butler during the Period of the Civil War,* 5 vols. (Norwood, Mass.: Plimpton, 1917), 5:5–8. For the Wade-Davis Manifesto, see Harold M. Hyman, ed., *The Radical Republicans and Reconstruction, 1861–1870* (Indianapolis: Bobbs-Merrill, 1967), 137–147.
21. Sumner to John Bright, Sept. 27, 1864, in Beverly Wilson Palmer, ed., *The Selected Letters of Charles Sumner,* 2 vols. (Boston: Northeastern University Press, 1990), 2:253. Andrew to Greeley, Sept. 3, 1864, in Henry G. Pearson, *Life of John A. Andrew,* 2 vols. (Boston: Houghton Mifflin, 1904), 2:163.
22. Glyndon Van Deusen, *Thurlow Weed: Wizard of the Lobby* (Boston: Little, Brown, 1947), 310–311; *Washington National Intelligencer,* Aug. 2, 1864; Smith to John Austin Stevens(?), Aug. 27, 1864, in *New York Sun,* June 30, 1889.
23. The *New York Sun* on June 30, 1889, published a large collection of letters relating to the proposed Cincinnati convention, including the call for it.
24. For a fuller account, see William C. Harris, "Conservative Unionists and the Presidential Election of 1864," *Civil War History* 38 (Dec. 1992): 298–318.
25. Paul Revere Frothingham, *Edward Everett: Orator and Statesman* (Boston: Houghton Mifflin, 1925), 462; *Washington National Intelligencer,* Sept. 20, 1864; *Boston Daily Advertiser,* Oct. 29, 1864.
26. Harris, "Conservative Unionists," 313–315. Prominent conservatives, including former president Fillmore, wrote public letters calling for the defeat of Lincoln as the only hope for peace and the restoration of the Union. Fillmore to Hiram Ketchum, Sept. 16, 1864, Millard Fillmore Papers, Buffalo and Erie County Historical Society (microfilm); *Louisville Daily Journal,* Sept. 30, 1864.
27. See, e.g., Joseph George Jr., "'Abraham Africanus I': President Lincoln Through the Eyes of a Copperhead Editor," *Civil War History* 14 (Sept. 1968): 333–335.
28. For the importance of race in the Democratic campaign, see David E. Long, *The Jewel of Liberty: Abraham Lincoln's Re-election and the End of Slavery* (Mechanicsburg, Pa.: Stackpole, 1994), ch. 9.
29. *Louisville Daily Journal,* Sept. 30, 1864. In its October 1864 issues the

Washington Constitutional Union, the newspaper of the Democratic party in the national capital, stressed nonracial charges against the Republicans and only attacked emancipation as an unconstitutional Radical commitment that would prolong the war. See also *Detroit Free Press,* October 1864 issues, shunning anti-black but not anti-emancipation rhetoric in the campaign.

30. *Detroit Free Press,* Nov. 2 and 3, 1864; George B. McClellan to Allan Pinkerton, Oct. 20, 1864, in Stephen W. Sears, ed., *The Civil War Papers of George B. McClellan: Selected Correspondence, 1860–1865* (New York: Ticknor and Fields, 1989), 614–615; McClellan to Robert C. Winthrop, Oct. 22, 1864, ibid., 615–616.

31. Frank L. Klement, *The Limits of Dissent: Clement L. Vallandigham and the Civil War* (New York: Fordham University Press, 1998), 292–294. For the impact of Holt's report and the Republican use of it, see Francis Lieber to Joseph Holt, Oct. 16, 1864; John Hamilton to Holt, Oct. 16, 1864; E. W. Dennis to Holt, Oct. 24, 1864; and R. W. Williams to Holt, Oct. 26, 1864, all in Joseph Holt Papers, LC. For the Democratic denial of a "Western Conspiracy," see *Washington Constitutional Union,* Nov. 1, 1864.

32. Entry for Sept. 27, 1864, *Strong Diary,* 3:494.

33. *Boston Daily Advertiser,* Oct. 7 and 17 (quoting Democrats), 1864; Washburne to Lincoln, Oct. 17, 1864, Lincoln Papers (microfilm); Nicolay and Hay, 9:372.

34. Dickinson to Lewis Cass, Sept. 26, 1864, in *Speeches, Correspondence, etc. of the late Daniel S. Dickinson of New York,* 2 vols. (New York: Putnam, 1867), 2:658; Van Deusen, *Thurlow Weed,* 311; entry for Sept. 21, 1864, *Welles Diary,* 2:155; *Boston Daily Advertiser,* Sept. 2, 1864; *Worcester* (Mass.) *Palladium,* as reported in *Washington National Intelligencer,* Sept. 13, 1864; Quincy (Ill.) *Daily Whig and Republican,* Oct. 27, 1864.

35. For the view that Blair's dismissal was tied to Frémont's withdrawal, see James M. McPherson, *Battle Cry of Freedom: The Civil War Era* (New York: Oxford University Press, 1988), 776.

36. Michael Burlingame, *The Inner World of Abraham Lincoln* (Urbana: University of Illinois Press, 1994), 174–175 (quotation), 222n185; entry for Dec. 18, 1864, *Hay Diary,* 246; Blair to Lincoln, Dec. 6, 1864, Lincoln Papers; entry for Feb. 21, 1865, *Welles Diary,* 2:243–244.

37. John C. Waugh, *Reelecting Lincoln: The Battle for the 1864 Presidency* (New York: Crown, 1997), 308–309 (quotation); *Speeches and Addresses Delivered in the Congress of the United States, and on Several Public Occasions, by Henry Winter Davis, of Maryland* (New York: Harper and Bros., 1867), 429–430.

38. Francis Lieber, *Lincoln or McClellan: Appeal to the Germans in Amer-*

ica (1864), in Frank Freidel, ed., *Union Pamphlets of the Civil War, 1861–1865,* 2 vols. (Cambridge, Mass.: Harvard University Press, 1967), 2:1128–34.

39. *The Liberator,* Sept. 16 and 23, 1864. For Douglass's criticism of Lincoln in 1864, see David W. Blight, *Frederick Douglass's Civil War: Keeping Faith in Jubilee* (Baton Rouge: Louisiana State University Press, 1989), 182–183.

40. William C. Harris, "Abraham Lincoln and Southern White Unionism," in Frank J. Williams, William D. Pederson, and Vincent J. Marsala, eds., *Abraham Lincoln: Sources and Style of Leadership* (Westport, Conn.: Greenwood, 1994), 136–138; Lincoln to the Senate and House of Representatives, Feb. 8, 1865, *Collected Works,* 8:270.

41. Lincoln to Abram Wakeman, July 25, 1864, *Collected Works,* 7:461 and n.

42. Lincoln to James G. Bennett, Feb. 20, 1865, *Collected Works,* 8:307. For Bartlett's report to Bennett on his conversation with Lincoln before the election, see ibid., 8:239–240n.

43. David Herbert Donald, *Lincoln* (New York: Simon and Schuster, 1995), 543.

44. Martin Duberman, *James Russell Lowell* (Boston: Houghton Mifflin, 1966), xix.

45. James Russell Lowell, "The President's Policy" (1864), in Lowell, *Political Essays* (Boston: Houghton Mifflin, 1904), 234–260; Lincoln to Messrs Crosby & Nichols, Jan. 16, 1864, *Collected Works,* 7:132 and n.

46. James Russell Lowell, "The Next General Election," *North American Review* (Oct. 1864): 569–571. Lowell, along with other New England intellectuals, appeared at Lincoln rallies in the Boston area; *Boston Daily Advertiser,* Oct. 13, 1864.

47. For an example of this improvement, see Reply to Members of the Presbyterian General Assembly, June 2, 1863, *Collected Works,* 6:244–245, 245n.

48. William Warren Sweet, *The Methodist Episcopal Church and the Civil War* (Cincinnati: Methodist Book Concern Press, 1912), 89–90; Response to Methodists, May 18, 1864, *Collected Works,* 7:350–351; *Christian Advocate and Journal,* May 26, 1864.

49. *Christian Advocate and Journal,* Sept. 15, 1864; Gilbert Haven, *National Sermons: Sermons, Speeches and Letters on Slavery and its War, From the Passage of the Fugitive Slave Bill to the Election of President Grant* (Boston: Lee and Shepard, 1869), 482.

50. John Hamilton to Joseph Holt, Oct. 16, 1864, Holt Papers; Sweet, *Methodist Episcopal Church,* 86, 111, 129.

51. Resolution of Lutheran General Synod of 1864, in McPherson, *Political*

History, 479 (this book contains several pro-Republican resolutions adopted by church organizations in the election year); Congregational pastor quoted in James H. Moorhead, *American Apocalypse: Yankee Protestants and the Civil War, 1860–1869* (New Haven: Yale University Press, 1978), 156; *Christian Advocate and Journal,* Nov. 17, 1864.

52. Nicolay and Hay, 9:354–355. Response to a Serenade, Oct. 19, 1864, *Collected Works,* 8:52–53.

53. Lincoln to Sherman, Sept. 19, 1864, *Collected Works,* 8:11 and n; Kenneth M. Stampp, *Indiana Politics during the Civil War* (Indianapolis: Indiana Historical Bureau, 1949), 252; McPherson, *Battle Cry of Freedom,* 804.

54. Lincoln to Isaac M. Schermerhorn, Sept. 12, 1864, *Collected Works,* 8:1–2. The draft was in pencil and unfinished.

55. Lincoln to Schermerhorn, Sept. 12, 1864, ibid., 8:2. This letter was sent to Schermerhorn.

56. Response to a Serenade, Oct. 19, 1864, *Collected Works,* 8:52; Estimated Electoral Vote, Oct. 13, 1864, ibid., 8:46; *Boston Daily Advertiser,* Dec. 20, 1864.

57. Response to a Serenade, Nov. 11, 1864, *Collected Works,* 8:100–101.

58. Mark E. Neely Jr., in *The Union Divided: Party Conflict in the Civil War North* (Cambridge, Mass.: Harvard University Press, 2002), provides a brilliant account of the political warfare in the North during the war. He convincingly challenges the argument long established in Civil War scholarship that the two-party system in the North contributed to Union victory. Neely writes that in many ways the reverse was true.

59. Entry for Nov. 9, 1864, *Strong Diary,* 3:511.

60. *Harper's Weekly,* Nov. 19, 1864; Emerson quoted in Waugh, *Reelecting Lincoln,* 357; James Russell Lowell to Aubrey de Vere, Dec. 27, 1864, in Sara Norton and M. A. DeWolfe Howe, eds., *The Letters of Charles Eliot Norton,* 2 vols. (New York: Houghton Mifflin, 1913), 1:282.

61. Motley to Lincoln, Nov. 28, 1864, Lincoln Papers; Marsh to William Pitt Fessenden, Nov. 23, 1864, William Pitt Fessenden Papers, LC.

62. *Christian Advocate and Journal,* Nov. 17, 1864; Beecher quoted in the *St. Louis Missouri Democrat,* Dec. 1, 1864 (despite the name, the *Missouri Democrat* was a Republican newspaper).

63. *Spectator* quoted in *Cincinnati Daily Gazette,* Jan. 24, 1865; Address of the Union and Emancipation Society of Manchester, n.d., in *The Liberator,* Dec. 30, 1864; see also *The Liberator,* Jan. 6, 1865.

64. Entry for Nov. 16, 1864, *Hay Diary,* 251; William C. Davis, *Lincoln's Men: How President Lincoln Became Father to an Army and a Nation* (New York: Free Press, 1999), 222–223; James M. McPherson, *Ordeal by Fire: The Civil War,* 2d ed. (New York: McGraw-Hill, 1993), 458.

65. R. J. M. Blackett, ed., *Thomas Morris Chester, Black War Correspon-*

dent: His Dispatches from the Virginia Front (Baton Rouge: Louisiana State University Press, 1989), 188. I am grateful to Professor John David Smith for bringing this important information to my attention. It is reasonable to conclude that the votes cast by the 5th Colored Troops in 1864 were the first by Ohio's African Americans.

66. *National Anti-Slavery Standard,* Nov. 26, 1864.
67. Davis quoted in Allan Nevins, *The War for the Union,* vol. 4: *The Organized War to Victory, 1864–1865* (New York: Scribner, 1971), 142.
68. The Final Test of Self-Government: An Address Delivered in Rochester, New York, on 13 Nov. 1864, in John W. Blassingame and John R. McKivigan, eds., *The Frederick Douglass Papers,* ser. 1: *Speeches, Debates and Interviews,* vol. 4: *1864–80* (New Haven: Yale University Press, 1991), 31–37; note from Sojourner Truth, *The Liberator,* Dec. 23, 1864.
69. *NYT,* Nov. 10, 1864; Oglesby to Lincoln, Nov. 20, 1864, Lincoln Papers.
70. As reported in Frederick W. Seward, *Seward at Washington, as Senator and Secretary of State: A Memoir of His Life, with Selections from His Letters, 1861–1872* (New York: Derby and Miller, 1891), 250.
71. *Boston Courier,* as reported in the *Boston Daily Advertiser,* Nov. 10, 1864. On the eve of the election, Democratic Senator Thomas A. Hendricks of Indiana wrote to a friend that "the most scandalous frauds" were discouraging McClellan supporters from voting. Thus the Democrats "will not give their full vote" and Lincoln would win the state by default, he declared. Hendricks to Jeremiah Black, Nov. 6, 1864, Jeremiah Black Papers, LC (microfilm). See also *Cincinnati Daily Enquirer,* Nov. 10, 1864, for similar charges. In the border states the loyalty oath was required of voters, which aided the Republican party though perhaps only enough to win Maryland.
72. McClellan to Manton M. Marble, Nov. 28, 1864, in Sears, ed., *Civil War Papers of McClellan,* 624. Barlow to McClellan, Nov. 9, 1864, ibid., 619n; *Register* quoted in Robert S. Harper, *Lincoln and the Press* (New York: McGraw-Hill, 1951), 224; see also *Chicago Times,* Nov. 8, 1864, for a similar reaction to Lincoln's re-election; Marble to McClellan, Nov. 13, 1864, Manton M. Marble Papers, LC; *New York World,* Nov. 9, 1864.
73. Extract of a Nov. 16, 1864, letter by Robert C. Winthrop (correspondent unknown), in *A Memoir of Robert C. Winthrop, Jr., Prepared for the Massachusetts Historical Society* (Boston: Little, Brown, 1897), 261.
74. *Washington National Intelligencer,* Nov. 22, 1864; *Louisville Daily Journal,* Oct. 24, 1864; Nov. 10, 1864; Jan. 16, 1865.
75. Davis to Confederate Congress, Nov. 7, 1864, in Dunbar Rowland, ed.,

Jefferson Davis, Constitutionalist: His Letters, Papers and Speeches, 10 vols. (Jackson: Mississippi Department of Archives and History, 1923), 6:397–398; *Savannah Republican* quoted in *New York World,* Nov. 10, 1864; entry for Nov. 17, 1864, in Frank E. Vandiver, ed., *The Civil War Diary of General Josiah Gorgas* (University: University of Alabama Press, 1947), 150.

76. Larry E. Nelson, *Bullets, Ballots, and Rhetoric: Confederate Policy for the United States Presidential Contest of 1864* (University: University of Alabama Press, 1980), 158–159.

77. Ibid., 159; entry for Nov. 15, 1864, in Beth G. Crabtree and James W. Patton, eds., *"Journal of a Secesh Lady": The Diary of Catherine Ann Devereux Edmondston, 1860–1866* (Raleigh: North Carolina Division of Archives and History, 1979), 635.

78. Quotation from Nevins, *War for the Union,* 4:119–120.

2. CAREWORN AND HAGGARD

1. Brooks, *Lincoln's Washington,* 17; Francis B. Carpenter, *The Inner Life of Abraham Lincoln: Six Months at the White House* (New York: Hurd and Houghton, 1868), 217; Arnold in Francis Fisher Browne, *The Every-Day Life of Abraham Lincoln: A Narrative and Descriptive Biography with Pen-Pictures and Personal Recollections by Those Who Knew Him* (Chicago: Browne and Howell, 1913), 545; Speed in David Herbert Donald, *Lincoln* (New York: Simon and Schuster, 1995), 568.

2. Browne, *Every-Day Life of Lincoln,* 545–546; Chambrun, *Impressions,* 100; *Washington Daily Chronicle,* July 26, 1864.

3. *Recollected Words,* 399, 506; Brooks, *Lincoln Observed,* 210.

4. *NYT,* Nov. 29, 1864.

5. Hay to William H. Herndon, Sept. 5, 1866, Herndon-Weik Collection, LC (microfilm).

6. Entry for Mar. 23, 1865, *Welles Diary,* 2:264.

7. *Recollected Words,* 503; William O. Stoddard, *Inside the White House in War Times: Memoirs and Reports of Lincoln's Secretary,* ed. Michael Burlingame (Lincoln: University of Nebraska Press, 2000), 109.

8. John Hay, "Life in the White House in the Time of Lincoln," in *Addresses of John Hay* (New York: Century, 1906), 326, 334; Carpenter, *Inner Life of Lincoln,* 223–225.

9. Pierce, *Memoir of Sumner,* 4:233; David R. Locke in Rice, *Reminiscences,* 447–448; entry for Feb. 7, 1865, *Welles Diary,* 2:238; Edwin C. Haynie, "At the Deathbed of Lincoln," *Century Magazine* 51 (1895–1896), 954.

10. Locke in Rice, *Reminiscences,* 442.

11. Entry for Jan. 1 [2?], 1865, Horatio Nelson Taft Diary, LC.

12. *New York Herald,* Jan. 4, 1865; entry for Jan. 2, 1865, *Welles Diary,* 2:219.

13. *Washington Daily National Republican,* Jan. 27, 1865; Chambrun, *Impressions,* 20–21, 33–34; *Recollected Words,* 123.

14. Justin G. Turner and Linda Levitt Turner, *Mary Todd Lincoln: Her Life and Letters* (New York: Knopf, 1972), 96–97, 161, 163.

15. Ibid., 145–146; Mary Todd Lincoln to Charles Sumner, Nov. 20, 24, 1864, ibid., 191–193. Lincoln thought highly of Banks and kept the general in Washington until April to lobby for his reconstruction plan; William C. Harris, *With Charity for All: Lincoln and the Restoration of the Union* (Lexington: University Press of Kentucky, 1997), 233, 246.

16. Douglass in Rice, *Reminiscences,* 195.

17. *Recollected Words,* 414; Browning to Isaac N. Arnold, Nov. 25, 1872, Isaac Newton Arnold Papers, Chicago Historical Society, Research Center; Matheny to J. A. Reed, Dec. 16, 1872, in James A. Reed, "The Later Life and Religious Sentiments of Abraham Lincoln," *Scribner's Monthly* (July 1873):337; Matheny interview, Dec. 9, 1873, in *Herndon's Informants,* 582–583.

18. Carpenter, *Inner Life of Lincoln,* 186–188; *Herndon's Informants,* 360; Richard N. Current, *The Lincoln Nobody Knows* (New York: Hill and Wang, 1992), 64; *Christian Advocate and Journal,* Apr. 27, 1865.

19. Carpenter, *Inner Life of Lincoln,* 202–203; Henry Champion Deming, *Eulogy of Abraham Lincoln, Before the General Assembly of Connecticut (June 8, 1865)* (Hartford: A. N. Clark, 1865), 41–42.

20. Stoddard, *Inside the White House,* 176.

21. Lincoln to Eliza P. Gurney, Sept. 4, 1864, *Collected Works,* 7:535. The statement about God's purpose was made to an old Illinois friend in 1864; Joseph Gillespie to William H. Herndon, Jan. 31, 1866, in *Herndon's Informants,* 182.

22. *National Baptist* (Philadelphia), Aug. 31, 1865, quoted in Lemuel Moss, *Annals of the United States Christian Commission* (Philadelphia: Lippincott, 1868), 214–215; see also *Collected Works,* 8:241 and 241–242n.

23. Moss, *Christian Commission,* 215–216.

24. Ibid., 217–218, 256; *Christian Advocate and Journal,* Feb. 16, 1865; Lincoln to George H. Stuart, Jan. 29, 1865, *Collected Works,* 8:245. Stuart in a letter to Josiah G. Holland, July 13, 1865, offers a slightly different account of Lincoln's attendance at the Christian Commission meeting; Allen C. Guelzo, "Holland's Informants: The Construction of Josiah Holland's 'Life of Abraham Lincoln,'" *Journal of the Abraham Lincoln Association* 23 (Winter 2002): 41–42.

25. Brooks, *Lincoln Observed,* 84; *Recollected Words,* 192; clipping from the *New Orleans Daily True Delta,* Jan. 1, 1864, Lincoln Papers.

26. "President Lincoln," *Littell's Living Age,* Feb. 18, 1865, excerpting *Macmillan's Magazine.*

27. Hay, "Life in the White House," 324–325; Stoddard, *Inside the White House,* 150.

28. Hay, "Life in the White House," 324; Hay to William H. Herndon, Sept. 5, 1866, Herndon-Weik Collection; Brooks, *Lincoln Observed,* 85; *Baltimore American and Commercial Advertiser,* Mar. 23, 1865, in Segal, *Conversations,* 375–378.

29. Entry for Dec. 24, 1864, *Welles Diary,* 2:201; Stoddard, *Inside the White House,* 170–171; *Christian Advocate and Journal,* Mar. 30, 1865. See Chapter 6 for the Beall and Kennedy cases.

30. Speed to Herndon, Jan. 12, 1866, in *Herndon's Informants,* 157–158.

31. Segal, *Conversations,* 372–373.

32. *Recollected Words,* 294.

33. Hay, "Life in the White House," 328; Stoddard, *Inside the White House,* 201; entries for Sept. 16, 1862, and Sept. 20, 1864, *Welles Diary,* 1:131, 136–137, 2:151.

34. Stoddard, *Inside the White House,* 182.

35. Entries for Oct. 1 and 7, 1864, *Welles Diary,* 2:166, 2:173–174.

36. Edward D. Neill, "Reminiscences of Lincoln's Last Year," in Theodore C. Blegen, ed., *Abraham Lincoln and His Mailbag: Two Documents by Edward D. Neill, One of Lincoln's Secretaries* (St. Paul: Minnesota Historical Society, 1964), 26.

37. Hay, "Life in the White House," 328, 331; Hay to Herndon, Sept. 5, 1866, Herndon-Weik Collection.

3. THE BURDEN OF PATRONAGE

1. The papers of Senator John Sherman, for example, in the Library of Congress, are replete with applications, letters of recommendation, and endorsements of Ohio Republicans seeking local federal positions after the election. No ambitious senator or representative would neglect to approach his party's president about these petitions.

2. Jean H. Baker, *Mary Todd Lincoln: A Biography* (New York: Norton, 1987), 202–203; Elizabeth J. Grimsley to Lincoln, Nov. 22, 1864, Lincoln Papers.

3. Francis B. Carpenter, *The Inner Life of Abraham Lincoln: Six Months at the White House* (New York: Hurd and Houghton, 1868), 276.

4. J. G. Randall and Richard N. Current, *Lincoln the President: Last Full Measure* (1955; Urbana: University of Illinois Press, 1991), 267–269; David M. Silver, *Lincoln's Supreme Court* (1957; Urbana: University of Illinois Press, 1998), 84–89, 74–75.

5. Frederick J. Blue, *Salmon P. Chase: A Life in Politics* (Kent, Ohio: Kent State University Press, 1987), 242; Charles Sumner to Francis Lieber,

Oct. 12, 1864, in Pierce, *Memoir of Sumner,* 4:207–209; Sumner to Chase, Oct. 24, 1864, in Beverly Wilson Palmer, ed., *The Selected Letters of Charles Sumner,* 2 vols. (Boston: Northeastern University Press, 1990), 2:24; Chase to Edwin M. Stanton, Oct. 13, 1864, *Chase Papers,* 4:432.

6. Wade quoted in entry for [July–Aug. 1863], *Hay Diary,* 77; *Recollected Words,* 2.

7. Entries for Sept. 14, 15, and 16, 1864, *Chase Papers,* 1:503–504; Chase to Kate Chase Sprague, Sept. 17, 1864; Chase to George S. Denison, Sept. 20, 1864, ibid., 4:432, 434.

8. Chase to George S. Denison, Nov. 11, 1864; Chase to Charles Sumner, Nov. 12, 1864; Samuel Hooper to Chase, Nov. 20, 1864; Schuyler Colfax to Chase, Dec. 5, 1864, ibid., 4:437–438, 439, 444–445.

9. *St. Louis Missouri Democrat,* Dec. 1, 1864; Lincoln quoted in Nicolay and Hay, 9:392.

10. Nicolay and Hay, 392–393; Allan Nevins, *The War for the Union,* vol. 4: *The Organized War to Victory, 1864–1865* (New York: Scribner, 1971), 118; entry for Nov. 26, 1864, *Welles Diary,* 2:181.

11. Entries for Oct. 17 and 18, 1864, *Browning Diary,* 1:688; entries for Nov. 22, Nov. 30, and Dec. 2, 1864, in Howard K. Beale, ed., "The Diary of Edward Bates, 1859–1866," in *Annual Report of the American Historical Association for the Year 1930* (Washington: Government Printing Office, 1930), 4:427–428, 429; *Collected Works,* 8:126n.

12. Edward Everett to Lincoln, Nov. 22, 1864, Lincoln Papers; Randall and Current, *Lincoln the President,* 272; entry for Nov. 26, 1864, *Welles Diary,* 2:181–182, 187.

13. Entries for Dec. 6 and 15, 1864, *Welles Diary,* 2:192, 196; *Recollected Words,* 162.

14. George S. Boutwell, *Reminiscences of Sixty Years in Public Affairs,* 2 vols. (1902; New York: Greenwood, 1968), 2:29; Brooks, *Lincoln Observed,* 154.

15. Entries for Nov. 9 and Dec. 18, 1864, *Hay Diary,* 246–247, 252.

16. *Sacramento Union,* Jan. 11, 1865; *Boston Journal,* Dec. 10, 1864; Dawes to his wife, Dec. 6, 1864, Henry L. Dawes Papers, LC.

17. Frank Blair to Montgomery Blair, Jan. 17, 1865, Blair Family Papers, LC (microfilm); Buchanan quoted in Nevins, *War for the Union,* 4:206.

18. Chase to Lincoln, Dec. 6, 1864, *Chase Papers,* 4:445; *Boston Journal,* Dec. 10, 1864; Blue, *Salmon P. Chase,* 245.

19. Chase to William Tecumseh Sherman, Jan. 2, 1865; Chase to Wendell Phillips, Feb. 7, 1865; Chase to Francis Lieber, Feb. 14, 1865, *Chase Papers,* 5:3–4, 10–11, 11–12.

20. Chase to Lincoln, Apr. 11, 1865, ibid., 5:15–16; Last Public Address, Apr. 11, 1865, *Collected Works,* 8:403.

21. Entry for Dec. 10, 1864, *Welles Diary,* 2:195–196.

22. Entry for Dec. 18, 1864, *Hay Diary,* 253–254.
23. Entry for Nov. 11, 1864, ibid., 249.
24. Entry for Feb. 21, 1865, *Welles Diary,* 2:243.
25. Ibid.; Harry J. Carman and Reinhard H. Luthin, *Lincoln and the Patronage* (New York: Columbia University Press, 1943), 325–326; Memorandum Concerning Maryland Appointments, Apr. 14, 1865, *Collected Works,* 8:411.
26. *Collected Works,* 7:268–269n; Carman and Luthin, *Lincoln and the Patronage,* 296, 314; Glyndon Van Deusen, *Thurlow Weed: Wizard of the Lobby* (Boston: Little, Brown, 1947), 310.
27. John G. Nicolay to Lincoln, Aug. 29, 30, 31, 1864, in Michael Burlingame, ed., *With Lincoln in the White House: Letters, Memoranda, and Other Writings of John G. Nicolay, 1860–1865* (Carbondale: Southern Illinois University Press, 2000), 154–156; entry for Sept. 5, 1864, *Welles Diary,* 2:136–137; Carman and Luthin, *Lincoln and the Patronage,* 314–315.
28. *Boston Journal,* Nov. 14, 1864; *Christian Advocate and Journal,* Dec. 1, 1864; *Boston Commonwealth,* Nov. 12, Dec. 17, 1864.
29. *New York Herald,* Mar. 4, 1865; *Recollected Words,* 442–443.
30. *Boston Commonwealth,* Nov. 12, 1864; *Boston Journal,* Nov. 14, 1864, Feb. 14, 1865; *New York World,* Dec. 9, 1864; *Cincinnati Daily Gazette,* Feb. 25, 1865.
31. Sarah F. Hughes, ed., *Letters and Recollections of John Murray Forbes,* 2 vols. (Boston: Houghton Mifflin, 1899), 2:122; see also *Boston Journal,* Mar. 1, 1865; George L. Stearns to Andrew Johnson, Jan. 16, 1865, in *The Papers of Andrew Johnson,* vol. 7, *1864–1865,* ed. Leroy P. Graf (Knoxville: University of Tennessee Press, 1986), 414–415, 415n.
32. Rice, *Reminiscences,* 241; *St. Louis Missouri Democrat,* Jan. 9, 1865.
33. Entry for Dec. 9, 1864, *Welles Diary,* 2:194–195; see also William P. Fessenden to Israel Washburn, Dec. 29, 1864, William Pitt Fessenden Papers, LC (microfilm). There is no evidence that Seward talked to Lincoln about Usher's situation in the cabinet.
34. Entry for Oct. 2, 1864, *Hay Diary,* 235; Allen Johnson and Dumas Malone, eds., *Dictionary of American Biography* (New York: Scribner, 1928), 9:182.
35. Holt to Lincoln, Nov. 30, 1864, Lincoln Papers; Rice, *Reminiscences,* 241. For Holt's Mississippi family, see J. R. Holt to "Uncle" (Joseph), Oct. 16, 1864, Joseph Holt Papers, LC.
36. Lincoln to James Speed, Dec. 1, 1864, *Collected Works,* 8:126; entries for Dec. 6 and 16, 1864, *Welles Diary,* 2:192, 197.
37. *Boston Commonwealth,* Dec. 17, 1864.
38. Gary Lee Williams, "James and Joshua Speed: Lincoln's Kentucky Friends" (Ph.D. diss., Duke University, 1971), 69, 119; *American Na-*

tional Biography, ed. John A. Garraty and Mark C. Carnes, 24 vols. (New York: Oxford University Press, 1999), 20:431–432.

39. Fessenden to Israel Washburn, Nov. 18, Dec. 29, 1864, Fessenden Papers; *Autobiography of Thurlow Weed,* 2 vols. (Boston: Houghton Mifflin, 1884), 1:622.

40. Carman and Luthin, *Lincoln and the Patronage,* 307.

41. Fessenden to Lincoln, Feb. 6, 1865, Letterbook, Fessenden Papers; Randall and Current, *Lincoln the President,* 277.

42. *Autobiography of Weed,* 1:620–622; James A. Rawley, *Edwin D. Morgan, 1811–1893: Merchant in Politics* (New York: Columbia University Press, 1955), 201–202; *Cincinnati Daily Gazette,* Feb. 25, 1865.

43. *Autobiography of Weed,* 1:622–623.

44. *St. Louis Missouri Democrat,* Feb. 28, 1865; *American National Biography,* 14:948–949. McCulloch's support of President Johnson against congressional Republicans during Reconstruction, however, would cost him powerful allies and obscure his important contributions to the postwar financial health of the country.

45. Entry for Mar. 3, 1865, *Welles Diary,* 2:251.

46. Elmo R. Richardson and Alan W. Farley, *John Palmer Usher: Lincoln's Secretary of the Interior* (Lawrence: University of Kansas Press, 1960), 50–52, 86; *Cincinnati Daily Gazette,* Feb. 25, Mar. 15, 1865.

47. Johnson Brigham, *James Harlan* (Iowa City: State Historical Society of Iowa, 1913), 189–190; *Philadelphia Press,* Mar. 13, 1865; *American National Biography,* 10:94.

48. Brigham, *James Harlan,* 194–196; *American National Biography,* 10:94.

49. Entry for Nov. 26, 1864, *Welles Diary,* 2:183.

50. Entry for Mar. 3, 1865, ibid., 2:251; *Philadelphia Press,* Mar. 13, 1865; Elizabeth Keckly, *Behind the Scenes; Or, Thirty Years a Slave, and Four Years in the White House* (New York: Oxford University Press, 1988), 157.

51. In March Lincoln told Edouard de Stoeckl, the Russian chargé d'affaires in Washington, that he hoped the war would be over by the end of the year, implying that he expected heavy fighting to continue until that time; Albert A. Woldman, *Lincoln and the Russians* (Cleveland: World Publishing, 1952), 153, quoting Stoeckl's dispatch to Prince Alexander Gortchakov, Apr. 10, 1865.

52. Last Public Address, Apr. 11, 1865, *Collected Works,* 8:403.

4. THE SEARCH FOR PEACE

1. Entry for Nov. 25, 1864, *Welles Diary,* 2:179.

2. Annual Message to Congress, Dec. 6, 1864, *Collected Works,* 8:137–139, 140–141.

3. Ibid., 146–147.
4. Ibid., 148–149.
5. Ibid., 149.
6. Ibid., 149–150, 151.
7. Ibid., 151–152.
8. Ibid., 152. Some historians have claimed that Lincoln in his annual message was threatening a harsher reconstruction policy; see Stephen B. Oates, *Abraham Lincoln: The Man Behind the Myth* (New York: Harper and Row, 1984), 140; Herman Belz, *Reconstructing the Union: Theory and Policy during the Civil War* (Ithaca: Cornell University Press, 1969), 248–249; James M. McPherson, *Battle Cry of Freedom: The Civil War Era* (New York: Oxford University Press, 1988), 843.
9. Annual Message to Congress, Dec. 6, 1864, *Collected Works*, 8:152.
10. *Washington National Republican*, Dec. 6, 1864; *Evening Post* quoted ibid., Dec. 9, 1864; *Gazette* quoted ibid., Dec. 10, 1864.
11. *St. Louis Missouri Democrat*, Dec. 16, 1864, citing the *Cincinnati Gazette*; Beverly Wilson Palmer, ed., *The Selected Papers of Thaddeus Stevens*, vol. 1: *January 1814–March 1865* (Pittsburgh: University of Pittsburgh Press, 1997), 512–513; *New York Independent* quoted in *The Liberator*, Dec. 23, 1864.
12. Lincoln to James H. Van Alen, Apr. 14, 1865, *Collected Works*, 8:413.
13. *St. Louis Missouri Democrat*, Dec. 16, 1864; *Boston Commonwealth*, Dec. 10, 1864; *New Orleans Tribune*, Dec. 21, 1864.
14. Lincoln to Stephen A. Hurlbut, Nov. 14, 1864, *Collected Works*, 8:106–107.
15. *Boston Commonwealth*, Dec. 10, 1864; *St. Louis Missouri Democrat*, Dec. 16, 1864, quoting the Washington correspondent of the *Cincinnati Gazette*. For a fuller account of the Lincoln-Banks effort to secure the seating of the Louisiana congressional delegation, see William C. Harris, *With Charity for All: Lincoln and the Restoration of the Union* (Lexington: University Press of Kentucky, 1997), 233–237.
16. Harris, *With Charity for All*, 237.
17. For a detailed account of the complicated proceedings over reconstruction legislation, see Belz, *Reconstructing the Union*, 250–265. My interpretation of the meaning of the congressional proceedings differs in some important aspects from Belz's.
18. *Chicago Tribune*, Feb. 1, 1865; *Boston Daily Advertiser*, Dec. 19, 28, 1864, Feb. 4, 1865; *Congressional Globe*, 38th Cong., 2d sess. (Jan. 24, 1865), 382–383; ibid. (Jan. 30, 1865), 434.
19. Zachariah Chandler to his wife, Jan. 16, 27, 1865, Zachariah Chandler Papers, LC (microfilm); *Boston Journal*, Jan. 26, 1865; *Philadelphia Press*, Jan. 27, 1865; Pierce, *Memoir of Sumner*, 4:211–212; Bruce Tap, *Over Lincoln's Shoulder: The Committee on the Conduct of the War* (Lawrence: University Press of Kansas, 1998), 207.

20. U.S. Congress, 38th Cong., 2d sess., *Senate Report* no. 127, 2–3.

21. Harris, *With Charity for All*, 244–245.

22. Washington correspondent (Noah Brooks?), Mar. 2, 1865, to *Sacramento Daily Union*, Apr. 10, 1865.

23. *Address of Hon. R. King Cutler, United States Senator of Louisiana (1865)*, in Henry Clay Warmoth Pamphlets, University of North Carolina Library, Chapel Hill.

24. *Harper's Weekly* 8 (Dec. 24, 1864), 818; "Occasional" (John W. Forney) to *Washington Daily Morning Chronicle*, Jan. 11, 1865; see also *Boston Journal*, Dec. 7, 1864; *Boston Daily Advertiser*, Dec. 7, 1864.

25. *Washington Daily Morning Chronicle*, Jan. 4, 1865; Larry E. Nelson, *Bullets, Ballots, and Rhetoric: Confederate Policy for the United States Presidential Contest of 1864* (University: University of Alabama Press, 1980), 164–165; *Boston Journal*, Feb. 16, 1865.

26. McPherson, *Political History*, Appendix, 457.

27. *Charlotte Western Democrat*, Nov. 29, 1864; *NYT*, Dec. 17, 1864; *Raleigh North Carolina Standard*, Jan. 4, 1865; Samuel F. Phillips to William H. Battle, Jan. 25, Feb. 4, 1865, Battle Family Papers, Southern Historical Collection, University of North Carolina, Chapel Hill.

28. Henry G. Connor, *John Archibald Campbell: Associate Justice, 1853–1861* (Boston: Houghton Mifflin, 1920), 161–163.

29. *Boston Journal*, Feb. 16, 1865, citing the *Raleigh Progress*, Feb. 3, 1865.

30. *New York Tribune*, Jan. 16, 1865; entries for Nov. 24, 26, Dec. 24, 1864, *Browning Diary*, 1:693–694, 695, 699.

31. Entry for Dec. 24, 1864, *Browning Diary*, 1:699; Pass for James W. Singleton, Jan. 5, 1865, *Collected Works*, 8:200. On the controversial and often illicit trade through the lines, see Chapter 6.

32. *New York Tribune*, Jan. 13, 1865.

33. Singleton's account of his mission appeared in several newspapers, including the *New York Times*, June 25, 1865.

34. *NYT*, June 25, 1865. About the same time Lee cautiously confided similar thoughts to Senator Robert M. T. Hunter of Virginia and General John B. Gordon. He refused, however, to communicate his views to Davis. Mark Grimsley, "Learning to Say 'Enough': Southern Generals and the Final Weeks of the Confederacy," in Mark Grimsley and Brooks D. Simpson, eds., *The Collapse of the Confederacy* (Lincoln: University of Nebraska Press, 2001), 48–50.

35. The account of the Singleton transaction and Lincoln's role in it has been pieced together from several sources. Entries for Jan. 30, 31, Feb. 1, 7, 21, 23, 1865, *Browning Diary*, 2:4–7; *NYT*, June 25, 1865; *New York Tribune*, Feb. 2, 6, 1865; *Boston Daily Advertiser*, Mar. 14, 1865; *St. Louis Missouri Democrat*, Mar. 18, 1865.

36. Lincoln to Grant, Feb. 7, 1865, *Collected Works*, 8:267.

37. Grant to Stanton, Mar. 8, 1865, *Grant Papers*, 14:113; *St. Louis Missouri Democrat*, Mar. 18, 1865; *NYT*, June 25, 1865; *Boston Daily Advertiser*, Mar. 14, 1865; entries for Mar. 11 and 16, 1865, *Browning Diary*, 2:10–12.

38. Grant to Singleton, Mar. 20, 1865, *Grant Papers*, 14:188.

39. Entry for Apr. 12, 1865, *Browning Diary*, 2:17; Matthew Page Andrews, "Singleton," *NYT*, Feb. 12, 1928; Pass for James W. Singleton, Apr. 13, 1865, *Collected Works*, 8:410.

40. Horace Greeley to Francis P. Blair Sr., Dec. 15, 1864, Blair Family Papers, LC (microfilm reel 17).

41. Blair to Greeley, Dec. 20, 1864, in William Ernest Smith, *The Francis Preston Blair Family in Politics*, 2 vols. (New York: Macmillan, 1933), 2:302.

42. Pass for Francis P. Blair Sr., Dec. 28, 1864, *Collected Works*, 8:188–189n; Nicolay and Hay, 10:96.

43. Davis to Blair, Jan. 12, 1865, *Collected Works*, 8:275 (italics added); on Blair's mission and Davis's reaction, see William C. Harris, "The Hampton Roads Peace Conference: A Final Test of Lincoln's Presidential Leadership," *Journal of the Abraham Lincoln Association* 21 (Winter 2000):34–36.

44. Smith, *Blair Family in Politics*, 2:311; *New York Herald*, Jan. 23, 1865.

45. Lincoln to Blair, Jan. 18, 1865, *Collected Works*, 8:220–221 (italics added).

46. *Boston Daily Advertiser*, Jan. 25, 1865; *NYT*, Jan. 10, 1865; see also Noah Brooks, *Washington in Lincoln's Time* (New York: Rinehart, 1958), 202.

47. Harris, "Hampton Roads Peace Conference," 39; James L. Bates to Stanton, Jan. 23, 1865, Edwin M. Stanton Papers, LC (microfilm); entry for Jan. 30, 1865, *Welles Diary*, 2:231–232.

48. *New York Herald*, Jan. 23, 1865; Brooks, *Washington in Lincoln's Time*, 202–203; Chandler to his wife, Jan. 25, 1865, Chandler Papers; Joseph Medill to Lincoln, Jan. 15, 1865, Lincoln Papers.

49. Alexander H. Stephens, *A Constitutional View of the Late War between the States*, 2 vols. (Philadelphia: National Publishing, 1870), 2:295; Lincoln to Thomas T. Eckert, Jan. 30, 1865, *Collected Works*, 8:277. For Davis's purpose in dispatching the peace commissioners, see William J. Cooper Jr., *Jefferson Davis, American* (New York: Knopf, 2000), 510–511.

50. Lincoln to Seward, Jan. 31, 1865, *Collected Works*, 8:250–251.

51. Eckert to Lincoln, Feb. 1, 1865, *Collected Works*, 8:281; Lincoln to the House of Representatives, Feb. 10, 1865, ibid., 8:281; Grant to Edwin M. Stanton, Feb. 1, 1865, ibid., 8:282. Grant's message was sent late on

February 1 but not received in Washington until 4:35 A.M. on February 2. It was immediately shown to Lincoln.

52. Theodore C. Blegen, ed., *Abraham Lincoln and His Mailbag: Two Documents by Edward D. Neill, One of Lincoln's Secretaries* (St. Paul: Minnesota Historical Society, 1964), 26–27; *New York Herald,* Feb. 4, 1865.

53. Stephens, *Constitutional View of the War,* 599–601.

54. Harris, "Hampton Roads Peace Conference," 48–49.

55. Stephens, *Constitutional View of the War,* 609–612; "Memorandum of the conversation at the conference in Hampton Roads," in John A. Campbell, *Reminiscences and Documents Relating to the Civil War during the Year 1865* (Baltimore: John Murphy, 1877), 15–16.

56. Stephens, *Constitutional View of the War,* 613–614.

57. Response to a Serenade, Feb. 1, 1865, *Collected Works,* 8:254.

58. For one historian's acceptance of the veracity of Stephens's account, see Ludwell H. Johnson, "Lincoln's Solution to the Problems of Peace Terms, 1864–1865," *Journal of Southern History* 34 (Nov. 1968):581–582. David Donald in his magisterial biography of Lincoln repeats Stephens's account without commenting on its accuracy; David Herbert Donald, *Lincoln* (New York: Simon and Schuster, 1995), 558.

59. Robert M. T. Hunter, "The Peace Commission of 1865," *Southern Historical Society Papers* 3 (1877):174. Stephens also reported Lincoln as saying that Northerners were as responsible for slavery as Southerners; *Constitutional View of the War,* 617.

60. Hunter, "Peace Commission of 1865," 176; Stephens, *Constitutional View of the War,* 611, 616–617 (quotation).

61. Hunter, "Peace Commission of 1865," 613; Campbell, "Memorandum," 15.

62. Harris, "Hampton Roads Peace Conference," 55.

63. Lincoln to the Senate and House of Representatives [Feb. 5, 1865], *Collected Works,* 8:260–261.

64. Francis Fessenden, *Life of William Pitt Fessenden,* 2 vols. (Boston: Houghton Mifflin, 1907), 2:8; entry for Feb. 6, 1865, *Welles Diary,* 2:237; [Endorsement], Feb. 5, 1865, *Collected Works,* 8:261.

65. William C. Harris, "Toward Appomattox, Toward Unconditional Surrender?" in Gabor S. Boritt, ed., *The Lincoln Enigma* (Oxford: Oxford University Press, 2001), 119; Annual Message to Congress, Dec. 3, 1861, *Collected Works,* 5:49 (quotation).

66. Gideon Welles, *Selected Essays by Gideon Welles: Civil War and Reconstruction,* comp. Albert Mordell (New York: Twayne, 1959), 182–183; Alexander K. McClure, *Abraham Lincoln and Men of War-Times: Some Personal Recollections of War and Politics during the Lincoln Administration* (Philadelphia: Times Publishing, 1892), 225.

67. Brooks, *Washington in Lincoln's Time,* 204–205, 206–207; *Congressional Globe,* 38th Cong., 2d sess. (Feb. 10, 1865), 733, 738.
68. *New York Tribune,* Feb. 7, 1865; *New York Herald,* Feb. 8, 1865; see also *NYT,* Feb. 7, 1865, and *Chicago Tribune,* Feb. 14, 1865, for similar praise.
69. *The Liberator,* Feb. 10, 1865.
70. Elizabeth Peabody to Horace Mann Jr., Feb. 1865, in Arlin Turner, ed., "Elizabeth Peabody Visits Lincoln, February 1865," *New England Quarterly* 48 (Mar. 1975): 124; for a similar tribute, see entry for Apr. 11, 1865, *Strong Diary,* 3:580.

5. THE HUMBLE INSTRUMENT OF GOD

1. Annual Message to Congress, Dec. 6, 1864, *Collected Works,* 8:149.
2. Lincoln to Albert G. Hodges, Apr. 4, 1864, *Collected Works,* 7:281–282. Hodges and other conservative Kentucky Unionists had come to Washington to indicate their opposition to the recruitment of black soldiers in their state. They reportedly went home satisfied with their interview with the president; ibid., 282–283n.
3. For more on the impact of the Emancipation Proclamation, see William C. Harris, "After the Emancipation Proclamation: Lincoln's Role in the Ending of Slavery," *North and South* 5 (Dec. 2001): 42–44.
4. James Rollins in Segal, *Conversations,* 363–364; Annual Message to Congress, Dec. 6, 1864, *Collected Works,* 8:149.
5. James M. McPherson, *Battle Cry of Freedom: The Civil War Era* (New York: Oxford University Press, 1988), 788.
6. Bancroft to Samuel S. Cox, Jan. 28, 1865, in M. A. DeWolfe Howe, ed., *The Life and Letters of George Bancroft,* 2 vols. (New York: Scribner, 1908), 2:157.
7. *New York World,* Dec. 21, 1864. *New York Atlas* quoted in *Washington Daily Chronicle,* Jan. 30, 1865; S. S. Cox to Marble, Dec. 21, 1864, Jan. 13, 1865; W. C. Kerr to Marble, Dec. 27, 1864, all in Manton M. Marble Papers, LC; James G. Blaine, *Twenty Years of Congress: From Lincoln to Garfield* (Norwich, Conn.: Henry Bill, 1884), 537.
8. *Boston Commonwealth,* Dec. 17, 1864.
9. Blaine, *Twenty Years of Congress,* 537; Laura Julian to her sister, Jan. 13, 1865, George W. Julian Papers, Indiana State Library, Indianapolis; "Castine," *Sacramento Daily Union,* Feb. 20, 1865.
10. John J. Janney in *Recollected Words,* 265; Samuel S. Cox, *Three Decades of Federal Legislation, 1855–1885* (Freeport, N.Y.: Books for Library Presses, 1970), 310; Cox to Marble, Feb. 2, 1865, Marble Papers.
11. Nicolay and Hay, 10:84–85.
12. LaWanda Cox and John H. Cox, in *Politics, Principle, and Prejudice,*

1865–1866 (New York: Free Press of Glencoe, 1963), 25, and James A. Rawley, in *Turning Points of the Civil War* (Lincoln: University of Nebraska Press, 1966), 201, have concluded erroneously that Bilbo played "a critically important role" in securing the passage of the Thirteenth Amendment.

13. Bilbo to Lincoln, Nov. 22, 1864, Jan. 26, 1865, Lincoln Papers; Bilbo to Seward, Jan. 10, 14, 23, 26, 1865, William H. Seward Papers, Rush Rhees Library, University of Rochester (microfilm); Lincoln to John A. Dix, Jan. 20, 1865, *Collected Works*, 8:226 and n. On the maneuvering to secure the passage of the amendment, see Michael Vorenberg, *Final Freedom: The Civil War, the Abolition of Slavery, and the Thirteenth Amendment* (Cambridge: Cambridge University Press, 2001), 180–204.

14. Segal, *Conversations*, 362–363.

15. Ibid., 363–364.

16. John Hogan to Andrew Johnson, June 19, 1865, Papers of Andrew Johnson, LC (microfilm).

17. Samuel S. Cox to Marble, Feb. 2, 1865, Marble Papers.

18. Elizabeth Peabody to Horace Mann Jr., Feb. 1865, in Arlin Turner, ed., "Elizabeth Peabody Visits Lincoln, February 1865," *New England Quarterly* 48 (Mar. 1975): 119–120; James M. Ashley to Lincoln, Jan. 31, 1865; Lincoln to Ashley, Jan. 31, 1865, both in *Collected Works*, 8:248 and n.

19. James M. Ashley to William H. Herndon, Nov. 23, 1866, group 4, reel 8, Herndon-Weik Collection, LC (microfilm).

20. *Congressional Globe*, 38th Cong., 2d sess. (Jan. 31, 1865), 189; Brooks, *Lincoln's Washington*, 410–411.

21. "Dixon," Feb. 1, 1865, to *Boston Daily Advertiser*, Feb. 4, 1865; David W. Blight, *Frederick Douglass's Civil War: Keeping Faith in Jubilee* (Baton Rouge: Louisiana State University Press, 1989), 186; Isaac Arnold, *The Life of Abraham Lincoln*, intro. James A. Rawley, 4th ed. (Lincoln: University of Nebraska Press, 1994), 365–366.

22. Response to a Serenade, Feb. 1, 1865, *Collected Works*, 8:254–255.

23. As reported in *The Liberator*, Feb. 10, 1865.

24. David Donald, *Charles Sumner and the Rights of Man* (New York: Knopf, 1970), ch. 5.

25. *Cincinnati Daily Gazette*, Feb. 1, 1865.

26. Lincoln to Conway, Mar. 1, 1865, *Collected Works*, 8:325.

27. McPherson, *Political History*, 594–595; Henry Steele Commager, ed., *Documents of American History*, 2 vols. (New York: Appleton-Century-Crofts, 1968), 1:451–452; William C. Harris, *With Charity for All: Lincoln and the Restoration of the Union* (Lexington: University Press of Kentucky, 1997), 253–254. On the Republican purposes behind the bill, see Herman Belz, "The Freedmen's Bureau of 1865 and

the Principle of No Discrimination according to Color," *Civil War History* 21 (Sept. 1975): 197–217. The life of the Freedmen's Bureau was extended indefinitely in 1866 and with greater authority.

28. *Quincy* (Ill.) *Daily Whig and Republican*, Mar. 4, 1865; *NYT*, Mar. 6, 1865; entry for Mar. 6, 1865, *Strong Diary*, 3:560; *New York Tribune*, Feb. 27 (quotation), Mar. 4, 1865.

29. Doolittle to his brother, Mar. 1865, in James R. Doolittle Papers, Wisconsin State Historical Society, Madison.

30. *NYT*, Mar. 4, 1865; *The Liberator*, Mar. 3, 1865.

31. *Cincinnati Daily Enquirer*, Mar. 4, 1865; *Louisville Journal*, Mar. 4, 1865; *New York Herald*, Mar. 4, 1865.

32. Entry for Mar. 4, 1865, *Welles Diary*, 2:251; *NYT*, Mar. 6, 1865.

33. Entry for Mar. 4, 1865, *Welles Diary*, 2:251–252; Chambrun, *Impressions*, 36–37. The most recent scholarly biography of Johnson does not identify his illness but says he was in "poor health" when he arrived in Washington in February and was "still feeling unwell" on inauguration day; Hans L. Trefousse, *Andrew Johnson: A Biography* (New York: Norton, 1989), 188–189.

34. *Recollected Words*, 320.

35. *New York Herald*, Mar. 8, 1865; *Chronicle* quoted ibid., Mar. 13, 1865.

36. *NYT*, Mar. 6, 1865; Margaret Leech, *Reveille in Washington, 1860–1865* (New York: Harper and Bros., 1941), 368.

37. Douglas L. Wilson, "A Note on the Text of Lincoln's Second Inaugural," *Documentary Editing* 24 (June 2002): 39–40. The inaugural address printed in *Collected Works*, 8:332–333, differs somewhat in spelling and punctuation from the speech that Lincoln read; the words are the same. I am indebted to Douglas Wilson for providing me with a copy of his article and also information on Lincoln's preparation of the address.

38. *NYT*, Mar. 6, 1865 (quotation); James Doolittle, "The Inauguration of Lincoln," Doolittle Papers; David Herbert Donald, *Lincoln* (New York: Simon and Schuster, 1995), 566; Chambrun, *Impressions*, 39. George Washington's first inaugural address is the shortest.

39. Randall M. Miller, Harry S. Stout, and Charles Reagan Wilson, eds., *Religion and the American Civil War* (New York: Oxford University Press, 1988), 10–11, 208, 223–224nn2,3; Ronald C. White Jr., *Lincoln's Greatest Speech: The Second Inaugural* (New York: Simon and Schuster, 2002); Lucas E. Morel, *Lincoln's Sacred Effort: Defining Religion's Role in American Self-Government* (Lanham, Md.: Lexington Books, 2000). While giving credit to Lincoln's religious emphasis in his second inaugural address, Allen C. Guelzo in his fine intellectual biography attributes it basically to a political strategy "against the Radicals and anyone else so full of themselves as to think both the questions

and answers obvious" regarding the war; *Abraham Lincoln: Redeemer President* (Grand Rapids, Mich.: Eerdmans, 1999), 419–420.

40. Address to the New Jersey Senate, Feb. 21, 1861, *Collected Works,* 4:236.

41. Tom Taylor to "Netta," Mar. 9, 1865, in Albert Castel, ed., *Tom Taylor's Civil War* (Lawrence: University Press of Kansas, 2000), 212; Brooks, *Lincoln's Washington,* 425; Salmon P. Chase to Mary Lincoln, Mar. 4, 1865, Lincoln Papers; *Recollected Words,* 56.

42. James Doolittle to his brother, Mar. 1865, Doolittle Papers; *NYT,* Mar. 6, 1865; Walter Lowenfels, comp., *Walt Whitman's Civil War* (1961; New York: Da Capo, 1989), 259; Leech, *Reveille in Washington,* 452.

43. Lowenfels, *Whitman's Civil War,* 259; *NYT,* Mar. 6, 1865; John G. Nicolay to Therena Bates, Mar. 5, 1865, in Michael Burlingame, ed., *With Lincoln in the White House: Letters, Memoranda, and Other Writings of John G. Nicolay, 1860–1865* (Carbondale: Southern Illinois University Press, 2000), 175; Leech, *Reveille in Washington,* 370; entry for Mar. 5, 1865, *Benjamin Brown French, Witness to the Young Republic: A Yankee's Journal, 1828–1870,* ed. Donald B. Cole and John J. McDonough (Hanover, N.H.: University Press of New England, 1989), 466; Elizabeth Keckly, *Behind the Scenes; Or, Thirty Years a Slave, and Four Years in the White House* (New York: Oxford University Press, 1988), 158. Keckly is mistakenly spelled "Keckley" on the title page of her book.

44. Keckly, *Behind the Scenes,* 160–161. In 1864 Lincoln had quietly received four black guests at a New Year's reception; none possessed the fame of Douglass or was greeted as enthusiastically; J. G. Randall and Richard N. Current, *Lincoln the President: Last Full Measure* (1955; Urbana: University of Illinois Press, 1991), 317–318. Accounts of Douglass at the reception vary slightly. I have largely followed Elizabeth Keckly's account, which Douglass related to her that night. For Douglass's own account of the incident, written years later, see *Life and Times of Frederick Douglass: His Early Life as a Slave, His Escape from Bondage, and His Complete History* (New York: Gramercy, 1993), 356–357.

45. *New York World,* Mar. 13, 1865.

46. This account of the ball has been derived from reports in the *Washington Daily Morning Chronicle,* Mar. 7, 1865, *New York Herald,* Mar. 8, 1865, and *NYT,* Mar. 5, 1865.

47. On this anticipated rupture, see Carl Schurz, *The Reminiscences of Carl Schurz,* vol. 3: *1863–1869* (New York: McClure, 1908), 109.

48. *New York Herald,* Mar. 8, 1865.

49. Ibid.; entry for Mar. 14, 1865, *Welles Diary,* 2:257; Keckly, *Behind the Scenes,* 157.

50. Arnold, *Life of Lincoln,* 404–405; Charles Francis Adams Jr., to Charles Francis Adams, Mar. 7, 1865, in Worthington C. Ford, ed., *A Cycle of Adams Letters, 1861–1865,* 2 vols. (Boston: Houghton Mifflin, 1920), 2:257–258.
51. *Washington National Intelligencer,* Mar. 6, 1865, quoted in Herbert Mitgang, ed., *Abraham Lincoln: A Press Portrait* (Athens: University of Georgia Press, 1989), 442.
52. *Boston Daily Advertiser,* Mar. 7, 1865; *Boston Journal,* Mar. 8, 1865.
53. *New York World,* Mar. 6, 1865; *Cincinnati Daily Enquirer,* Mar. 7, 1865; *Detroit Free Press,* Mar. 5, 1865. The Confederate press printed the inaugural address but apparently did not comment on it.
54. Bryant quoted in Robert S. Harper, *Lincoln and the Press* (New York: McGraw-Hill, 1951), 317; *Boston Commonwealth,* Mar. 18, 1865; *New York Tribune,* Mar. 6, 1865.
55. *Spectator,* Mar. 18, 1865; *Saturday Review,* Mar. 18, 1865; *Times* (London), Mar. 17, 1865; all in *Littell's Living Age,* Apr. 8, 1865.
56. Lincoln to Weed, Mar. 15, 1865, *Collected Works,* 8:356.

6. BEYOND THE BATTLEFIELD

1. Segal, *Conversations,* 379–380; *Recollected Words,* 370.
2. *Memoir of John Yates Beall: His Life; Trial; Correspondence; Diary; and Private Manuscript Found among His Papers* (Montreal: John Lovell, 1865); the charges and specifications are printed on pages 95–96.
3. Mrs. Roger A. Pryor (Sara A. Pryor), *Reminiscences of Peace and War* (New York: Macmillan, 1904), 340–341; *Memoir of Beall,* 68–73; *New York Herald,* Feb. 18, 1865; entry for Feb. 23, 1865, *Browning Diary,* 2:7–8; Thaddeus Stevens to Lincoln, Feb. 24, 1865, Lincoln Papers. Probably one reason Lincoln refused to commute the sentence was his mistaken belief that Beall had been involved in the plot to burn New York hotels at the time of the fall election; Pryor, *Reminiscences,* 340–341.
4. Dix to Edwin M. Stanton, Feb. 14, 1865, Edwin M. Stanton Papers, LC (microfilm); *Memoir of Beall,* 87.
5. *Recollected Words,* 41; Emanuel Hertz, *Abraham Lincoln: A New Portrait,* 2 vols. (New York: Horace Liveright, 1931), 2:949.
6. Oscar A. Kinchen, *Confederate Operations in Canada and the North* (North Quincy, Mass.: Christopher, 1970), 155–156.
7. General Orders no. 24, Headquarters, Department of the East, Mar. 20, 1865; Confession of Robert C. Kennedy, Mar. 25, 1865 (dictated a few hours before his execution), both in OR, ser. 2, vol. 8, 414–416, 428–429; NYT, Nov. 26, 29, 1864; *New York Tribune,* Mar. 27, 1865; Rob-

ert C. Kennedy to Lincoln, Mar. 14, 1865, Lincoln Papers; John W. Headley, *Confederate Operations in Canada and New York* (New York: Neale, 1906), 450–451.

8. See, e.g., *Detroit Free Press*, Nov. 12, 18, 24, Dec. 6, 1864.

9. On the St. Albans raid and its aftermath, see Robin W. Winks, *Canada and the United States* (Baltimore: Johns Hopkins Press, 1960), 298–301; Brian Jenkins, *Britain and the War for the Union*, 2 vols. (Montreal: McGill-Queens University Press, 1974–1980), 2:357, 360–363; Reginald C. Stuart, "St. Albans, Vermont, Raid," in *Encyclopedia of the American Civil War*, ed. David Heidler and Jeanne Heidler, 5 vols. (Santa Barbara, Calif.: ABC-Clio, 2000), 4:1845–46. For the Confederate purposes in the raid, see the *Annual Cyclopedia and Register of Important Events of the Year 1864* (New York: Appleton, 1869), 97, and *Detroit Free Press*, Nov. 12, 1864, citing the *Stansend* (Canada) *Journal*.

10. Chandler to Forbes, Dec. 26, 1864, Zachariah Chandler Papers, LC. *New York World*, Dec. 16, 1864, Mar. 21, 1865 (quotation); Calvin Day to Gideon Welles, Jan. 19, 1865, Gideon Welles Papers, LC (microfilm).

11. Winks, *Canada and the United States*, 318; *NYT*, Dec. 16, 1864; *New York Herald*, Dec. 17, 18, 1864.

12. Annual Message to Congress, Dec. 6, 1864, *Collected Works*, 8:141.

13. Entry for Dec. 16, 1864, *Welles Diary*, 2:198; Seward to Adams, Dec. 13, 19, 1864, in *Papers Relating to Foreign Affairs Accompanying the Annual Message of the President, to the First Session Thirty-Ninth Congress, 1865*, pt. 1 (Washington: Government Printing Office, 1866), 35, 49–51; General Orders no. 97, Dec. 14, 1864, Headquarters, Department of the East, in Morgan Dix, comp., *Memoirs of John Adams Dix*, 2 vols. (New York: Harper and Bros., 1883), 2:112–113.

14. Stanton to Dix, Dec. 15, 1864, Stanton Papers.

15. *Annual Cyclopedia, 1864*, 361; Jenkins, *Britain and the War for the Union*, 2:363; Pierce, *Memoir of Sumner*, 4:209; Winks, *Canada and the United States*, 323–324.

16. *New York World*, Dec. 16, 1864; Jenkins, *Britain and the War for the Union*, 2:368; Rufus King to Seward, Mar. 11, 1865, William H. Seward Papers, Rush Rhees Library, University of Rochester; Nicolay and Hay, 8:25n.

17. Charles Francis Adams to Charles Francis Adams Jr., Feb. 10, 1865, in Worthington C. Ford, ed., *A Cycle of Adams Letters, 1861–1865*, 2 vols. (Boston: Houghton Mifflin, 1920), 2:253–255.

18. Nicolay and Hay, 8:25–26; Winks, *Canada and the United States*, 314, 320, 329, 333; Stuart, "St. Albans, Vermont, Raid," 1846.

19. Adams to Charles Francis Adams Jr., Mar. 24, 1865, in Ford, *Cycle*

of Adams Letters, 2:258–259; Letter from "Occasional," *Philadelphia Press,* Mar. 29, 1865.

20. Lincoln to Banks, Aug. 5, 1863; Lincoln to Grant, Aug. 9, 1863, *Collected Works,* 6:364, 374; entry for Aug. 9, 1863, *Hay Diary,* 71.

21. Annual Message to Congress, Dec. 6, 1864, *Collected Works,* 8:137.

22. For documents relating to the Davis resolution see McPherson, *Political History,* 349–354; see also *Speeches and Addresses Delivered in the Congress of the United States and on Several Public Occasions, by Henry Winter Davis of Maryland* (New York: Harper and Bros., 1867), 472–479.

23. McPherson, *Political History,* 350; *Speeches and Addresses of Davis,* 456.

24. McPherson, *Political History,* 600; *Boston Commonwealth,* Dec. 24, 1864.

25. *Speeches and Addresses of Davis,* 473–475.

26. *Congressional Globe,* 38th Cong., 2d sess. (Dec. 20, 1864), 50–51.

27. The roll call votes are found in McPherson, *Political History,* 600. In 1865 Edward McPherson, clerk of the House, compiled and published many important documents relating to the war.

28. *NYT,* Dec. 20, 1864.

29. *Boston Daily Advertiser,* Dec. 24, 1864.

30. *New York Herald,* Jan. 25, Jan. 8, Feb. 27, 1865.

31. Quoted in Lynn M. Case and Warren F. Spencer, *The United States and France: Civil War Diplomacy* (Philadelphia: University of Pennsylvania Press, 1970), 561.

32. Chambrun, *Impressions,* 48 (quotation), 85–86; Case and Spencer, *United States and France,* 561–563.

33. The British and French also were at odds regarding European affairs, particularly the French role in the unification of Italy in 1859–1860.

34. Belmont to Seward, Mar. 2, 1865; Bigelow to Seward, Mar. 2, 1865, both in Seward Papers; Bigelow to Morgan, Mar. 3, 1865; Seward to Bigelow, Mar. 6, 1865, both in John Bigelow, *Retrospectives of an Active Life,* 3 vols. (New York: Baker and Taylor, 1909), 2:353, 360.

35. When asked in 1863 by a representative of Brigham Young what his policy toward the Mormons would be, Lincoln replied: "You go back and tell Brigham Young that if he will let me alone, I will let him alone." Mormons were delighted with this response, which ended thirty-three years of federal interference in their affairs. George U. Hubbard, "Abraham Lincoln as Seen by the Mormons," *Utah Historical Quarterly* 31 (Winter 1963): 103.

36. For the conflict on the Plains, see Alvin M. Josephy Jr., *The Civil War in the American West* (New York: Knopf, 1991), 289–291.

37. David A. Nichols, "Lincoln and the Indians," in Gabor S. Boritt, ed., *The Historian's Lincoln: Pseudohistory, Psychohistory, and History* (Urbana: University of Illinois Press, 1998), 155–158; Lincoln to Alfred

Sully, Nov. 19, 1864, *Collected Works*, 8:116 and n. For an extended unsympathetic treatment of Lincoln's Indian policy, see David A. Nichols, *Lincoln and the Indians: Civil War Policy and Politics* (Columbia: University of Missouri Press, 1978). Hans Trefousse has an insightful critique of Nichols's criticisms in Boritt, *Historian's Lincoln*, 170–174.

38. Speech to Indians, Mar. 27, 1863, *Collected Works*, 6:151–152 and 152n.

39. Annual Message to Congress, Dec. 1, 1862, *Collected Works*, 5:526.

40. Annual Message to Congress, Dec. 8, 1863, *Collected Works*, 7:47–48; *Secretary of the Interior's Report for 1863* (Washington: Government Printing Office, 1864), v–vi; Annual Message to Congress, Dec. 6, 1864, *Collected Works*, 8:146–147.

41. See, e.g., Lincoln to John Evans, Mar. 16, 1865, *Collected Works*, 8:356 and n; J. G. Knapp to Doolittle, Dec. 18, 1864, James R. Doolittle Papers, Wisconsin State Historical Society, Madison.

42. Dr. Anson G. Henry to his wife, Mar. 13, 1865, in Harry E. Pratt, comp., *Concerning Mr. Lincoln: In Which Abraham Lincoln Is Pictured as He Appeared to Letter Writers of His Time* (Springfield, Ill.: Abraham Lincoln Association, 1944), 116–120; Segal, *Conversations*, 373–375. On Dole's tenure, see Harry Kelsey, "William P. Dole and Mr. Lincoln's Indian Policy," *Journal of the West* 10 (July 1971): 484–492; Donavan L. Hofsommer, "William Palmer Dole, Commissioner of Indian Affairs, 1861–1865," *Lincoln Herald* 75 (Fall 1973): 97–114.

43. Henry B. Whipple, "My Life among the Indians," *North American Review* 150 (Apr. 1890): 438.

44. Josephy, *Civil War in the American West*, 306–310; testimony of Samuel G. Colley, in "Condition of the Indian Tribes," U.S. Senate *Report* no. 156, 39th Cong., 2d sess., 27–29.

45. *New York Herald*, Jan. 11, 19, 1865; *NYT*, Feb. 21, Mar. 11, 31, 1865; Annual Message to Congress, Dec. 6, 1864, *Collected Works*, 8:146–147.

46. *New York Herald*, Jan. 14, 1865; *Congressional Globe*, 38th Cong., 1st sess. (Jan. 9, 1865), 158; (Jan. 13, 1865), 255 (Sumner quotation); Sumner to Doolittle, Feb. 4, 1865, Doolittle Papers.

47. *Congressional Globe*, 38th Cong., 1st sess. (Jan. 13, 1865), 250; *Chicago Tribune*, Jan. 14, 1865.

48. "Condition of the Indian Tribes," 1–5; Nichols, *Lincoln and the Indians*, 210.

49. *St. Louis Missouri Democrat*, Mar. 9, 1865; Johnson Brigham, *James Harlan* (Iowa City: State Historical Society of Iowa, 1913), 189–190; Kelsey, "Dole," 484–485, 488–490.

50. Proclamation Concerning Trade with the Indians, Mar. 17, 1865, *Collected Works*, 8:359.

51. Proclamation Forbidding Intercourse with Rebel States, Aug. 16, 1861, *Collected Works,* 4:487–488; License of Commercial Intercourse, Mar. 31, 1863, ibid., 6:157.
52. G. F. Allen to Trumbull, Feb. 16, 1864, Lyman Trumbull Papers, LC; Banks to Edwin M. Stanton, Feb. 2, 1864, Nathaniel P. Banks Papers, LC; James M. McPherson, *Battle Cry of Freedom: The Civil War Era* (New York: Oxford University Press, 1988), 621.
53. Grant to Edward R. S. Canby, Mar. 7, 1865, *OR,* ser. 1, vol. 48, pt. 4, 829–830; entries for July 5 (quotation), Sept. 9, 1864, *Welles Diary,* 2:66, 129.
54. Gabor S. Boritt, *Lincoln and the Economics of the American Dream* (1978; Urbana: University of Illinois Press, 1994), 243; entry for July 5, 1864, *Welles Diary,* 2:66; Harold F. Williamson, *Edward Atkinson: The Biography of an American Liberal, 1827–1905* (Boston: Old Corner Book Store, 1934), 13–15.
55. *Washington National Intelligencer,* Jan. 19, 1864, quoting *New York Commercial Advertiser; Washington Daily Morning Chronicle,* Feb. 24, 1865; *Boston Daily Advertiser,* Jan. 12, 1864; *New York Herald,* Jan. 14, 1865; *New York World,* Feb. 18, 1865; *NYT,* Mar. 3, 1865 (quotation).
56. Sickles to Lincoln, May 31, 1864, Lincoln Papers.
57. Cadwallader C. Washburn to Elihu B. Washburne, Apr. 23 (quotation), May 16, Aug. 25, 1864, in Gaillard Hunt, *Israel, Elihu, and Cadwallader Washburn: A Chapter in American Biography* (1925; New York: Da Capo, 1969), 144, 346–347.
58. Banks to Stanton, Feb. 2, 1864, Banks Papers; Canby to Stanton, Dec. 7, 1864, *OR,* ser. 1, vol. 41, pt. 4, 786–787. See *Philadelphia Press,* Jan. 6, 1865, for an example of newspaper commentary on the report.
59. See McPherson, *Battle Cry of Freedom,* 637, 668; David Herbert Donald, Jean H. Baker, and Michael F. Holt, *The Civil War and Reconstruction* (New York: Norton, 2001), 365; Stanley S. McGowen, "Vicksburg Campaign," in *Encyclopedia of the American Civil War,* 4:2027.
60. Butler to Dibble, Feb. 1, 1864, in *Private and Official Correspondence of Gen. Benjamin F. Butler during the Period of the Civil War,* 5 vols. (Norwood, Mass.: Plimpton, 1917), 3:353.
61. George H. Gordon, *Diary of Events in the War of the Great Rebellion, 1863–1865* (Boston: James R. Osgood, 1882), 376, 380–381, 388; "Trade with the Rebellious States," U.S. House *Report* no. 24, 38th Cong., 2d sess., 4.
62. Entry for Sept. 9, 1864, *Welles Diary,* 2:138–140.
63. *New York Herald,* Jan. 14, 1865.
64. Lincoln to Canby, Dec. 12, 1864, *Collected Works,* 8:163–164. For an excellent analysis of Lincoln's faith in the financial importance of cotton

to the Union cause, see Boritt, *Lincoln and the Economics of the American Dream*, 206.

65. The *New York Times*, Feb. 18, 1865, published a list with the number of bales of "some of the principal holders of permits to trade in the insurrectionary states."

66. Patterson to Lamon, Dec. 30, 1864, Jan. 3, 1865, Ward Hill Lamon Papers, Huntington Library, San Marino, Calif.; Lamon to Lincoln, Mar. 23, Feb. 18, 1865, Lincoln Papers.

67. Cotton Permit for Fergus Peniston, Jan. 4, 1865, *Collected Works*, 8:196–197 and n; for a similar permit for Thomas C. Durant, vice president of the Union Pacific Railroad, see Order for Hanson A. Risley, Nov. 30, 1864, *Collected Works, Supplement* (1974), 268–269.

68. Hahn to Lincoln, Jan. 29, 1864, and Bullitt to Lincoln, Apr. 29, 1864, Lincoln Papers; Lincoln to Canby, Aug. 9, 1864, *Collected Works*, 7:488–489, 489n.

69. Entry for Sept. 27, 1864, *Welles Diary*, 2:159–161.

70. Entry for Oct. 3, 1864, ibid., 167; Lincoln to Farragut, Nov. 11, 1864, *Collected Works*, 8:103 and 103–104n.

71. Pass for Augustus R. Wright, Nov. 14, 1864, *Collected Works, Supplement*, 266 and n; *NYT*, Feb. 18, 1865; *Testimony Taken by the Joint Select Committee to Inquire into the Condition of Affairs in the Late Insurrectionary States: Georgia* (Washington: Government Printing Office, 1872), 1:90–91.

72. Entry for Apr. 12, 1865, *Browning Diary*, 2:17; Browning to Major O'Beirne, May 25, 1865, Orville H. Browning Papers, Illinois State Library, Springfield; transcription of William C. Bibb articles in the *San Antonio Messenger*, Apr.–May 1893, Carl Sandburg Civil War Collection, University of Illinois, Urbana-Champaign.

73. Transcription of Bibb articles, Sandburg Collection.

74. Thomas C. Teasdale, *Reminiscences and Incidents of a Long Life* (St. Louis: National Baptist Pub. Co., 1887), 198–200.

75. Lincoln to Canby, Mar. 18, 1865, *Collected Works*, 8:363; Teasdale, *Reminiscences*, 199–200, 202 (endorsement), 206–207; Pass for Thomas C. Teasdale, Mar. 18, 1865, *Collected Works*, 8:365. Though the original has not been found, the document endorsing Teasdale's mission, if authentic, must hold the distinction of being the only one containing the autographs of both Civil War presidents.

76. *Boston Commonwealth*, Jan. 25, 1865; see also *Philadelphia Press*, Jan. 6, 1865; *Chicago Tribune*, Mar. 7, 1865.

77. "Trade with the Rebellious States," 1–2.

78. *New York Herald*, Mar. 13, 1865; Forbes to Edward Atkinson, Mar. 8, 1865, in Williamson, *Atkinson*, 20.

79. Entry for Mar. 31, 1865, "George W. Julian's Journal—Assassination of

Lincoln," *Indiana Magazine of History* 11 (December 1915): 329; Lincoln to Grant, Mar. 8, 1865, *Collected Works*, 8:343–344 and 344n; Grant to Stanton, Mar. 10, 1865; Stanton to Grant, Mar. 11, 1865, both in *Grant Papers*, 14:118–119n; Grant's order is in *Collected Works*, 8:344–345n.

80. Grant to Canby, Feb. 13, 1865, *OR*, ser. 1, vol. 48, pt. 4, 829–830.

81. Washington correspondent to *Boston Daily Advertiser*, Mar. 27, 1865; entry for Apr. 14, 1865, *Welles Diary*, 2:280–281.

82. *Calendar of Francis Harrison Pierpont Letters and Papers in West Virginia Depositories* (Charleston: West Virginia Historical Records Survey, Federal Works Progress Administration, 1940), 323–324; entry for Mar. 31, 1865, "Julian's Journal," 339.

7. AT THE FRONT

1. Brooks D. Simpson, *Ulysses S. Grant: Triumph over Adversity, 1822–1865* (Boston: Houghton Mifflin, 2000), 413–414; Donald C. Pfanz, *The Petersburg Campaign: Abraham Lincoln at City Point, March 20–April 9, 1865* (Lynchburg, Va.: H. E. Howard, 1989), 1–2; Lincoln to Grant, Mar. 20, 1865, *Collected Works*, 8:367.

2. John S. Barnes, "With Lincoln from Washington to Richmond in 1865," *Appleton's Magazine* 9 (May 1907): 515–520. Three aides accompanied Mrs. Lincoln to City Point.

3. *Chicago Tribune*, Mar. 24, 1865; *New York Herald*, Mar. 29, Apr. 2, 1865; *New York Tribune*, Mar. 30, 1865; see also *Louisville Journal*, Apr. 7, 1865.

4. Entry for Mar. 23, 1865, *Welles Diary*, 2:264.

5. Lincoln to Edwin M. Stanton, Mar. 25, 1865, *Collected Works*, 8:373; Pfanz, *Petersburg Campaign*, 5–6.

6. Judkin Browning, "Battle of Fort Stedman," in *Encyclopedia of the Civil War*, ed. David Heidler and Jeanne Heidler, 5 vols. (Santa Barbara, Calif.: ABC-Clio, 2000), 2:753; report of General John G. Parke, Mar. 25, 1865, *OR*, ser. 1, vol. 46, pt. 3, 109–110.

7. Barnes, "With Lincoln," 521; Horace Porter, *Campaigning with Grant* (New York: Century, 1906), 406; Pfanz, *Petersburg Campaign*, 7–8 (quotation).

8. Lincoln to Stanton, Mar. 25, 1865, *Collected Works*, 8:374; Barnes, "With Lincoln," 521; Lyman to Elizabeth Lyman, Mar. 26, 1865, in George R. Agassiz, ed., *Meade's Headquarters, 1864–1865: Letters of Colonel Theodore Lyman from the Wilderness to Appomattox* (Boston: Atlantic Monthly Press, 1922), 325.

9. Lyman to Elizabeth Lyman, Mar. 26, 1865; *New York Herald*, Mar. 28, 1865; *St. Louis Missouri Democrat*, Apr. 8, 1865.

10. Barnes, "With Lincoln," 522; Segal, *Conversations,* 375.

11. Porter, *Campaigning with Grant,* 410.

12. Ibid., 413; Barnes, "With Lincoln," 522; *New York Herald,* Mar. 29, 1865.

13. *Philadelphia Inquirer,* as reported in the *Louisville Journal,* Apr. 7, 1865.

14. David Herbert Donald, *Lincoln* (New York: Simon and Schuster, 1995), 572–573; Barnes, "With Lincoln," 523–524, 743; Lincoln to Stanton, Apr. 1, 1865, *Collected Works,* 8:381; Lincoln to Mary Todd Lincoln, Apr. 2, 1865, ibid., 8:384.

15. Porter, *Campaigning with Grant,* 220.

16. Pfanz, *Petersburg Campaign,* 23; Katherine Helm, *The True Story of Mary, Wife of Lincoln* (New York: Harper and Bros., 1928), 88 (quotation).

17. Entry for Mar. 27, 1865, David S. Sparks, ed., *Inside Lincoln's Army: The Diary of Marsena Rudolph Patrick, Provost Marshal General, Army of the Potomac* (New York: Thomas Yoseloff, 1964), 483.

18. Porter, *Campaigning with Grant,* 417–419; Sherman to Isaac N. Arnold, Nov. 28, 1872, Isaac Newton Arnold Papers, Chicago Historical Society; a copy of this letter was kindly given to me by Mark L. Bradley.

19. Simpson, *Grant,* 418; Sherman to Arnold, Nov. 28, 1872, Arnold Papers.

20. William C. Harris, "Toward Appomattox, Toward Unconditional Surrender?" in Gabor S. Boritt, ed., *The Lincoln Enigma* (Oxford: Oxford University Press, 2001), 122–123; Mark L. Bradley, *This Astounding Close: The Road to Bennett Place* (Chapel Hill: University of North Carolina Press, 2000), 46–47.

21. Harris, "Toward Appomattox," 123.

22. *Memoirs of General William T. Sherman,* 2 vols. (New York: Appleton, 1913), 2:327. For the controversy over Sherman's terms to Johnston, see John F. Marszalek, *Sherman: A Soldier's Passion for Order* (New York: Free Press, 1993), 346–349.

23. Porter, *Campaigning with Grant,* 425.

24. Ibid.

25. Ibid., 426; Simpson, *Grant,* 419–420.

26. Elizabeth Keckly, *Behind the Scenes; Or, Thirty Years a Slave, and Four Years in the White House* (New York: Oxford University Press, 1988), 171. On one occasion, however, Lincoln angrily refused to meet with Vice President Johnson, who had come to City Point to see him. Perhaps he was still upset with Johnson because of his embarrassing performance at the inauguration ceremony; David Dixon Porter, *Incidents and Anecdotes of the Civil War* (New York: Appleton, 1885), 284–285; *Recollected Words,* 297.

27. Porter, *Campaigning with Grant*, 426.
28. Lincoln to Stanton, Mar. 30, 1865, *Collected Works*, 8:377; *Grant Papers*, 14:273; *New York Herald*, Mar. 30, Apr. 3, 4, 1865; Barnes, "With Lincoln," 744.
29. Lincoln to Stanton, Apr. 2, 1865, *Collected Works*, 8:382 and n; Lincoln to Grant, Apr. 2, 1865, ibid., 8:383 and n; Stanton to Lincoln, Apr. 3, 1865; Lincoln to Stanton, Apr. 4, 1865, ibid., 8:384–385n, 385; on the fall of Petersburg, see Noah Andre Trudeau, *The Last Citadel: Petersburg, Virginia, June 1864–April 1865* (Boston: Little, Brown, 1991), ch. 17.
30. *New York Herald*, Apr. 5, 1865; Pfanz, *Petersburg Campaign*, 53–54; Porter, *Campaigning with Grant*, 450–451.
31. Pfanz, *Petersburg Campaign*, 56.
32. Trudeau, *Last Citadel*, 412; *New York Herald*, Apr. 7, 1865; Porter, *Incidents and Anecdotes*, 291.
33. Lincoln to Stanton, Apr. 3, 1865, *Collected Works*, 8:385; *New York Herald*, Apr. 7, 1865; George H. Gordon, *Diary of Events in the War of the Great Rebellion, 1863–1865* (Boston: James R. Osgood, 1882), 398–399; Porter, *Incidents and Anecdotes*, 294.
34. R. J. M. Blackett, ed., *Thomas Morris Chester, Black War Correspondent: His Dispatches from the Virginia Front* (Baton Rouge: Louisiana State University Press, 1989), 294–295, 297; Coffin in Rice, *Reminiscences*, 180–181.
35. Barnes, "With Lincoln," 748–749; Coffin in Rice, *Reminiscences*, 183; *New York Herald*, Apr. 7, 1865; *Boston Daily Advertiser*, Apr. 7, 1865; Ernest B. Furgurson, *Ashes of Glory: Richmond at War* (New York: Knopf, 1996), 344–345.
36. Porter, *Incidents and Anecdotes*, 299–300, 302.
37. C. G. Chamberlayne, ed., "Abraham Lincoln in Richmond," Memorandum of Gustavus A. Myers, Apr. 1865, *Virginia Magazine of History and Biography* 41 (Oct. 1933): 320–322; Campbell to Horace Greeley, Apr. 26, 1865, Campbell Family Papers, Duke University Library, Durham, N.C.
38. *Recollected Words*, 172, 182 (quotation), 339, 404.
39. Harris, "Toward Appomattox," 125; "George W. Julian's Journal—Assassination of Lincoln," *Indiana Magazine of History* 11 (Dec. 1915): 333; Lincoln to Weitzel, Apr. 12, 1865, *Collected Works*, 8:406–407.
40. Pierce, *Memoir of Sumner*, 4:234; Barnes, "With Lincoln," 750; Lincoln to Seward, Apr. 5, 1865, *Collected Works*, 8:387 and n; entries for Mar. 28, 30, Apr. 4, 5, 1865, *Welles Diary*, 2:268–269, 274–275; *New York Herald*, Apr. 3, 1865.
41. Lincoln to Seward, Apr. 5, 1865; Lincoln to Grant, Apr. 6, 1865, *Collected Works*, 8:387, 388 and n.
42. *New York Independent*, quoted in Francis B. Carpenter, *The Inner Life*

of *Abraham Lincoln: Six Months at the White House* (New York: Hurd and Houghton, 1868), 287–288; letters of Apr. 9, 22, 1865, to *Green Mountain Freeman* (Montpelier, Vt.), in Emil and Ruth Rosenblatt, eds., *Hard Marching Every Day: The Civil War Letters of Private Wilbur Fisk* (Lawrence: University of Kansas Press, 1992), 322–323.

43. *Recollected Words*, 396 (quotation); Carpenter, *Inner Life of Lincoln*, 289.

44. Carpenter, *Inner Life of Lincoln*, 288.

45. This account was printed in the *Raleigh Tri-Weekly Standard*, Mar. 26, 1867.

46. Barnes, "With Lincoln," 521; Porter, *Incidents and Anecdotes*, 311–312 (quotation).

47. Septima M. Collis, *A Woman's War Record, 1861–1865* (New York: Putnam, 1889), 62–67. Septima was the wife of General Collis and lived with him at City Point. Rufus Barringer offered substantially the same account of the meeting; see "Reminiscences of Paul B. Barringer," Paul B. Barringer Papers, North Carolina Division of Archives and History, Raleigh.

48. Collis, *A Woman's War Record*, 69–70.

49. Lincoln to Grant, Apr. 7, 1865, *Collected Works*, 8:392.

50. Keckly, *Behind the Scenes*, 169–170.

51. Chambrun, *Impressions*, 78, 81, 82 (quotation); Pfanz, *Petersburg Campaign*, 88.

52. Chambrun, *Impressions*, 83–84 (quotation); Pierce, *Memoir of Sumner*, 4:235.

53. Pierce, *Memoir of Sumner*, 4:235; Frederick W. Seward, *Seward at Washington, as Senator and Secretary of State* (New York: Derby and Miller, 1891), 271–272; Margaret Leech, *Reveille in Washington, 1860–1865* (New York: Harper and Bros., 1941), 381.

54. Entry for Apr. 10, 1865, *Welles Diary*, 2:278; Edward D. Neill, "Reminiscences of Lincoln's Last Year," in Theodore C. Blegen, ed., *Abraham Lincoln and His Mailbag: Two Documents by Edward D. Neill, One of Lincoln's Secretaries* (St. Paul: Minnesota Historical Society, 1964), 38; William H. Crook, *Through Five Administrations: Reminiscences of Colonel William H. Crook, Body-Guard to President Lincoln*, comp. and ed. Margarita Spalding Gerry (New York: Harper and Bros., 1910), 60–61.

55. Response to Serenade, Apr. 10, 1865, *Collected Works*, 8:393, 393–394n (quoting the *Washington National Intelligencer*, Apr. 11, 1865).

56. Last Public Address, Apr. 11, 1865, *Collected Works*, 8:399–400.

57. Ibid., 400–404.

58. Don E. Fehrenbacher, *Lincoln in Text and Context* (Stanford: Stanford University Press, 1987), 118.

59. Annual Message to Congress, Dec. 1, 1862, *Collected Works*, 5:531.

60. Last Public Address, Apr. 11, 1865, *Collected Works*, 8:403–405; Harris, "Toward Appomattox," 129.
61. *Philadelphia Press*, Apr. 14, 1865.
62. *New York Herald*, Apr. 13, 1865; *NYT*, Apr. 13, 1865; *Chicago Tribune*, Apr. 14, 1865; *New York Tribune*, Apr. 12, 1865; *Detroit Free Press*, Apr. 14, 1865.
63. *Philadelphia Press*, Apr. 14, 1865; Brooks, *Lincoln's Washington*, 436–439.

8. MARTYRDOM

1. W. Emerson Reck, *A. Lincoln: His Last 24 Hours* (1987; Columbia: University of South Carolina Press, 1994), 15–16.
2. Colfax in Segal, *Conversations*, 391–393; *Recollected Words*, 113–114. Colfax apparently recorded this conversation soon after the assassination.
3. Colfax in Segal, *Conversations*, 393.
4. Lincoln to James H. Van Alen, Apr. 14, 1865, *Collected Works*, 8:413 and n (for quotation from Van Alen's letter to Lincoln, undated).
5. David Homer Bates, *Lincoln in the Telegraph Office* (New York: Century, 1907), 366–367.
6. Entry for Apr. 14, 1865, *Welles Diary*, 2:280–283. Welles actually wrote this account three days later.
7. Ibid., 2:280–282; Gideon Welles, *Selected Essays by Gideon Welles: Civil War and Reconstruction*, comp. Albert Mordell (New York: Twayne, 1959), 193.
8. Seward in *Recollected Words*, 398; *Washington Daily Chronicle*, Apr. 15, 1865; entry for Apr. 14, 1865, *Welles Diary*, 2:281.
9. Charles A. Dana, *Recollections of the Civil War: With the Leaders at Washington and in the Field in the Sixties* (New York: Appleton, 1898), 273–274.
10. Ibid., 274–276.
11. Earl Schenck Miers, ed., *Lincoln Day by Day: A Chronology, 1809–1865*, 3 vols. (Washington: Sesquicentennial Commission, 1960), 3:329; David Herbert Donald, *Lincoln* (New York: Simon and Schuster, 1995), 593.
12. Miers, *Lincoln Day by Day*, 3:329; William H. Crook, *Through Five Administrations: Reminiscences of Colonel William H. Crook, Body-Guard to President Lincoln*, comp. and ed. Margarita Spalding Gerry (New York: Harper and Bros., 1910), 65; John T. Stuart, "Conversation" with John Nicolay, June 24, 1875, John Hay Collection, Hay Library, Brown University; Chambrun, *Impressions*, 84. In a September 1866 interview with William H. Herndon, Mary Lincoln said that

"Mr Lincoln up to 1865 wanted to live in Springfield and be buried there," but "changed his notion . . . and never settled on any place particularly—intended moving & travelling some"; *Herndon's Informants*, 359.

13. *Washington Daily Chronicle*, Apr. 17, 1865; Edwin C. Haynie, "At the Deathbed of Lincoln," *Century Magazine* 51 (1895–1896), 954.

14. Reck, *Lincoln: His Last 24 Hours*, 53–57; Card of Admission for George Ashmun, Apr. 14, 1865, *Collected Works*, 8:413. Several people later claimed to have spoken to Lincoln as he left for Ford's Theatre. Senator William M. Stewart said that the president wrote a note inviting him to return the next morning, but that he dropped the note as he was leaving the White House. It has not been found. Reck, *Lincoln: His Last 24 Hours*, 59.

15. Donald, *Lincoln*, 595.

16. Thomas R. Turner, *The Assassination of Abraham Lincoln* (Malabar, Fla.: Krieger, 1999), 15, 119; William Hanchett, *The Lincoln Murder Conspiracies* (Urbana: University of Illinois Press, 1983), 54–55. Terry Alford, the author of a forthcoming biography of Booth, has kindly provided me with important information on the assassination.

17. Turner, *Assassination*, 15–16.

18. Entry for Apr. 14, 1865 (written three days later), *Welles Diary*, 2:283–287; Turner, *Assassination*, 21–23.

19. Chambrun, *Impressions*, 106 (quotation); *Cincinnati Daily Gazette*, Apr. 17, 1865; *Washington Chronicle*, Apr. 24, 1865; entry for Apr. 17, 1865, *Strong Diary*, 3:586–587.

20. Wilbur Fisk to *Green Mountain Freeman* (Montpelier, Vt.), Apr. 20, 1865, in Emil Rosenblatt and Ruth Rosenblatt, eds., *Hard Marching Every Day: The Civil War Letters of Private Wilbur Fisk* (Lawrence: University of Kansas Press, 1992), 323; William C. Davis, *Lincoln's Men: How President Lincoln Became Father to an Army and a Nation* (New York: Free Press, 1999), 239–241.

21. Mark L. Bradley, *This Astounding Close: The Road to Bennett Place* (Chapel Hill: University of North Carolina Press, 2000), 163–164.

22. William C. Harris, *With Charity for All: Lincoln and the Restoration of the Union* (Lexington: University Press of Kentucky, 1997), 267–268; *Cincinnati Daily Enquirer*, Apr. 20, 1865.

23. Entry for Apr. 23, 1865, Beth G. Crabtree and James W. Patton, eds., *"Journal of a Secesh Lady": The Diary of Catherine Ann Devereux Edmondston, 1860–1866* (Raleigh: North Carolina Division of Archives and History, 1979), 702. On the probable effect of Lincoln's assassination on Southern reconstruction, see Harris, *With Charity for All*, epilogue; see also Herman Belz, *Reconstructing the Union: Theory and Policy during the Civil War* (Ithaca: Cornell University Press,

1969), 302–311; LaWanda Cox, *Lincoln and Black Freedom: A Study in Presidential Leadership* (Columbia: University of South Carolina Press, 1981), 142, 150–155.

24. Wade quoted in "The Reconstruction Period, 1865–1869," manuscript, Henry L. Dawes Papers, LC; Hans L. Trefousse, *Andrew Johnson: A Biography* (New York: Norton, 1989), 197–198; entry for Apr. 15, 1865, "George W. Julian's Journal—Assassination of Lincoln," *Indiana Magazine of History* 11 (Dec. 1915): 335; Henry Winter Davis to Samuel F. Du Pont, Apr. 22, 1865, Samuel F. Du Pont Papers, Eleutherian Mills Historical Library, Greenville, Del.; Chandler to his wife, Apr. 23, 1865, Zachariah Chandler Papers, LC.

25. Address after the assassination of President Lincoln, Tremont Temple, Boston, Apr. 23, 1865, in *Speeches, Lectures, and Letters by Wendell Phillips,* 2d ser. (Boston: Lee and Shepard, 1900), 446–453; Rice, *Reminiscences,* 47–69, 101–138, 139–160, 185–195, 255–291, 307–314; Grimes to his wife, Apr. 16, 1865, in William Salter, *The Life of James W. Grimes* (New York: Appleton, 1876), 278.

26. Frederick Douglass, "Our Martyred President: An Address Delivered in Rochester, New York, on 15 Apr. 1865," in John W. Blassingame and John R. McKivigan, eds., *The Frederick Douglass Papers,* ser. 1: *Speeches, Debates, and Interviews,* vol. 4: *1864–80* (New Haven: Yale University Press, 1991), 74–79.

27. Robert S. Harper, *Lincoln and the Press* (New York: McGraw-Hill, 1951), 357; *Detroit Free Press,* Apr. 16, 1865; see also *Washington Constitutional Union,* Apr. 15, 17, 1865, for Democratic outrage and call for vengeance.

28. *Cincinnati Daily Enquirer,* Apr. 17, 18 (citing the *Dayton Empire*), 19 (quotation), 1865.

29. *Cincinnati Daily Gazette,* Apr. 17, 1865.

30. *Washington Constitutional Union,* Apr. 26, 1865; Harper, *Lincoln and the Press,* 349–350; entries for Apr. 15, 27, 1865, Nicholas B. Wainwright, ed., *A Philadelphia Perspective: The Diary of Sidney George Fisher Covering the Years 1834–1871* (Philadelphia: Historical Society of Pennsylvania, 1967), 493–496; *Philadelphia Press,* Apr. 20, 1865; William D. Foulke, *Life of Oliver P. Morton, Including his Important Speeches,* 2 vols. (Indianapolis: Bowen-Merrill, 1899), 1:439.

31. Daniel C. Eddy, *The Martyr President: A Sermon Preached Before the Baldwin Place Church, Apr. 16, 1865* (Boston: Graves and Young, 1865), 19.

32. *Christian Advocate and Journal,* Apr. 20, 27, 1865.

33. Ibid., Apr. 27, May 4 (quotations), 1865; Resolution of Cleveland Congregational Conference, Apr. 19, 1865, in *The Papers of Andrew Johnson,* ed. Leroy P. Graf, vol. 7, *1864–1865* (Knoxville: University of Tennessee Press, 1986), 586n.

34. David B. Chesebrough, *"No Sorrow like Our Sorrow": Northern Protestant Ministers and the Assassination of Lincoln* (Kent, Ohio: Kent State University Press, 1994), 55, 68–69. Chesebrough analyzed 340 sermons by Protestant ministers.

35. Ibid., 139n7. Though most Jews supported the war, ably served the Union cause, and appreciated Lincoln's fair-mindedness toward them, they became convenient scapegoats for many Northerners when the war effort faltered; Bertram W. Korn, *American Jewry and the Civil War* (Cleveland: World Publishing, 1961), chs. 7–8.

36. Eddy, *Martyr President*, 9, 18; Chesebrough, *"No Sorrow like Our Sorrow,"* 69.

37. *Christian Advocate and Journal*, May 4, 1865.

38. Ralph Morrow, *Northern Methodism and Reconstruction* (East Lansing: Michigan State University Press, 1956), ch. 8; James H. Moorhead, *American Apocalypse: Yankee Protestants and the Civil War, 1860–1869* (New Haven: Yale University Press, 1978), 184–189.

39. Entries for Apr. 18, 19, 1865, *Welles Diary*, 2:292; Brooks, *Lincoln's Washington*, 454–455; entry for Apr. 19, 1865, *Strong Diary*, 3:590.

40. Brooks, *Lincoln's Washington*, 455–456; entry for Apr. 19, 1865, *Welles Diary*, 2:293.

41. *Philadelphia Press*, Apr. 19, 1865; Nicolay and Hay, 10:318–319.

42. *Christian Advocate and Journal*, May 4, 1865.

43. Henry S. Wilson to Bluford Wilson, Apr. 23, 1865, in Harry E. Pratt, comp., *Concerning Mr. Lincoln: In Which Abraham Lincoln Is Pictured as He Appeared to Letter Writers of His Time* (Springfield, Ill.: Abraham Lincoln Association, 1944), 126–128; *NYT*, Apr. 24, 1865.

44. *NYT*, Apr. 26, 1865.

45. *Philadelphia Press*, Apr. 26, 1865; for more on the cortege in New York, see *NYT*, Apr. 25, 26, 1865.

46. *NYT*, Apr. 28, 1865; Nicolay and Hay, 10:321–322; Stephen B. Oates, *With Malice toward None: The Life of Abraham Lincoln* (New York: Harper and Row, 1977), 473–474; Jay Winik, *April 1865: The Month That Saved America* (New York: HarperCollins, 2001), 358; Mark E. Neely Jr., *The Lincoln Encyclopedia* (New York: McGraw-Hill, 1982), 122.

47. Henry P. H. Brownell to his parents, Apr. 30, 1865; Julia Kirby to Joseph Duncan, May 7, 1865, both in Pratt, *Concerning Mr. Lincoln*, 129–131.

48. Matthew Simpson, *Funeral Address Delivered at the Burial of President Lincoln, At Springfield, Illinois, May 4, 1865* (New York: Carlton and Porter, 1865), 9–12.

49. Ibid., 13–14, 20.

50. Ibid., 21.

51. *Washington Daily Chronicle*, May 5, 1865.

52. Excerpts from the *Times,* Apr. 29, 1865, and the *Liverpool Shipping Gazette,* n.d., in *Littell's Living Age* 85 (Apr.–June 1865): 355–357; Bright to Sumner, Apr. 29, 1865, in Pierce, *Memoir of Sumner,* 4:240.

53. *Times,* Apr. 29, 1865, and *London Examiner,* n.d., in *Littell's Living Age* 85 (Apr.–June 1865): 356, 365.

54. James B. Eads to Gideon Welles, May 3, 1865, Gideon Welles Papers, LC; Bigelow quoted in Lynn M. Case and Warren F. Spencer, *The United States and France: Civil War Diplomacy* (Philadelphia: University of Pennsylvania Press, 1970), 571–572; Merrill D. Peterson, *Lincoln in American Memory* (New York: Oxford University Press, 1994), 25.

55. Judd quoted in Harold Hyman, ed., *Heard Round the World: The Impact Abroad of the Civil War* (New York: Knopf, 1969), 161; Albert A. Woldman, *Lincoln and the Russians* (Cleveland: World Publishing, 1952), 262.

56. *Constitution* and *Le Pays* quoted in Harper, *Lincoln and the Press,* 360–361; Peterson, *Lincoln in American Memory,* 25; *Times* (London), Apr. 27, 29, 1865, in *Littell's Living Age* 85 (Apr.–June 1865): 353, 356.

57. *London Review,* n.d., in *Littell's Living Age* 85 (Apr.–June 1865): 369; *Daily Post* quoted in Harper, *Lincoln and the Press,* 362.

58. *Philadelphia Press,* Apr. 18, 1865 (quotation); Peterson, *Lincoln in American Memory,* 25–26; *The Assassination of Abraham Lincoln, Late President of the United States of America, and the Attempted Assassination of William H. Seward: Expressions of Condolence and Sympathy Inspired by These Events* (Washington: Government Printing Office, 1866); included in the 717 pages of condolences were 69 pages of messages from Americans.

59. Henry Champion Deming, *Eulogy of Abraham Lincoln, Before the General Assembly of Connecticut (June 8, 1865)* (Hartford: A. N. Clark, 1865), 12–13, 18, 20, 45, 56–57.

60. Bancroft to his wife, Dec. 15, 16, 1861, Feb. 24, 1864, in M. A. DeWolfe Howe, ed., *The Life and Letters of George Bancroft,* 2 vols. (New York: Scribner, 1908), 2:144–146, 155–156; Roy P. Basler, *The Lincoln Legend: A Study in Changing Conceptions* (New York: Octagon, 1969), 93 (quotation).

61. George Bancroft, "Memorial Address on the Life and Character of Abraham Lincoln," in *Memorial Addresses Delivered Before the Two Houses of Congress on the Life and Character of Abraham Lincoln, James A. Garfield, and William McKinley* (Washington: Government Printing Office, 1903), 27, 72–74; John Hay to William H. Herndon, Sept. 5, 1866, Herndon-Weik Collection, LC. Bancroft's denunciation of Palmerston and European nations did not go unnoticed. While some Europeans applauded his remarks, the British, French, and Austrian

ministers in Washington lodged a protest with the Johnson administration; Lilian Handlin, *George Bancroft: The Intellectual as Democrat* (New York: Harper and Row, 1984), 284–285.

62. Whitman's "Lilacs" may be found in Walter Lowenfels, comp., *Walt Whitman's Civil War* (1961; New York: Da Capo, 1989), 326–333; William W. Betts Jr., ed., *Lincoln and the Poets: An Anthology* (Pittsburgh: University of Pittsburgh Press, 1965), 41–42.

63. Lowell's "Ode" was published in the *Atlantic Monthly* 16 (Sept. 1865): 364–371.

64. William Cullen Bryant to Frances Bryant, Sept. 7, 1864, in William Cullen Bryant II and Thomas G. Voss, eds., *The Letters of William Cullen Bryant*, vol. 4: *1858–1864* (New York: Fordham University Press, 1984), 402–403 and n; Parke Godwin, *A Biography of William Cullen Bryant, With Extracts from His Private Correspondence*, 2 vols. (New York: Russell and Russell, 1883), 2:229.

65. *NYT*, Apr. 26, 1865; *Christian Advocate and Journal*, May 4, 1865.

ACKNOWLEDGMENTS

Many people have contributed to the preparation of this book. I have received considerable help from colleagues in the Department of History, North Carolina State University, and from friends elsewhere. I owe a special debt to John David Smith, Alexander J. De Grand, Jennifer Fleischner, Douglas L. Wilson, and Terry Alford for reading parts or all of the manuscript and offering many useful suggestions. Throughout my study of Lincoln, John David and Alex have provided encouragement and assistance. I suspect that they, along with others, have sometimes grown tired of hearing about Abraham Lincoln. John Sellers, Michael Musick, Mark Bradley, Alex Christopher Meekins, and Michael Burlingame shared important information on source materials with me. I am also thankful for the valuable critique of the work by two anonymous readers for Harvard University Press.

As every author knows, good editors are essential. I am grateful to Joyce Seltzer and Camille Smith of Harvard University Press for their careful and skillful editing. I benefited immensely from their suggestions and encouragement. In addition, Joyce's assistant David Lobenstine provided guidance in the early stages of the publication process.

During the several years of research and writing that yielded this book, graduate assistants Nancy Kaiser, Michael Thomas Smith, Javan D. Frazier, and Jennifer Davis aided me. They seemed to have a sixth sense for locating materials I needed. Sehoya and James Cotner helped me navigate the frustrating world of computer technology, and Paul Betz ably formatted the final draft. Norene Miller, Deborah Kroll, and Julie Rabinowitz also assisted me. As always, my wife Betty gave important and caring support.

Librarians, archivists, and curators of manuscript collections are often the unsung heroes of scholarly research and writing. I received splendid help from the staff of the D. H. Hill Library at North Carolina State University. Mimi Riggs, Marihelen Stringham, and Darby Orcutt, especially, with great efficiency and cheerfulness, tracked down valuable research materials for me. I am thankful for the aid of Mary Burkee of the Rare Book and Special Collections Library at the University of Illinois at Urbana-Champaign, Olga Tsapina of the Manuscript Department of the Huntington Library, Nancy M. Martin of the Rare Books and Special Collections Department of the Rush Rhees Library at the University of Rochester, Mary-Jo Kline of the John Hay Library at Brown University, and the staffs of the Perkins Library at Duke University, the University of North Carolina Library, the Chicago Historical Society, the State Historical Society of Wisconsin, the Thomas Cooper Library at the University of South Carolina, the William and Mary Library, the Cornell University Library, the Manuscript Division of the Library of Congress, and the Illinois State Historical Library. Cindy Van Horn of the Lincoln Museum in Fort Wayne, Indiana, kindly furnished the illustrations.